Library of
Southern Civilization
Lewis P. Simpson, Editor

The
FLUSH TIMES
of
ALABAMA
and
MISSISSIPPI

The
FLUSH TIMES
of
ALABAMA
and
MISSISSIPPI

◆

A Series of Sketches

JOSEPH G. BALDWIN

With an Introduction and Notes by

JAMES H. JUSTUS

◆LOUISIANA STATE UNIVERSITY PRESS◆
BATON ROUGE *and* LONDON

New material copyright © 1987 by Louisiana State
University Press
All rights reserved
Manufactured in the United States of America
10   9   8   7   6   5   4   3   2   1
Library of Congress Cataloging-in-Publication Data
Baldwin, Joseph G. (Joseph Glover), 1815–1864.
The flush times of Alabama and Mississippi.

(The Library of Southern civilization)
Reprint. Originally published: New York :
Appleton, 1853.
Introd. includes bibliographical references.
1. Alabama—Social life and customs—Anecdotes,
facetiae, satire, etc.   2. Mississippi—Social life and
customs—Anecdotes, facetiae, satire, etc.   3. Law—
Alabama—Anecdotes, facetiae, satire, etc.   4. Law—
Mississippi—Anecdotes, facetiae, satire, etc.
5. Baldwin, Joseph G. (Joseph Glover), 1815–1864—
Anecdotes.   I. Justus, James H.   II. Title.
F326.6.B34   1987   976.1'05   87-10918
ISBN 0-8071-1141-1 (pbk.)

CONTENTS

A NOTE ON THE TEXT

The Flush Times of Alabama and Mississippi was published by D. Appleton and Company of New York on or just before December 11, 1853. It sold well—there were ten editions in the nineteenth century—though it probably failed to meet the projection touted by the editor of the *Southern Literary Messenger,* who in the February, 1854, number estimated that continuing demand for the volume would ensure sales of "20,000 copies" during the first six months after publication.

Although there are some typographical and spelling errors (Baldwin frequently misremembered the names of fictional characters and was inconsistent in the spelling and accenting of foreign phrases), the first edition contains fewer than do succeeding editions. Later editions also incorporate a few substantive changes, but there is no evidence that Baldwin had any hand in them. The present edition is a reproduction of a copy of the first edition in the University Library of Western Illinois University.

ON THE NOTES

Joseph Glover Baldwin is the most consciously literary of his peers in humor of the Old Southwest. Most of his favorite authors—Shakespeare, Scott, Irving, Johnson, Lamb, Dickens—make their appearance in *Flush Times*, but Baldwin's familiarity with literature ranges widely, from Vergil, Ovid, and Cicero to Sterne, Byron, and Bulwer-Lytton, and his pages are peppered with allusions to authors whose works have now been largely forgotten: Samuel Foote, Sarah Stickney Ellis, James Beattie. Many of his literary references are embedded as phrases in his own prose, and even the passages he chooses to quote are usually modified, sometimes radically, to suit his context. Any future critical edition of *Flush Times* will take note of Baldwin's pervasive literariness, since it has an important bearing on such larger matters as authorial intention, genre, and audience; because of limited space, however, only those allusions to earlier authors which affect meaning that would otherwise be lost are noted here. Latin terms, especially legal Latin, have been briefly explained, as have most references to topical issues and historical figures. As a cheerful amalgam

of memoir and fiction, Baldwin's sketches are richly popu-
lated both by real professionals whose names in the early
1850s would have been familiar to readers (S. S. Prentiss,
John A. Quitman, John J. Crittenden) and by imaginary
ones, those inspired by literature as well as the author's
time and place (Major Willis Wormley, Cave Burton, Paul
Beechim). Many of his characters are modeled, with considerable creative latitude, on friends and acquaintances
who are identified only by initials (Squire A., H. G——y,
Hon. J.F.T.); in the expedient belief that little literary relevance would result from such discovery, no attempt has
been made to identify these historical models in *The Flush
Times of Alabama and Mississippi*. Certain historical names,
I regret to say, have stubbornly resisted reasonable efforts at
identification.

INTRODUCTION

When Joseph Glover Baldwin rode into Mississippi in April of 1836, he was only one among thousands of ambitious young men from the seaboard states seeking their fortunes in the newly opened lands of the Old Southwest. By 1853, when he recreated that arrival in *The Flush Times of Alabama and Mississippi*, those lands had already entered America's imaginative consciousness. Because of hundreds of sketches that celebrated the scenery, people, and habits of the lower states, the Old Southwest—a region stretching from the Savannah River to the Mississippi—was concept and metaphor as much as it was geography.

Baldwin's arrival in the new country almost coincided with the publication of Augustus Baldwin Longstreet's *Georgia Scenes* (1835), the volume usually credited as the first to exploit the southern backwoods in the vernacular realism we now call "humor of the Old Southwest." Although Longstreet's characters do not literally belong to the new lands (they reflect rural and village life in backcountry Georgia, no longer a frontier), this collection of sketches was, as Edgar Allan Poe predicted, "a sure omen of better days" for southern writing. *Georgia Scenes* became the conspicuous model for many amateur writers, a remarkable group of lawyers, doctors, editors, and other professionals who in the nearly three decades before the Civil War turned to literature in order to capture the flavor of life as they lived and observed it in the frontier South. Written by men for an appreciative masculine audience, their sketches, many of them never collected and some of the authors still unknown, appeared first in local newspapers and then nationally, through the journalistic exchange system, in such lively newspapers as the New Orleans *Picayune* and the St. Louis *Reveille*. The best of them, as well as the merely representative, found their way into William T. Porter's popular, influential, and long-lasting weekly, the New York *Spirit of the Times*. Dozens of collections issued from the presses—some, like *Georgia Scenes*, bore regional imprints, but many were enterprises of Philadelphia and New York publishers.

Since these writers were amateurs, the quality of their sketches varied widely. The heart of each contribution, however, was the amusing incident and the colorful character whose nonstandard language as well as his ungenteel actions became a staple whether the author wrote from Alabama, Arkansas, or east Tennessee. Yeoman farmers, backwoodsmen, hunters, riverboatmen, preachers, widows, and casual confidence men were popular figures in anecdotes that frequently turned on confrontation—with their peers, with naïfs, with Yankees and other travelers. All the sketches were brief, ranging from the column "filler" to the fairly elaborate piece interweaving situation, character, time and place, and language in complex episodes that resembled the formal short story. The authors typically disguised their contributions with initials or pseudonyms ("Sugartail," "Omega," "N. of Arkansas"), partly because of long tradition reaching back to the eighteenth-century British essayists and partly because of a reluctance to be identified as "writing men" in a country and a region that assigned little value to such dilettantes.

Although derived in spirit from the personal essay and the American example of Washington Irving, the humorous sketch in the South was triggered by the sporting letter from gentlemen, usually on country estates, who recounted recent experiences in field and stream. The hunting letter, because it often described forays into the backwoods, quickly evolved into verbal portraits of memorable or eccentric local characters, complete with stylistic attempts to capture their speech. Although South Carolinians and cultivated Georgians frequently wrote such sporting literature, those who settled temporarily in the new country became the most distinctive contributors. From the end of the second war with England to 1836, when by federal fiat the final great removal of the southern Indian nations opened up all the Mississippi Territory to white settlement, the area attracted not only migrants escaping the worn-out soil and narrowing economic opportunities of the older states but also land speculators, drifters, gamblers, wage earners, adventurers, and confidence artists of various stripes. By 1852 when Baldwin, by then a successful lawyer, began contributing his work to the prestigious *Southern Literary Messenger*, his

sketches had been preceded by several published col-
lections delineating life in the region: William Tappan
Thompson's *Major Jones's Courtship* (1843), Johnson Jones
Hooper's *Some Adventures of Captain Simon Suggs* (1845),
Thomas Bangs Thorpe's *Mysteries of the Backwoods* (1846),
John S. Robb's *Streaks of Squatter Life* (1847), Joseph M.
Field's *The Drama in Pokerville* (1847), Henry Clay Lewis'
Odd Leaves from the Life of a Louisiana "Swamp Doctor"
(1850), and Joseph B. Cobb's *Mississippi Scenes* (1851).
Authenticated as social history by memorial reconstruc-
tion, Baldwin's Old Southwest is also shaped by literary
convention.

In his preface to *Flush Times*, Baldwin indirectly acknowledges his familiarity with earlier volumes, and in conception and style, one sketch, "Simon Suggs, Jr.," specifically pays homage to Hooper. Picturing himself as Falstaff,
a genial roister quietly banking on the indulgence of that
"Sovereign," the reading public, with brassy insouciance he
claims originality: "No other work with which he is acquainted, has been published in the United States designed
to illustrate the periods, the characters, and the phases
of society." Most of the previous books, beginning with
Georgia Scenes, had in fact done just that, and some of them
had been expressly "designed" to do so. Nowhere in his
preface does Baldwin suggest the true originality of his
book: that his "Series of Sketches" (he also calls his uneven
chapters "pieces," "leaves," "papers," and "articles") is
unified by the voice of an authorial narrator whose whiggish
and lawyerly sensibility presides over the re-creation of a

riotous social carnival, shading it with both moral evalua-
tion and humorous indulgence.

The book is hardly comprehensive; "the periods, the
characters, and the phases of society" depicted in *Flush
Times* have been rigorously selected. The importance of
place has its source not in the makeshift amenities of hard-
scrabble communities—the local conditions that appalled
and delighted so many visitors in their accounts of travel in
the Old Southwest—but in the ramifications of an economic
system based on paper money, credit, confidence, and unre-
strained speculation. Baldwin's interest is not the physical
new country or the "mercurial and reckless population" it
attracts, but the promissory atmosphere that lawyers rightly
perceived was made to order for them.

Before he sets out from his Virginia home, the narrator
hears of "that sunny land of most cheering and exhilarating
prospects of fussing, quarrelling, murdering, violation of
contracts, and the whole catalogue of *crimen falsi*—in fine,
of a flush tide of litigation in all of its departments, civil and
criminal." The author heightens the restlessness and risk
taking that inform the humor of many of his contemporaries
into a general spirit of chicanery, but the dramatic examples
of ignorance, swindling, mendacity, and theft of the public
treasury all involve lawyers, not their clients. While Baldwin's narrator manages to suggest the shape and color of society generally, the tales we hear from him deal specifically
with the bench and bar—other lawyers and their clients,
judges and their friends, court recorders, jurors, appreciative courtroom audiences. The figures of the Old South-

west most familiar to readers by the 1850s—hunters, hog merchants, ring-tailed roarers, gamblers, circuit riders—presumably escaped litigation: they are either missing from Baldwin's canvas entirely or are only incidentally chalked in as background. Even when he wants to metaphorize the "whirling vortex of a new and seething population" without hierarchy or order, the narrator finds a Miltonic vividness in the contentious competition of codes and statutes imported from older states, especially their uncertain relevance to conditions in the new: "Nothing was settled. Chaos had come again, or rather, had never gone away. Order, Heaven's first law, seemed unwilling to remain where there was no other law to keep it company."

Into this "California of Law, whose surface strife only indicated the vast *placers* of legal dispute waiting in untold profusion," Baldwin enters as a Virginian willing himself to succeed in a society that is as morally questionable as it is professionally promising. Along his route the narrator pointedly dismisses the simpler "picayune standard" he observes as the norm in east Tennessee in favor of the "wild spend-thriftism" farther south, a milieu that puts a premium on extravagance and calculation. It is worth noting that even from his legal perspective, the dubious ethics of the Alabama and Mississippi of 1836 spill over professional boundaries, characterizing an entire society grown decadent before it has ceased being primitive. The operative referents of humor so common in other collections—*frontier, backwoods, wilderness*—are rare in *Flush Times*. What distinguishes Baldwin's society is what lawyerly ambition has helped to shape; the recurring words in his lexicon are *humbug, pretentiousness, fraud.*

In *Georgia Scenes*, in which Longstreet describes sports, entertainments, social events, joking, and mutual conning as normative, a cheerful spirit lightens even the pretentiousness of the society matron and the village *bon vivant.* Baldwin's premise is that his Flush Times society is neither rural nor urban; to thrive there requires a gambler's shrewdness, and innocence is always hostage to greed, as we hear in the narrator's cynical maxim, "He who does not go ahead is run over and trodden down."

Like an eighteenth-century satirist, Baldwin's persona excoriates the "vulgarity—ignorance—fussy and arrogant pretension—unmitigated rowdyism—bullying insolence" of an era vitiated by "the reign of humbug, and wholesale insanity"; but the very energy of his style suggests an emotional engagement with his subject: "What country could boast more largely of its crimes? What more splendid role of felonies! What more terrific murders! What more gorgeous bank robberies! What more magnificent operations in the land offices! . . . Such superb forays on the treasuries, State and National! . . . Such august defalcations! . . . And in INDIAN affairs!—the very mention is suggestive of the poetry of theft—the romance of a wild and weird larceny! What sublime conceptions of super-Spartan roguery! Swindling Indians by the nation!" Although this spirited invective is perhaps the most extreme in the book, many of Baldwin's effective passages evoke similar aspects of his time and place, notably competitiveness and self-interest, and they are effective in part because the author's persona never quite exempts himself from the general corruption "that halcyon period" comes to symbolize—"Larceny grew not only respectable, but genteel," "Swindling was raised to the dignity of the fine arts," "Felony came forth." We are never to assume that in his bold personifications the narrator numbers himself literally among the worst of the malefactors, but we see him fully participating in the more pervasive sort: "Avarice and hope joined partnership."

The quintessential fraud in this society is Ovid Bolus, whose portrait so resembles a seventeenth-century "Character" out of Overbury and Webster that it might be titled "The Liar." The maliciousness and wit of the original genre are suggested in the *discordia concors* of the name that links the ancient artist of fabled transformations and the lowly pill out of nineteenth-century barnyard medicine. An Irvingesque iteration and accretion make definitive this portrait of a slick operator who in "every house . . . left an autograph, in every ledger a souvenir," before his sudden departure for the Brazos. It is unimportant that a South Carolinian who settled briefly in Kemper County during Baldwin's Mississippi stay inspired the creation of Ovid Bolus, but that he was a lawyer is significant. Although not all the characters in *Flush Times* are drawn with the same emphasis as this great liar is, the memorable ones are lawyers, and all are meant to suggest the larger society they service with such expedience. "The bar of every country is, in some sort," writes Baldwin, "a representative of the character of the people of which it is so important an 'institution'"—which is why portraits of and anecdotes about lawyers both at work and at play constitute the resonating subject of his book.

A ponderous generalization underlines the sustained satire of "Simon Suggs, Jr., Esq.": "There is a tone and spirit of morality attaching to the profession of the law so elevating and pervasive in its influence, as to work an almost instantaneous reformation in the character and habits of its disciples." Its mock solemnity precedes the biography of the hero and the most salient detail of his professionalism. After some judicious emending of a law license he has won at faro in Alabama, Suggs presents himself in Arkansas as a counselor-at-law and solicitor in chancery. The fictive son of Hooper's shifty captain thus assumes in even newer country the same exalted role played by Ovid Bolus, who, unconfined by "mere lingual" lying, "acted lies as well." So "elevating" is his profession that the older swindler escaped his creditors by slipping off to Texas; Suggs's "reformation" comes with his appointment as Choctaw agent to negotiate claims on the federal treasury, a "responsible and lucrative office" that requires his presence in Washington each winter.

The narrator's bemusement with Bolus and Suggs tends to neutralize the indignation he allows himself in a few other sketches in *Flush Times*—for example, in the three essays "The Bench and the Bar," "How the Times Served the Virginians," and "The Bar of the South-West." Few praiseworthy instances emerge in the specific profiles and anecdotes, but the deficiencies are softened by the comic or mock-neutral terms. Frank Glendye, though "a great brick," is also an irresponsible drunkard who damages his client's case by failing to show up in court to argue it. Innocent of legal learning, W.B.T., a former Methodist preacher who had fallen from grace ("not a high fall"), depends upon his sonorous voice to carry him through shaky cases. One prosecutor, a former "old-field schoolmaster," brings only his pedantry and conceit to his adopted profession; and one judge is characterized totally by his nagging, unprofessional curiosity. The "slangwhanging" Cave Burton of Kentucky, known as the Blowing Cave, is lumbering, ignorant, and insensitive to everything but his appetite. Fond of juries, he feeds them "little scraps of gossip, or hearsay, or neighborhood reports," and the narrator is compelled to judge the man, despite his natural conviviality, a "monstrous demagogue." Another sketch is an amusing exposé of an old shyster who, "having clung to the bar after being at least twice stricken from the roll," comes from Mississippi to hustle a potential client being held for murder in an Alabama jail. And though more gently handled, the Virginia lawyers in exile in the new country—gentlemanly orators more articulate about *amor patriae* than about Blackstone—come across in Baldwin's account as genial dolts.

In this extensive gallery, only the narrator and his immediate friends escape the full onus of incompetence, mendacity, or fraud; but their opportunism, quirks, and practical jokes are prominent enough to suggest their easy accommodation to the shabby professionalism of their era. Even some of the lawyers whom Baldwin regards as honestly gifted are tainted. In "My First Appearance at the Bar," structured as any lawyer's generic combat story, the passing of time cannot fully

erase the remembered nastiness with which a tough professional demolishes a "lawyerling." The narrator's profile of
Caesar Kasm, a skillful but malicious eccentric (who later
dies of apoplexy while abusing someone else's client), is as
unsentimental as the old crank himself. Despite his function in the sketch—to initiate the greenhorn—the authorial
tone invites us to regard Old Sar Kasm as the embodiment
not of strength but of mean-spiritedness. And in almost a
sidebar detail in "The Bench and the Bar," the narrator betrays his reservations about Jim T., the peer he and his
friends most admire, when he describes how the arrogant
young man browbeats a colleague who is devoted to him.
Even the narrator, we learn, is granted a license to practice
law by a circuit judge who asks him "not a single legal
question."

Of all the profiles of Flush Times lawyers only that of
"Hon. Francis Strother [Lyons]" is ostensibly proffered as a
model. The man's personal rectitude, civility, scholarly aptitude, and devotion to his work are climactically ratified by
his public service in which, as commissioner of the state
banks of Alabama, he restores solvency, order, and responsibility to a chaotic economy created by "both intelligent
and ignorant rascality," thereby redeeming the state from
"that hell-carnival" known as Flush Times. But in an anecdote Strother, while protesting, goes to the head of a line of
men waiting for a shave. Baldwin cannot avoid demonstrat-
ing even in this gentlemanly model the subtle practice of
social control exercised by a privileged class. Baldwin's
other real-life portrait, the more interesting "Hon. S. S.

Prentiss," dramatizes a brilliant talent's succumbing to the disorder and dissipation nourished by his time and place. If Strother is "the type of a class" rapidly disappearing in the hurly-burly of progress, Prentiss hauntingly comes to stand as "a type of his times, a representative of the qualities of the people, or rather of the better qualities of the wilder and more impetuous part of them." The narrator's syntactic waffling is a correlative to Baldwin's own moral ambivalence about the era during which he himself thrives as a "representative" figure.

The deliberately strong aura of retrospect in *Flush Times* is evidence enough that Baldwin was much too busy *during* those years to record his impressions. Chronology confirms that evidence. For the fifteen years he spent in the new states—from 1836, when he arrived, to 1852, when his sketches began appearing in print—he was as restless as the population in general. In mid-1837 he moved from Mississippi, where in fifteen months he had earned a reputation as a good young lawyer, and took up residence in Gainesville, Alabama. His successful partnership there with Jonathan Bliss was still prospering in 1850, when Baldwin dissolved it and moved on to Livingston, where he eventually joined with T. B. Wetmore in a new law partnership. Sometime in 1853 he went to Mobile and practiced briefly before moving back to Livingston in early 1854. In these years he also made trips to Texas (1839 and 1850) and to Philadelphia (for the 1848 Whig national convention) and other eastern cities and watering places. Despite the legal and economic chaos so vividly depicted in his sketches, Baldwin found the times normal enough to marry, have children, maintain an extensive and stable domestic establishment, serve a term in the Alabama legislature, run (unsuccessfully) for the U.S. Congress, and carry on a thriving law practice. By the time he first found enough leisure to describe and evaluate the Flush Times, probably in 1851, they were over.

His collection of pieces, which Appleton of New York published in December, 1853, included seventeen sketches that his friend John R. Thompson had accepted and published in the *Southern Literary Messenger*, enriched by nine others. Implicit throughout *Flush Times* is a then-and-now contrast that protects the imaginative latitude of an author who is also a social historian. The relative stability of the present allows Baldwin a certain creative license in depicting the gross instability of the recent past, especially its moral and professional shortcomings. That latitude begins with the title. Logically the term *Flush Times*, which Baldwin apparently coined, should refer to the general spirit of speculation and the conduct of business on credit in the years just *prior* to the national economic collapse of 1837. But his is a metaphorical use that connotes the prevailing social and professional attitudes of both *boom* and *bust*. Of the twenty-six sketches, only ten are dated, most of them in 1836 and 1837; one sketch is set "in the times we write of" and another in "184—"; the action in some pieces is reported as having taken place "fifteen years ago"; and in several sketches the setting is simply during "Flush Times."

Significantly, the only explicitly contemporary sketch is

"Simon Suggs, Jr., Esq." In the correspondence between
the two con men that constitutes the preliminaries to "A
Legal Biography," dated November and December, 1852,
the vanity-press editor quotes some puffery that could serve
as a comic epigraph for most of the sketches in *Flush
Times*—the self-serving aphorism "that the lawyer's distinction was preferable to all others, since it was impossible to
acquire in our profession, a false or fraudulent reputation."
Designed to flatter the ego and lighten the pocketbook of his
mark, the tactic is no longer feasible in Alabama, which
young Suggs has forsaken for the greener fields of Rackinsack, Arkansas. By the 1850s, Baldwin suggests, scoundrel
time in *his* Southwest is over.

But it is not merely a matter of conditions then and conditions now, the pattern in which fraud, larceny, and rascality
in Alabama and Mississippi are refined out with the passage
of a few years and replaced by civil order, economic stability, and respect for institutions. For Baldwin, paradox is
more germane than is contrast. The very climate that attracted Ovid Bolus and Hooper's Simon Suggs, Sr., also attracted at the same time, so Baldwin assures us, a cadre of
estimable and gifted lawyers "not equalled, as a whole, by
the same number of lawyers in any other quarter of the
Union." The Age of Brass, that is, with its shinplaster morals is transformed into a golden age: in "the years [between]
1833 and 1845, the bar was most numerous, and, we think,
on the whole, most able." Again, the hedging syntax, which
tends to undercut the otherwise confident assertion, is but
one indication of Baldwin's general ambivalence as he at-

tempts to convert an age of improbity and venality, what he elsewhere describes as "the ante-type of California—without the gold," into a stunning historical moment in which the best legal minds of his generation clustered together. It is an artful turn worth following.

Halfway through the table of contents (though about two-thirds through the book) Baldwin positions his two "serious" character studies of famous contemporaries, his tributes to Strother and Prentiss. Unlike most of the other profiles of semi-fictional or fictively disguised acquaintances, these portraits are earnest exercises in the biographer's art, combining historically verifiable facts and personal judgments of their characters and careers, and they flank the most revealing of Baldwin's three formal essays. "The Bar of the South-West" functions as an apologia in which the author deliberately recasts his first version of the drama of Flush Times with stalwart feature players who morally and professionally reinforce the stars, Strother and Prentiss. While he does not downplay the irresponsibility, dishonesty, and chaos, Baldwin now supplies a motif that makes the action a providential trial. The climate of chicanery that felled even the great Prentiss now becomes a salubrious test of all worthy young men. Although the "free manners and not over-puritanic conversation" may have been deleterious to the young lawyer's spiritual nature ("we leave this moral problem to be solved by those better able to manage it"), the narrator declares that "if the subject *were* able to stand the trial, his moral constitution, like his physical after an attack of yellow fever, would be apt to be the better for it."

If up to this point we have been led to think of southwestern lawyers as a band of opportunists, a point Baldwin himself has made with considerable wit and skill, now we are invited to reconsider. Not only does he pronounce the first quarter of his century the "great judicial era of the United States"; he also declares that distinction best illustrated by the profession "in the States of Tennessee, Alabama, Mississippi and Louisiana." (He tentatively adds Texas and California to that earned "preëminence," but neglects to mention Arkansas, the bailiwick of Simon Suggs, Jr.) If, as we suspect, the previously demonstrated rascality of the age may have been literarily enhanced, then perhaps the unlikely preeminence of the age is now being validated by rhetoric more than by documentary evidence.

"The Bar of the South-West" is a paean to the "almost perfect equality" of opportunity that the Flush Times offered to young lawyers—and by implication to all young newcomers. With Emersonian fervor Baldwin defends the heady age just ended because it allowed talent to flourish without traditional society's restraints. With Virginia clearly in mind, Baldwin notes that in such a society "the chains of habitude and mode and fashion fetter" the young man: he is "cramped by influence, prejudice, custom, opinion," and he lives with surveillance and "under a sense of *espionage*." Vivified, however, by "the law of liberty," he no longer must endure that network of arbitrary forces that trammel him— "wealth, family, influence, class, caste, fashion, coterie and adventitious circumstances of all sorts." In the freedom of the new country he no longer has to fritter away his powers "upon non-essentials—upon the style and finish of a thing rather than upon its strength and utility—upon modes" rather than ends.

Baldwin's attitude toward Virginia is ancestral but not pious, just as his attitude toward the Southwest is critical but not moralistic. His brief characterization of Strother as "a gentleman of the Old School with the energy of the New" could with justice apply also to Baldwin himself. His praise of the revolutionary generation in *Party Leaders* (1855), his second book, reflects national consensus more than commonwealth pride, and he is remarkably detached when he discriminates among the generation that followed. He pillories the complacent colonial snobs, corrupted by "mimic forms of royalty" that "infected the manners of the gentry," a class whose descendants—nameless old fogies who hover over several chapters of *Flush Times*—erected arbitrary barriers to the professional and intellectual development of its young men. Although he declares that there was "no character more attractive than that of a young Virginian, fifteen years ago, of intelligence, of good family, education and breeding," Baldwin makes it clear that he and others of his generation could succeed only outside Virginia, as part of its "surplus talent." His healthy objectivity can be seen in an especially instructive observation in *Party Leaders* about Henry Clay and his wishy-washy Virginia supporters. When Clay became John Quincy Adams' secretary of state, the response of the Jacksonians, who made capital of the deal that squeezed them out, was politically understandable. But Baldwin says that Clay's former Virginia allies were ungenerously seeking social revenge. These old-line politicians still regarded the Kentucky Whig as "a specimen of the parvenu, as a new man, as a hoosier, and a hoosier meant 'half-horse, half-alligator, and a little touch of the snapping-turtle.' He had come from the backwoods, at a time when they were a wilderness." In addition, Clay "had not borne himself very humbly" amid the Virginians. His want of respect had been annoying "to the second-rate men of Congress," those oracles back home "whom he handled sometimes not very gently." And though he considers Jefferson's belief in the common man excessively idealistic, he applauds his influence on popular government, which, imperfectly conducted as it is, nevertheless *"elevates the masses,"* since opportunity means that the "chilling distance . . . between the higher and lower classes" can be bridged.

Baldwin's experience in the speculative climate of the Southwest in the 1830s oddly confirms both the idealistic "error" and the salubrious influence that he attributes to Jefferson. If lines of class and caste were more routinely crossed in these chaotic years than they were in more socially stable eras, *Flush Times* itself gives us no striking instance of how self-government elevates the *masses*. Those best served by fledgling self-government were Prentiss and Strother, already exceptional men who could turn the times to their advantage while also benefiting the general public. The masses of men in *Flush Times* are neither elevated nor degraded by politics; they function mostly as supernumeraries in anecdotes about court cases and the leisure-time pleasures of lawyers.

Interestingly, however, when the narrator laments the corruption in taste and thought among his contemporaries who address "ignorant juries," the observation stems less from class snobbery than from professional concern. His point is that the meanest of forensic tricks—"humbug, rant, cant and hypocrisy," "demagoguism and flimsy perversions," "interminable wordiness and infinite repetition, exaggeration, bathos and vituperation," "low wit and buffoonery"—were more common in the courts of the older states and among the older, more traditional counselors than they were at "the new bar" in Alabama and Mississippi. The very vulgarity of the new society discouraged such histrionics, for the eager young lawyers could not condescend to canny clients and juries and audiences, a watchful, skeptical people in whom "the organs of Reverence" were almost entirely wanting.

Baldwin describes how, in this young man's country, a pragmatic competitiveness among lawyers led to the development of a style marked by "readiness, precision, plainness, pertinency, knowledge of law, and a short-hand method of getting at and getting through with a case," an economical style that he sees paralleled by the community generally. The new population, "standing knee-deep in exploded humbugs," had little patience with the older states' legal niceties, and few jurors wanted "their ears fed with vain repetitions, mock sentimentality, or tumid platitudes." Their skeptical countenance "stops curiously the flow of the current when the humbugger sees the intended humbuggee looking him . . . in the eye, and seeming to say by the expression of his own, 'Squire, do you see any thing green here?'" While older lawyers' cant might be overlooked, "the juniors with us had no such immunity." Baldwin stresses the word-of-mouth reputations that passed from one set of eager litigants to another. If the young lawyer tried inappropriate tricks, that fact was "rehearsed in his presence" until he learned better. "If he made himself *very* ridiculous, he was carried around the circuit, like a hung jury in old times, for the especial divertisement of the brethren."

A skeptic might point out that the young men, by escaping the "tedious novitiate" back home, not only shed an old-fashioned style in the undisciplined Southwest but also evaded a more stringent curriculum of reading law. Baldwin's encomium to this "class of men" in the years from 1833 to 1845 who "ennobled the profession of the law," curiously relates to general aspects of character, not to professional qualities: *faithful, chivalrous, reliable, trustworthy, loyal,* and *honorable*. Such diction contributes little to our sense of these young men as lawyers. It is only when Baldwin acknowledges the exceptions that his pen becomes vigorous in his citation of their less attractive attributes: "Bullying insolence, swaggering pretension, underhanded arts, low detraction, unworthy huckstering for fees, circumvention, artful dodges, ignoring engagements, facile obliviousness of arrangements, and a smart sprinkling . . . of pettifogging, quibbling and quirking." The pungence of the exceptions stylistically overpowers the blandness of the rule. Furthermore, the specific profiles in *Flush Times* illustrate not the generalizations but the anomalies.

The wit and style of Baldwin the humorist are inextricably tied to his richly ambivalent sensibility in confronting both the society he admired but left and the society he scorned but entered. Like many of his fellow humorists, Baldwin betrays his whiggish sympathies for the values of the southern professional and planter classes, and it is easy enough to find textual evidence in his writing that reflects that biographical fact. "The Old Folks at Home" would have seen significance in Baldwin's dedicating his two published books to Virginians years after he had ceased to live among them: *Flush Times* to "My Friends in the Valley of the Shenandoah" and *Party Leaders* to his uncle and mentor, Briscoe G. Baldwin. Despite the splendid comic drama of "How the Times Served the Virginians," in which the proud, impractical, and honorable immigrants finally succumb to the freewheeling speculative economy spawned by the Jacksonian ethos, Baldwin remained suspicious of democracy and shared the belief of his class that political leadership should be in the hands of the educated few. Yet both Baldwin's career and his writing reveal a complexity that mere political orientation cannot fully explain. If he was active in the Whig cause before the party dissolved, he then chose to be a Democrat, not a Republican. There is little to suggest that he was doctrinaire in either role.

More than any of his contemporaries among the humorists, Baldwin stylistically announces his patrician origins. A Tidewater urbanity makes his narrating voice one of the most cultivated of the era. But this style, with its far-ranging diction, its allusiveness, its elegant periods, is not the whole story. In one memorable passage in "How the Times Served the Virginians," a romantic evocation of Williamsburg and the College of William and Mary, that voice seems to anticipate the nostalgic rhythms of Thomas Nelson Page, but even this soft-focus indulgence is wry, not sentimental, nostalgia. Generally Baldwin's is a style in which Virginia elegance is invigorated by the locutions and blunt constructions of the frontier. It is a style that effectively articulates the balanced sympathies of the man himself. His ancestry does not prevent mockery from lacing his affectionate references to Virginians. He can also artfully exaggerate both the lowest and highest qualities of character among his fellow lawyers in Alabama and Mississippi. While the authorial narrator is not the most interesting character in *Flush Times*, he is the most complex, and that style is one measure of Baldwin's healthy ambivalence both to the Old Dominion and to the Old Southwest.

In the moral order of Baldwin's world, judicial tics and ethical shortcuts, unprofessional rivalry, and grasping self-interest loom larger than do professional courtesy, scholarly expertise, and administrative efficiency. While the virtues of this world may emerge as more than perfunctory strengths, the narrator is emotionally engaged only when he confronts the spectacle of its weaknesses. Although he is not much interested in the Southwest as a vale of soul making, he consciously casts the new country as a crucible in which character is tested, and he is notably unsentimental in the process. There are few real victims, for example, worth his or our tears. Naïveté and innocence, no less than active trick-

ery, involve roughhewn testing. Except for "poor Ben O.,"
Baldwin makes no provision for ensuring the reader's customary sympathy for the underdog, and he refuses to linger
even on poor Ben's traducing by Ovid Bolus, a sharper wit.
All participants in the life of their time play now prosecution, now defense—or effortlessly turn themselves into witnesses, judges, jurors. The games most worth the candle
before 1837 simultaneously profit and entertain the players;
after the crash, ending the reckless cycle of credit and
speculation, they test one's mettle.

In Baldwin's retrospect, the great event toward which the
Rag Empire inexorably moved was Andrew Jackson's Specie
Circular, which effectively destroyed local paper as currency of exchange. This form of providence, a secular intrusion from Beyond that cast a fragile human system into
disarray, was itself a trial for the human animal, offering
chances for recovery or for the forging of new accommodations to destiny in which some men rose and others fell.
Some merely went to Texas. Baldwin moved on to the final
phase of his career, not because of failure but because of
continued ambition, and his destination was not Rackinsack, Arkansas, or the Brazos in Texas, but the very different frontier of post−gold rush California. A specialist in
civil law, he would find time there in the midst of a prosperous practice and a term on the state supreme court to
begin "The Flush Times of California." Although the manu-
script was never finished, Baldwin's first book on the original Flush Times continued to be read, partly because of his
generation's nostalgia for a period of social chaos that seemed

increasingly benign as an entire nation lurched closer to civil conflict. But *Flush Times* remained a classic long after its author's death in 1864 not simply because it was sprightly social history. It was also a fascinating memoir by a man of uncommon subtlety of mind who projected his own sensibility into the record. If the explicit drama of this book is the triumph of society over disorder through the agency of civilizing institutions, the covert victory is the survival and success of the autobiographical narrator, ratified by the publication and popularity of the account itself.

Except for the Strother and Prentiss profiles, however, that account generally reads more like fiction than like history or autobiography and for reasons other than the preponderance of character studies and anecdotes. Whether we choose to designate his second self as persona or narrator or autobiographical hero or "Baldwin," his intricate use of himself as character is a major fictive act that radiates strongly throughout *Flush Times*. The author puts his chief character through paces that will allow him to earn the role of hero: Baldwin the writer, the self presently in power as he calls up his retrospective self along with its historical context, in effect validates his identity by linking that earlier self with the worst excesses of his era. But he only links; he does not equate. The present self cannot but be a revisionist historian-autobiographer. While there is nothing to make us suppose that Baldwin was one of the scoundrels, his literary act is itself a kind of cultural redemption for the Flush Times. He readily submits his naïve self to professional humiliation ("My First Appearance at the Bar"); he admits that there was a touch of fraudulence in his getting a license to

practice, but not being asked legal questions also demonstrates the ineptness of his betters ("The Bench and the
Bar"); he includes himself among the opportunists in his vi-
gnettes of ignorance and expedience, but to remove some of
the taint he also comes to share the glory he himself causes
to be shed all around ("The Bar of the South-West").

Baldwin's writing, which has been described as "gentle," is
sometimes regarded as an anomaly, presumably because it
lacks the verbal pugnacity of the half horse–half alligators
whose vernacular idioms trigger the tall tale and invigorate
much of the writing of the frontier in general. But Big Bears
are not the only inhabitants of the literary Southwest, and
neither are their rhetorical fireworks the stylistic norm. The
complex issue of realism in southwestern humor is too often
reduced to the degree to which the backwoods figures and
their dialect dominate the sketches in which they appear.
Given such a measurement, Baldwin seems to be uncon-
cerned with realism, since we hear the voice of the authorial
narrator more often than we hear the competing voices of
even his most colorful characters. Compared with George
Washington Harris' invention of backwoods rococo for his
Sut Lovingood—one of the great linguistic achievements in
American literature—Baldwin's version of yeoman speech
is modestly functional. Moreover, the tension of classes and
values implied by the linguistic contrast between gentleman
and backwoodsman is neither as explicit nor as pervasive in
Flush Times as it is in such pieces as Thorpe's "The Big
Bear of Arkansas" and "The Indefatigable Bear-Hunter."
    While frontier brag and the braggart's hijinks in the tall

tale were important contributions to the language and kinetic narratives of American literary realism, we should not forget that most Old Southwest authors promoted their vernacular characters within and through a prose that was relentlessly mainstream. The impact of Addison and other essayists and of Irving and the Knickerbocker school is especially evident in the more literarily ambitious of the humorists. The enclosing style in Longstreet, Hooper, Thorpe, and Baldwin is conservative (even a trifle old-fashioned in its "correctness"), allusive, and self-consciously witty in its projection of an authorial persona. Such a genteel style may seem oddly suited to, say, the anecdote as practical joke, until we remember that the humor of the Old Southwest resists the kind of taxonomy favored by generic purists. This cultural phenomenon comprises many modes, some of them undeniably refractory. The story of frontier humor, like that of much of American literature, is the story of unstable forms. The folk tale, the sporting letter, the sketch, the essay, the travel account, the memoir, the newspaper filler, the ethnic joke, the tall tale that shades imperceptibly into fantasy: all these and more flow into the genre we have chosen to call southwestern humor.

Not all these modes find their way into Baldwin's writing. The most common are the character study and the anecdote of varying length and complication, as well as the complexly structured essay. The sketches in *Flush Times* feature anecdotal whimsy rather than physical action because Baldwin's primary interest is not narrative but character, especially as it develops into representative figures in the legal fraternity. There are rascals, frauds, and confidence men among his portraits, but the flashier braggarts whose competitive rhetoric threatens mayhem are conspicuously missing.

Flush Times is the most richly textured of all the volumes of southwestern humor, and none of the others depends so heavily on legal Latin, which punctuates these sketches as insistently as do the allusions to Shakespeare, Byron, Johnson, Irving, Goldsmith, and Lamb. Both devices attest to the intimate alliance between American literature and the law, one with longer-lasting relevance in the South than elsewhere in the nation. Unlike *Georgia Scenes*, for which Longstreet deliberately created two personas, the better to encompass the variety and tone of life in the more remote counties of Georgia, *Flush Times* is intensely specialized, dominated by a single, well-read, semi-autobiographical narrator—projected, however, at different stages during his eighteen years in the Old Southwest.

The substance of the book is what the narrator himself sees and reports. Although the devices vary—segments of action reduced to mere authorial summary ("Sharp Financiering"), or related by internal narrators ("Cave Burton, Esq., of Kentucky"), or literally dramatized ("Samuel Hele, Esq.")—the voice of Baldwin's persona is dominant, and his authority and control are never threatened by alternate narrators. Experience outside his ken, moreover, is rigorously omitted. Eschewing the folkloristic exaggeration of the tall tale, its marvelous creatures in the wild, and its stylized rhetoric whose extended play is often thought to be the measure of the distinctive backwoods idiom, Baldwin's anecdotes never stray from the possible and only occasionally from the plausible.

In only two sketches—the most action we see in the book—does Baldwin depict raucous physicality, and in each case the social chaos is muted by the containing techniques of the narrator. Cave Burton's Earthquake Story, in which a sequence of disruptive accidents brings a courthouse to the verge of anarchy, is an inset piece that climaxes an otherwise rambling, desultory narrative. And in "Justification after Verdict," in which a naïf's faux pas in a restaurant creates the kind of slapstick havoc later made famous by the silent film, the action is twice removed, reaching us not as a witness' testimony but as the court stenographer's *notes* of the testimony. Although both sketches are structured as farce, as are the rambunctious pranks of Sut Lovingood, Baldwin's farce is mediated by and subordinated to the regulated pace of the narrator's own strategies and style.

The realism of Baldwin's work is in the integrity of the narrator's sensibility itself, not in the explosive bursts of ring-tailed roaring. While his ear for rural dialects was as acute as Longstreet's or Thorpe's, vernacular segments in his sketches are coherently related to the general purpose of the pieces rather than being conspicuous bravura exercises. In view of the standardized practice in the nineteenth-century popular press of representing southern speech by a mere handful of orthographical tricks, Baldwin is unusually discriminating in the portraits of his southwestern characters. Even the backwoods vernacular that he is sometimes charged with ignoring makes its logical and tactful appearance. The transcriptlike exchange between the lawyer and the aspirant in "Examining a Candidate for License" would be pointless without it; so too the grievance that the narrator must deal with in "Old Uncle John Olive" and the drunken candor of Ned Ellett in "Jonathan and the Constable." The compulsive patter of the country con man of "John Stout, Esq., and Mark Sullivan" demonstrates the marginal survival techniques of small-change frauds. And despite the overlay of epistolary formulas, the letters from Simon Suggs, Jr., to an eastern editor who requested a biographical sketch are triumphant reminders of the oral origins of the vernacular tradition: "Im obleeged to you for your perlite say so, and so forth. I got a friend to rite it—my own ritin being mostly perfeshunal."

In addition to the language of such occasional ne'er-do-wells and habitués of the doggeries as Jonas Sykes ("An Affair of Honor"), Baldwin uses a variety of idioms and speech rhythms to indicate educational and class distinctions among lawyers as well as their litigious clients: the shrewd and witty Irish, both at the bar and in the docket ("Jo. Heyfron," "Scan. Mag."); the garrulousness of a lawyer whose appetite is greater for oysters than for the finer points of law ("Cave Burton, Esq., of Kentucky"); a Georgia militia major, a sturdy "dimmycrat," who fears that his cowardice in the courtroom will disgrace his party ("The Bench and the Bar"); a pretentious schoolmaster whose pedantic testimony in court reflects Baldwin's scorn for one of Virginia's legacies—inflated public address ("Assault and Battery"); and

the testy, plain-speaking squire who cynically appropriates
the language of courtly paternalism to counter the propriety
of a Yankee schoolmarm infected with the ideas of Harriet
Beecher Stowe ("Samuel Hele, Esq.").

In Baldwin's portraits the colorful denizens of the backwoods are not dominant because historically they were not.
Flush Times delineates that cultural moment in which hordes
of heterogeneous, ambitious outsiders not only thronged to
the new lands but also set the tone for the socially unstable
communities they quickly contrived. Some of the settlers
may have been what gentlemen in the older states would
have considered backwoodsmen, but most who came to the
Southwest "brought property—many of them a great deal,"
as Baldwin accurately observes: "Nearly every man was a
speculator; at any rate, a trader."

Insofar as he faithfully captures this moment, *Flush Times*
is dependable social history. It is memorable because it is a
work of art that happily exploits imaginative skills to supple-
ment and indeed reshape memorial reconstruction. Baldwin's governing aesthetic metaphor in *Flush Times* is his
"gallery of daubs," and he frequently refers to the image of
his canvas, of paintings and portraits, of charcoal sketches,
of nibbing his pen to a fine hair-stroke, of the difficulty
in transcribing mental pictures into anything but coarse
copies—in effect admitting the importance of imagination
in the writing of social history. "A writer usually catches
something from, as well as communicates something to, his
subject," he writes at the end of "The Bar of the South-
West." If "some old fogy" should charge the writer with

being "little better than a romancer in prose," he can just blame it on the author's subject matter—"two or three regiments of lawyers." A genial exaggeration in itself, the phrase also locates the source of lying as a high art in the very profession whose lore unifies this book. We should not forget that Baldwin chose "Ovid Bolus, Esq." as his initial sketch. Like Bolus, whose lying narratives presume to be circumstantial realism, Baldwin contrives his with enough sly inventiveness "to make the several facts of the narrative fall in very gracefully with the principal scheme." His famous liar operates with such freedom because he had long ago "torn down the partition wall between his imagination and his memory," and if Baldwin never goes as far as Bolus, he too at times makes little distinction between "the impressions made upon his mind by what came *from* it, and what came *to* it."

By a cheerfully unsystematic union of those two kinds of impressions, the inventive memoirist creates as well as finds a landscape, envisions as well as describes the dynamics of a people who for a cultural moment happened to occupy that space. For his given geography, Baldwin shapes elliptical, stylized, generic settings. While counties and towns occur by name, usually disguised, none is depicted. In his economy of description, no settlement, village, or town is unique. The first stop in his migration from Virginia was "on the thither side of the state line of Alabama, in the charming village of P."; his first appearance at the bar was "in the town of H——, State of Alabama"; he argues a case in "the Kemper Court." Like Baldwin, he is mobile, indif-

ferent to coherent chronology or particularized places. Even
when the autobiographical narrator is merely a background
presence, in those sketches formally structured as anecdote
or profile, place names are perfunctory: "the Circuit court of
N * * * * * * Mississippi"; "the flourishing village of M.";
"the S. Circuit Court"; "the neighborhood of M——ville."
The more explicit the place names—Screamersville, Splitskull—the more satiric their function.

With their emphasis on the bench and bar, the anecdotes, profiles, and essays in *Flush Times* betray no aware-
ness of natural geography or that persistent interest in landscape, either aesthetic or utilitarian, so often revealed by
visitors and settlers alike in the 1830s. Unlike Thomas
Bangs Thorpe, for example, Baldwin is not fascinated by
the symbiotic relationship of physical place and human
character. There is in fact scarcely a passage of scenic description that would enable the reader to imagine what frontier Alabama and Mississippi even *looked* like. Only when
he is surveying the bar and evaluating his contemporaries
does he even bother to distinguish Alabama and Mississippi. These states in the years just before and after 1837
are of a piece: while the region may be unique, its specific
locales are much too similar for differentiation.

If the professional focus in the book diminishes the impact of physical geography, it also affects noticeably the
form and function of individual sketches. As we have seen,
the times served some Virginians by forcing them to invent
a cleaner, more practical legal style—hence Baldwin's emphasis on the contrast between their courtroom manner at

home and in exile. But the simpler style in legal argumenta-
tion encouraged by a rough society also nourished, for
better or worse, another kind of theater. If, as Baldwin
claims, the traditional "Fourth of Julyisms" were so routed
that they flourished mostly on the stump and at political
barbeques, the victory had formal implications in his writing. Stripped of oratorical encumbrances, courtroom dra-
mas became in substance efficient legal versions of the
fight, the sporting contest, the card game, and in form the
generic equivalent of the anecdote or practical joke. *Flush
Times* is rich in those forms (and in the structurally interesting essays), but not in complex narratives. Significantly, the
only example of the shaggy tale is Cave Burton's Earthquake
Story, in which the teller, humiliated by the brisk efficiency
of his fellows who act rather than tell, stands out as the man
of appetite done in by his own mouth. With its longueurs
and looping irrelevancies, the rambling, shaggy tale thus
parallels the rhetorical humbug of the old-style courtroom
performance.

If courtroom drama in the new country historically became commensurate with the kind played out publicly and
regularly in the community at large, literarily its frequency
in *Flush Times*—humor as both source and scene—suggests the pervasiveness of winning and losing as a cultural
model in the Old Southwest. As we might expect, the courtroom dominates Baldwin's world: formal or makeshift, it is
the central stage for his players' competition. But the forensic emphasis spills over into such subsidiary stages as the
boardinghouse, doggery, stagecoach inn, and dining room—

arenas where the combative skills of the courtroom continue. Furthermore, the drama on the main stage cannot be enacted in private. Nor can that on the secondary stages. Designed for its maximum impact as exposure, and facilitated by schemes, tricks, and maneuvers, the game of winning and losing is played in public, where its players are redeemed or defeated. In the Baldwin model, there is no private occasion because there is no private space.

The politics of the balloting station are no different from those of the hustings. Such private virtues as integrity and honor are insufficient as constituent identity until openly challenged and tested. As we see in "Squire A. and the Fritters" and "Cave Burton, Esq., of Kentucky," the convivial board is also the competitive board—another opportunity for concocting stratagems at the expense of one of the parties present. The organic family has scarcely more impact in Baldwin than it has in Hemingway. Only the cheerful Major Wormley and his adoring wife and daughters, a family out of Goldsmith transposed to a ragtag Alabama plantation, glow with domestic sentiment, and even that glow is supplied by a patronizing lawyer more in rhythm with the frontier sharper than with other displaced Virginians. The family hearth must serve also as public accommodation. Even the bedroom reflects the nineteenth-century necessity of multiple occupancy of rooms and beds. Jonathan in "Jonathan and the Constable" uses his bedroom as an extension of his office, and his younger roommate—the narrator "possuming sleep"—eavesdrops while the drunk constable gives a candid judgment of Jonathan's lawyering.

Even in the mildest cases of personal discomfiture, "blabbing this thing all over town" is a social given, not an idle threat.

Indeed, the one mystery in *Flush Times*—the one in which *what happened?* generates the action—is worth noting in this light. Although it derives from the standard motif of the provincial in the city, "Justification after Verdict" is skillfully constructed and rich in character relationships. The narrator's client, Paul Beechim, is charged with the public beating of Phillip Cousins after the two former friends return from a trip to New Orleans. While accepting the guilty verdict, Beechim refuses to divulge the circumstances that might mitigate his punishment. This is the only sketch in which privacy seems to take precedence over the drama of public revelation. But that priority is of course overturned, as it must be in this world of full disclosure. The secret is breached in court by a third party, a fellow villager who had also been in New Orleans at the time of the mysterious incident. The assault, he reveals, was Beechim's retaliation for being humiliated by Cousins at a fashionable restaurant.

Self-deluded, Beechim is an extreme example of the provincial who thinks himself a cosmopolitan, and is guilty therefore of pride as well as narrow experience. Knoxville, which he regards "at once the Athens and Paris of America," is his model of refinement during his exile in the new country. "Rusticity and vulgarity were abominations to him," notes the narrator, and though he was "an excellent fellow," his "high-church Knoxvillism" invites irreverence.

In this variation the bumpkin drinks the water from his finger bowl—Beechim is told it is "sop" for his fresh pineapple. Baldwin's hotel scene is at once funny and painful. Beechim is generally unobservant, but the eyes of other diners—"ladies, dandies, foreigners, moustached fellows"—are predictably drawn to the mess he makes on his plate. Their laughter escalates when the gulled diner finishes his course and observes primly and loudly, "'I think the pine-apple very good, but don't you think the sauce is rather insipid?'" In his rush to escape the scene of his humiliation, Beechim creates enough havoc to make the next morning's *Picayune* ("no names given"). The judge declares, "Justification complete!" when the truth comes out, but the price of public exoneration is exposure. Before the embarrassed Beechim leaves town he tells his lawyer: "You have saved my body but you have ruined my character. . . . But . . . if—you—can—help—it—don't—let—this—thing—get—back—to—Knoxville." The incident now enters local lore, perpetuated by public repetition and, in a larger context, by Baldwin's written version, which will itself surely "get—back—to—Knoxville."

Our emotional response to this anecdote is complex. Like all dupes in such stories, the central figure gets his comeuppance for inadequate self-knowledge, and if pride goes before his fall, it continues afterward as well. Yet his anguished cry—"you have ruined my character"—is an accurate self-assessment, since Beechim knows that all private aspects of character must be submitted to public verification. We grudgingly admire his retaliation, along with the

official court that exposes him, in part because the wag
ceases to be a character after his joke in New Orleans. Although bloodied by a cane, Cousins is literally not a party to
the court action and disappears from the story. His punishment, which in some stories would follow the biter-bit pattern, is in Baldwin's sketch only a passing necessity of the
narrative, presumably unworthy of comment either by a
spokesman within the sketch or by the narrator. The verdict
seems less an expression of even comic justice than an occasion for public entertainment, so much so that the judge's
final words, "The Court adjourns for refreshment," seem almost redundant.

Flush Times is primarily Baldwin's gallery of lawyers of
widely varying talents (ranging from the brilliant to the ignorant) and professional ethics (ranging from the conscien-
tious to the fraudulent). Somewhere in the middle range are
the author and his friends who act on their breaks in the
exciting new country. Although they may be honest and
skillful, they are also opportunistic: "It was a merry time for
us craftsmen," the narrator remembers, "and we brightened
up mightily, and shook our quills joyously, like goslings in
the midst of a shower." He looks back upon those times of
judicial and economic confusion "with the pious gratitude
and serene satisfaction with which the wreckers near the
Florida Keys contemplate the last fine storm."

It is this voice that makes *Flush Times* distinctive. Despite Baldwin's good ear for vernacular rhythms and a hand
for reproducing them accurately, his real achievement is the
creation of a literary self, a persona whose wit, ambivalence,

and elegant control are themselves an effective stylistic medium of psychological realism. The complex spectacle of frontier experience supplied Baldwin not only materials that could be transformed into humor but also the primary biographical occasion for humanizing motive and act.

The
FLUSH TIMES
of
ALABAMA
and
MISSISSIPPI

Simeon Suggs Jr.

THE

FLUSH TIMES

OF

ALABAMA AND MISSISSIPPI.

A Series of Sketches.

BY

JOSEPH G. BALDWIN.

NEW-YORK:
D. APPLETON AND COMPANY,
200 BROADWAY.
LONDON: 16 LITTLE BRITAIN.
M.DCCC.LIII.

PREFACE.

———•••———

Some of these papers were published in the Southern Literary Messenger, and having met with a favorable reception from the Public, and a portion of the Press, the author has yielded to the solicitations of his own vanity, and other flattering friends, and collected them in a volume with other pieces of the same general character. The scheme of the articles he believes to be original in design and execution,—at least, no other work with which he is acquainted, has been published in the United States designed to illustrate the periods, the characters, and the phases of society, some notion of which is attempted to be given in this volume. The author, under the tremor of a

first publication, felt strongly inclined to offer a
sneaking apology for the many errors and imperfections of his work ; such as the fact that the articles
were written in 'haste, under the pressure of professional engagements and amidst constant interruptions ;
and that he has no time or opportunity for correction
and revision. But he anticipated the too ready answer to such a plea : " If you had no time to write
well, why did you write at all ? Who constrained you ?
If you were not in dress to see company, why come
unbidden into the presence of the public ? Why not,
at least, wait until you were fit to be presented ? "
He confesses that he sees no way to answer these
tough questions, unless the apology of Falstaff for
rushing into the presence of *King* Hal, " before he
had time to *have* made new liveries "—" stained with
travel and sweating with desire to see him,"—be a
good one—as, " inferring the zeal he had to see him "
—" the earnestness of affection "—" the devotion : "
but in poor Jack's case, " *not to deliberate, not to remember, not to have patience to shift him,*" was not
a very effectual excuse for his coming out of sorts ;
and we are afraid, that that other Sovereign, the

Public, is not more facile of approach, or more credulous of excuses ; for, unfortunately, the ardor of an author's greeting is something beyond the heat of the Public's reception of him, or, as Pat expresses it, the reciprocity of feeling is all on one side.

Without apology, therefore, he gives these leaves to the winds,—with that feeling of comfort and composure which comes of the knowledge that, let the venture go as it may, he loses little who puts but little at hazard.

The author begs to return to the accomplished Editor of the Messenger, JNO. R. THOMPSON, ESQ., his acknowledgments, for revising and correcting this work as it passed through the press.

LIVINGSTON, *Ala.*, 1853.

CONTENTS.

———●●●———

OVID BOLUS, ESQ.,

ATTORNEY AT LAW AND SOLICITOR IN CHANCERY.

A Fragment.

———◆◆———

*　　*　　*　　*　　*　　*　　*

AND what history of that halcyon period, ranging from the
year of Grace, 1835, to 1837; that golden era, when shin-
plasters were the sole currency; when bank-bills were " as
thick as Autumn leaves in Vallambrosa," and credit was a
franchise,—what history of those times would be complete,
that left out the name of Ovid Bolus? As well write the
biography of Prince Hal, and forbear all mention of Falstaff.
In law phrase, the thing would be a " deed without a
name," and void; a most unpardonable *casus omissus*.

　I cannot trace, for reasons the sequel suggests, the early
history, much less the birth-place, pedigree, and juvenile
associations of this worthy. Whence he or his forbears got
his name or how, I don't know: but for the fact that it is to
be inferred he got it in infancy, I should have thought he

borrowed it: he borrowed every thing else he ever had, such things as he got under the credit system only excepted: in deference, however, to the axiom, that there is *some* exception to *all* general rules, I am willing to believe that he got this much honestly, by *bona fide* gift or inheritance, and without false pretence.

I have had a hard time of it in endeavoring to assign to Bolus his leading vice: I have given up the task in despair; but I have essayed to designate that one which gave him, in the end, most celebrity. I am aware that it is invidious to make comparisons, and to give pre-eminence to one over other rival qualities and gifts, where all have high claims to distinction: but, then, the stern justice of criticism, in this case, requires a discrimination, which, to be intelligible and definite, must be relative and comparative. I, therefore, take the responsibility of saying, after due reflection, that in my opinion, Bolus's reputation stood higher for lying than for any thing else: and in thus assigning pre-eminence to this poetic property, I do it without any desire to derogate from other brilliant characteristics belonging to the same general category, which have drawn the wondering notice of the world.

Some men are liars from interest; not because they have no regard for truth, but because they have less regard for it than for gain: some are liars from vanity, because they would rather be well thought of by others, than have reason for thinking well of themselves: some are liars from a sort of necessity, which overbears, by the weight of temptation, the

sense of virtue : some are enticed away by the beguile-
ments of pleasure, or seduced by evil example and education.
Bolus was none of these : he belonged to a higher department
of the fine arts, and to a higher class of professors of this
sort of Belles-Lettres. Bolus was a natural liar, just as
some horses are natural pacers, and some dogs natural set-
ters. What he did in that walk, was from the irresistible
promptings of instinct, and a disinterested love of art. His
genius and his performances were free from the vulgar alloy
of interest or temptation. Accordingly, he did not labor a
lie : he lied with a relish : he lied with a coming appetite,
growing with what it fed on : he lied from the delight of invention and the charm of fictitious narrative. It is true he
applied his art to the practical purposes of life ; but in so far
did he glory the more in it ; just as an ingenious machinist
rejoices that his invention, while it has honored science, has
also supplied a common want.

Bolus's genius for lying was encyclopediacal : it was what
German criticism calls many-sided. It embraced all subjects
without distinction or partiality. It was equally good upon
all, " from grave to gay, from lively to severe."

Bolus's lying came from his greatness of soul and his
comprehensiveness of mind. The truth was too small for
him. Fact was too dry and common-place for the fervor of
his genius. Besides, great as was his memory—for he even
remembered the outlines of his chief lies—his invention was
still larger. He had a great contempt for history and histo-
rians. He thought them tame and timid cobblers ; mere

tinkers on other people's wares,—simple parrots and magpies of other men's sayings or doings; borrowers of and acknowledged debtors for others' chattels, got without skill; they had no separate estate in their ideas: they were bailers of goods, which they did not pretend to hold by adverse title; buriers of talents in napkins making no usury; barren and unprofitable non-producers in the intellectual vineyard—*nati consumere fruges*.

He adopted a fact occasionally to start with, but, like a Sheffield razor and the crude ore, the workmanship, polish and value were all his own: a Thibet shawl could as well be credited to the insensate goat that grew the wool, as the author of a fact Bolus honored with his artistical skill, could claim to be the inventor of the story.

His experiments upon credulity, like charity, began at home. He had long torn down the partition wall between his imagination and his memory. He had long ceased to distinguish between the impressions made upon his mind by what came *from* it, and what came *to* it: all ideas were facts to him.

Bolus's life was not a common man's life. His world was not the hard, work-day world the groundlings live in: he moved in a sphere of poetry: he lived amidst the ideal and romantic. Not that he was not practical enough, when he chose to be: by no means. He bought goods and chattels, lands and tenements, like other men; but he got them under a state of poetic illusion, and paid for them in an imaginary way. Even the titles he gave were not of the *earthy*

sort—they were sometimes *clouded*. He gave notes, too,—
how well I know it!—like other men; he paid them like
himself.

How well he asserted the Spiritual over the Material!
How he delighted to turn an abstract idea into concrete cash
—to make a few blots of ink, representing a little thought,
turn out a labor-saving machine, and bring into his pocket
money which many days of hard exhausting labor would not
procure! What pious joy it gave him to see the days of
the good Samaritan return, and the hard hand of avarice relax its grasp on land and negroes, pork and clothes, beneath
the soft speeches and kind promises of future rewards—
blending in the act the three cardinal virtues, Faith, Hope,
and Charity; while, in the result, the chief of these three
was *Charity* !

There was something sublime in the idea—this elevating the spirit of man to its true and primeval dominion
over things of sense and grosser matter.

It is true, that in these practical romances, Bolus was
charged with a defective taste in repeating himself. The
justice of the charge must be, at least, partially acknowledged : this I know from a client, to whom Ovid sold a tract of
land after having sold it twice before : I cannot say, though,
that his forgetting to mention this circumstance made any
difference, for Bolus originally had no title.

There was nothing narrow, sectarian, or sectional, in
Bolus's lying. It was on the contrary broad and catholic.
It had no respect to times or places. It was as wide, illimit-

able, as elastic and variable as the air he spent in giving it
expression. It was a generous, gentlemanly, whole-souled
faculty. It was employed often on, and in behalf of, objects
and occasions of this sort, but no more and no more zeal-
ously on these than on others of no profit to himself. He
was an Egotist, but a magnificent one : he was not a liar because an egotist, but an egotist because a liar. He usually
made himself the hero of the romantic exploits and adventures he narrated ; but this was not so much to exalt himself, as because it was more convenient to his art. He had
nothing malignant or invidious in his nature. If he exalted
himself, it was seldom or never to the disparagement of others, unless, indeed, those others were merely imaginary persons, or too far off to be hurt. He would as soon lie for
you as for himself. It was all the same, so there was something doing in his line of business, except in those cases in
which his necessities required to be fed at your expense.

He did not confine himself to mere lingual lying: one
tongue was not enough for all the business he had on hand.
He acted lies as well. Indeed, sometimes his very silence
was a lie. He made nonentity fib for him, and performed
wondrous feats by a " masterly inactivity."

The *personnel* of this distinguished Votary of the Muse,
was happily fitted to his art. He was strikingly handsome.
There was something in his air and bearing almost princely,
certainly quite distinguished. His manners were winning,
his address frank, cordial and flowing. He was built after
the model and structure of Bolingbroke in his youth, *Ameri-*

canized and *Hoosierized* a little by a "raising in," and an
adaptation to, the Backwoods. He was fluent but choice of
diction, a little sonorous in the structure of his sentences to
give effect to a voice like an organ. His countenance was
open and engaging, usually sedate of expression, but capable
of any modifications at the shortest notice. Add to this his
intelligence, shrewdness, tact, humor, and that he was a ready
debater and elegant declaimer, and had the gift of bringing
out, to the fullest extent, his resources, and you may see that
Ovid, in a new country, was a man apt to make no mean impression. He drew the loose population around him, as the
magnet draws iron filings. He was the man for the "boys,"
—then a numerous and influential class. His generous profusion and free-handed manner impressed them as the bounty
of Cæsar the loafing commonalty of Rome: Bolus was no
niggard. He never higgled or chaffered about small things.
He was as free with his own money—if he ever had any of
his own—as with yours. If he never paid borrowed money,
he never asked payment of others. If you wished him to loan
you any, he would hand you a handful without counting it:
if you handed him any, you were losing time in counting it,
for you never saw any thing of it again: Shallow's funded
debt on Falstaff were as safe an investment: this would have
been an equal commerce, but, unfortunately for Bolus's friends,
the proportion between his disbursements and receipts was
something scant. Such a spendthrift never made a track
even in the flush times of 1836. It took as much to support
him as a first class steamboat. His bills at the groceries

were as long as John Q. Adams' Abolition petition, or, if
pasted together, would have matched the great Chartist memorial. He would as soon treat a regiment or charter the
grocery for the day, as any other way; and after the crowd
had heartily drank—some of them "laying their souls in
soak,"—if he did not have the money convenient—as when
did he?—he would fumble in his pocket, mutter something
about nothing less than a $100 bill, and direct the score, with
a lordly familiarity, to be charged to his account.

Ovid had early possessed the faculty of ubiquity. He
had been born in more places than Homer. In an hour's discourse, *he* would, with more than the speed of Ariel, travel
at every point of the compass, from Portland to San Antonio,
some famous adventure always occurring just as he "rounded
to," or while stationary, though he did not remain longer
than to see it. He was present at every important debate
in the Senate at Washington, and had heard every popular
speaker on the hustings, at the bar and in the pulpit, in the
United States. He had been concerned in many important
causes with Grymes and against Mazereau in New Orleans,
and had borne no small share in the fierce forensic battles,
which, with singular luck, *he* and Grymes always won in the
courts of the Crescent City. And such frolics as they had
when they laid aside their heavy armor, after the heat and
burden of the day! Such gambling! A negro *ante* and
twenty on the call, was moderate playing. What lots of
"Ethiopian captives" and other plunder *he raked down*
vexed Arithmetic to count and credulity to believe; and, had

it not been for Bolus's generosity in giving "the boys" a chance to win back *by doubling off on the high hand*, there is no knowing what changes of owners would not have occurred in the Rapides or on the German Coast.

The Florida war and the Texas Revolution, had each furnished a brilliant theatre for Ovid's chivalrous emprise. Jack Hays and he were great chums. Jack and he had many a hearty laugh over the odd trick of Ovid, in lassoing a Camanche Chief, while galloping a stolen horse bare-backed, up the San Saba hills. But he had the rig on Jack again, when he made him charge on a brood of about twenty Camanches, who had got into a mot of timber in the prairies, and were shooting their arrows from the covert, Ovid, with a six-barrelled rifle, taking them on the wing as Jack rode in and flushed them !

It was an affecting story and feelingly told, that of his and Jim Bowie's rescuing an American girl from the Apaches, and returning her to her parents in St. Louis ; and it would have been still more tender, had it not been for the unfortunate necessity Bolus was under of shooting a brace of gay lieutenants on the border, one frosty morning, before breakfast, back of the fort, for taking unbecoming liberties with the fair damosel, the spoil of his bow and spear.

But the girls Ovid courted, and the miraculous adventures he had met with in love beggared by the comparison, all the fortune of war had done for him. Old Nugent's daughter, Sallie, was his narrowest escape. Sallie was accomplished to the romantic extent of two ocean steamers, and

1*

four blocks of buildings in Boston, separated only from immediate "perception and pernancy," by the contingency of
old Nugent's recovering from a confirmed dropsy, for which
he had been twice ineffectually tapped.   The day was set—
the presents made— *enperle* of course—the guests invited :
the old Sea Captain insisted on Bolus's setting his negroes
free, and taking five thousand dollars apiece for the loss.
Bolus's love for the "peculiar institution" wouldn't stand it.
Rather than submit to such degradation, Ovid broke off the
match, and left Sallie broken-hearted ; a disease from which
she did not recover until about six months afterwards, when
she ran off with the mate of her father's ship, the Sea Serpent,
in the Rio trade.

Gossip and personal anecdote were the especial subjects
of Ovid's elocution.   He was intimate with all the notabili-
ties of the political circles.   He was a privileged visitor of
the political green-room.   He was admitted back into the
laboratory where the political thunder was manufactured, and
into the office where the magnetic wires were worked.   He
knew the origin of every party question and movement, and
had a finger in every pie the party cooks of Tammany baked
for the body politic.

One thing in Ovid I can never forgive.   This was his
coming it over poor Ben O.   I don't object to it on the score
of the swindle.   That was to have been expected.   But swindling Ben was degrading the dignity of the art.   True, it illustrated the universality of his science, but it lowered it to
a beggarly process of mean deception.   There was no skill

in it. It was little better than crude larceny. A child could have done it; it had as well been done to a child. It was like catching a cow with a lariat, or setting a steel trap for a pet pig. True, Bolus had nearly practised out of custom. He had worn his art threadbare. Men, who could afford to be cheated, had all been worked up or been scared away. Besides, Ford couldn't be put off. He talked of money in a most ominous connection with blood. The thing could be settled by a bill of exchange. Ben's name was unfortunately good—the amount some $1,600. Ben *had* a fine tract of land in S——r. He has not got it now. Bolus only gave Ben one wrench—that was enough. Ben never breathed easy afterwards. All the V's and X's of ten years' hard practice, went in that penful of ink. Fie! Bolus, Monroe Edwards wouldn't have done that. He would sooner have sunk down to the level of some honest calling for a living, than have put his profession to so mean a shift. I can conceive of but one extenuation; Bolus was on the lift for Texas, and the desire was natural to qualify himself for citizenship.

The genius of Bolus, strong in its unassisted strength, yet gleamed out more brilliantly under the genial influence of "the rosy." With boon companions and "reaming suats," it was worth while to hear him of a winter evening. He could "gild the palpable and the familiar, with golden exhalations of the dawn." The most common-place objects became dignified. There was a history to the commonest articles about him: that book was given him by Mr. Van Buren

—the walking stick was a present from Gen. Jackson : the thrice-watered Monongahela, just drawn from the grocery hard by, was the last of a distillation of 1825, smuggled in from Ireland, and presented to him. by a friend in New Orleans, on easy terms with the collector; the cigars, not too fragrant, were of a box sent him by a schoolmate from Cuba, in 1834—*before* he visited the Island.   And talking of Cuba —he had met with an adventure there, the impression of which never could be effaced from his mind.   He had gone, at the instance of Don Carlos y Cubanos, (an intimate classmate in a Kentucky Catholic College,) whose life he had saved from a mob in Louisville, at the imminent risk of his own.   The Don had a sister of blooming sixteen, the least of whose charms was two or three coffee plantations, some hundreds of slaves, and a suitable garnish of doubloons, accumulated during her minority, in the hands of her uncle and guardian, the Captain General.   All went well with the young lovers—for such, of course, they were—until Bolus, with his usual frank indiscretion, in a conversation with the Priest, avowed himself a Protestant.   Then came trouble.   Every effort was made to convert him ; but Bolus's faith resisted the eloquent tongue of the Priest, and the more eloquent eyes of Donna Isabella.   The brother pleaded the old friendship —urged a seeming and formal conformity—the Captain General urged the case like a politician—the Señorita like a warm and devoted woman.   All would not do.   The Captain General forbade his longer sojourn on the Island.   Bolus took leave of the fair Señorita : the parting interview held in the orange bower, was affecting : Donna Isabella, with dishevelled hair, threw herself at his feet ; the tears streamed from her eyes : in liquid tones, broken by grief, she implored him to relent,—reminded him of her love, of her trust in him, and of the consequences—now not much longer to be concealed— of that love and trust ; ("though I protest," Bolus would say, "I don't know what she meant exactly by *that*.") "Gentlemen," Bolus continued, "I confess to the weakness—I wavered—but then my eyes happened to fall on the breast-pin with a lock of my mother's hair—I recovered my courage : I shook her gently from me. I felt my last hold on earth was loosened—my last hope of peace destroyed. Since that hour, my life has been a burden. Yes, gentlemen, you see before you a broken man—a martyr to his Religion. But, away with these melancholy thoughts : boys, pass around the jorum." And wiping his eyes, he drowned the wasting sorrow in a long draught of the poteen ; and, being much refreshed, was able to carry the burden on a little further,— *videlicet*, to the next lie.

It must not be supposed that Bolus was destitute of the tame virtue of prudence—or that this was confined to the avoidance of the improvident habit of squandering his money in paying old debts. He took reasonably good care of his person. He avoided all unnecessary exposures, chiefly from a patriotic sense, probably, of continuing his good offices to his country. His recklessness was, for the most part, lingual. To hear him talk, one might suppose he held his carcass merely for a target to try guns and

knives upon; or that the business of his life was to draw
men up to ten paces or less, for sheer improvement in marks-
manship.   Such exploits as he had gone through with,
dwarfed the heroes of romance to very pigmy and sneaking
proportions.   Pistol at the Bridge when he bluffed at honest Fluellen, might have envied the swash-buckler airs, Ovid
would sometimes put on.   But I never could exactly identify the place he had laid out for his burying-ground.   Indeed, I had occasion to know that he declined to understand several not very ambiguous hints, upon which he
might, with as good a grace as Othello, have spoken, not to
mention one or two pressing invitations which his modesty
led him to refuse.   I do not know that the base sense of
fear had any thing to do with these declinations: possibly
he might have thought he had done his share of fighting,
and did not wish to monopolize : or his principles forbade it
—I mean those which opposed his paying a debt: knowing
he could not cheat that inexorable creditor, Death, of his
claim, he did the next thing to it; which was to delay and
shirk payment as long as possible.

It remains to add a word of criticism on this great *Ly-*
ric artist.

In lying, Bolus was not only a successful, but he was a
very able practitioner.   Like every other eminent artist, he
brought all his faculties to bear upon his art.   Though
quick of perception and prompt of invention, he did not
trust himself to the inspirations of his genius for *improvis-*
ing a lie, when he could well premeditate one.   He delibe-

rately built up the substantial masonry, relying upon the occasion and its accessories, chiefly for embellishment and collateral supports: as Burke excogitated the more solid parts of his great speeches, and left unprepared only the illustrations and fancy-work.

Bolus's manner was, like every truly great man's, his own. It was excellent. He did not come blushing up to a lie, as some otherwise very passable liars do, as if he were making a mean compromise between his guilty passion or morbid vanity, and a struggling conscience. Bolus had long since settled all disputes with *his* conscience. He and it were on very good terms—at least, if there was no affection between the couple, there was no fuss in the family; or, if there were any scenes or angry passages, they were reserved for strict privacy and never got out. My own opinion is, that he was as destitute of the article as an ostrich. Thus he came to his work bravely, cheerfully and composedly. The delights of composition, invention and narration, did not fluster his style or agitate his delivery. He knew how, in the tumult of passion, to assume the "temperance to give it smoothness." A lie never ran away with him, as it is apt to do with young performers: he could always manage and guide it; and to have seen him fairly mounted, would have given you some idea of the polished elegance of D'Orsay, and the superb *menage* of Murat. There is a tone and manner of narration different from those used in delivering ideas just conceived; just as there is a difference between the sound of the voice in reading and in speaking. Bolus knew

this, and practised on it. When he was narrating, he put
the facts in order, and seemed to speak them out of his
memory ; but not formally, or as if by rote. He would stop
himself to correct a date; recollect he was wrong—he was
that year at the White Sulphur or Saratoga, &c. : having
got the date right, the names of persons present would be
incorrect, &c. : and these he corrected in turn. A stranger
hearing him, would have feared the marring of a good story
by too fastidious a conscientiousness in the narrator.

His zeal in pursuit of a lie under difficulties, was remarkable. The society around him—if such it could be
called—was hardly fitted, without some previous preparation, for an immediate introduction to Almack's or the classic precincts of Gore House. The manners of the nation
were rather plain than ornate, and candor rather than polish,
predominated in their conversation. Bolus had need of
some forbearance to withstand the interruptions and cross-
examinations, with which his revelations were sometimes received. But he possessed this in a remarkable degree. I
recollect, on one occasion, when he was giving an account of
a providential escape he was signally favored with, (when
boarded by a pirate off the Isle of Pines, and he pleaded masonry, and gave a sign he had got out of the Disclosures of
Morgan,) Tom Johnson interrupted him to say that he had
heard *that* before, (which was more than Bolus had ever
done.) B. immediately rejoined, that he had, he believed,
given him, Tom, a *running* sketch of the incident. " Rather," said Tom, " I think, a *lying* sketch." Bolus scarcely

smiled, as he replied, that Tom was a wag, and couldn't help
turning the most serious things into jests; and went on with
his usual brilliancy, to finish the narrative. Bolus did not
overcrowd his canvas. His figures were never confused,
and the subordinates and accessories did not withdraw attention from the main and substantive lie. He never squandered his lies profusely : thinking, with the poet, that
" bounteous, not prodigal, is kind Nature's hand," he kept
the golden mean between penuriousness and prodigality ;
never stingy of his lies, he was not wasteful of them, but
was rather forehanded than pushed, or embarrassed, having,
usually, fictitious stock to be freshly put on 'change, when
he wished to " make a raise." In most of his fables, he in-
culcated but a single leading idea; but contrived to make
the several facts of the narrative fall in very gracefully with
the principal scheme.

The rock on which many promising young liars, who
might otherwise have risen to merited distinction, have split,
is vanity : this marplot vice betrays itself in the exultation
manifested on the occasion of a decided hit, an exultation
too inordinate for mere recital, and which betrays authorship ; and to betray authorship, in the present barbaric,
moral and intellectual condition of the world is fatal. True,
there seems to be some inconsistency here. Dickens and Bul-
wer can do as much lying, for money too, as they choose, and
no one blame them, any more than they would blame a lawyer regularly *fee'd* to do it; but let any man, gifted with the
same genius, try his hand at it, not deliberately and in writ-

ing, but merely orally, and ugly names are given him, and
he is proscribed! Bolus heroically suppressed exultation
over the victories his lies achieved.

Alas! for the beautiful things of Earth, its flowers, its
sunsets—its lovely girls—its lies—brief and fleeting are
their date. Lying is a very delicate accomplishment. It
must be tenderly cared for, and jealously guarded. It must
not be overworked. Bolus forgot this salutary caution.
The people found out his art. However dull the commons
are as to other matters, they get sharp enough after a while,
to whatever concerns their bread and butter. Bolus not
having confined his art to political matters, sounded, at last,
the depths, and explored the limits of popular credulity.
The denizens of this degenerate age, had not the disinterestedness of Prince Hal, who " cared not how many fed at his
cost;" they got tired, at last, of promises to pay. The
credit system, common before as pump-water, adhering, like
the elective franchise to every voter, began to take the
worldly wisdom of Falstaff's mercer, and ask security; and
security liked something more substantial than plausible
promises. In this forlorn condition of the country, returning to its savage state, and abandoning the refinements of a
ripe Anglo-Saxon civilization for the sordid safety of Mexican or Chinese modes of traffic; deserting the sweet simplicity of its ancient truthfulness and the poetic illusions of
Augustus Tomlinson, for the vulgar saws of poor Richard
—Bolus, with a sigh like that breathed out by his great pro-
totype after his apostrophe to London, gathered up, one

bright moonlight night, his articles of value, shook the dust from his feet, and departed from a land unworthy of his longer sojourn. With that delicate consideration for the feelings of his friends, which, like the politeness of Charles II., never forsook him, he spared them the pain of a parting interview. He left no greetings of kindness; no messages of love : nor did he ask assurances of their lively remembrance. It was quite unnecessary. In every house he had left an autograph, in every ledger a souvenir. They will never forget him. Their connection with him will be ever regarded as

——" The *greenest* spot
In memory's waste."

Poor Ben, whom he had honored with the last marks of his confidence, can scarcely speak of him to this day, without tears in his eyes. Far away towards the setting sun he hied him, until, at last, with a hermit's disgust at the degradation of the world, like Ignatius turned monk, he pitched his tabernacle amidst the smiling prairies that sleep in vernal beauty, in the shadow of the San Saba mountains. There let his mighty genius rest. It has earned repose. We leave Themistocles to his voluntary exile.

MY FIRST APPEARANCE AT THE BAR.

HIGGINBOTHAM
        vs.   } *Slander.*
SWINK.

DID you ever, reader, get a merciless barrister of the old
school after you when you were on your first legs—in the
callow tenderness of your virgin epidermis ? I hope not. I
wish I could say the same for myself; but I cannot: and
with the faint hope of inspiring some small pity in the
breasts of the seniors, I now, one of them myself, give in
my lively experience of what befell me at my first appearance on the forensic boards.

I must premise by observing that, some twenty years
ago—more or less—shortly after I obtained license to practise law in the town of H———, State of Alabama, an unfortunate client called at my office to retain my services in
a celebrated suit for slander. The case stands on record,
Stephen O. Higginbotham vs. *Caleb Swink.* The aforesaid Caleb, " greatly envying the happy state and condition
of said Stephen," who, " until the grievances," &c., " never
had been suspected of the crime of hog-stealing," &c., said,

" in the hearing and presence of one Samuel Eads and other good and worthy citizens," of and concerning the plaintiff, " you" (the said Stephen meaning) " are a noted hog thief, and stole more hogs than all the wagons in M—— could haul off in a week on a turnpike road." The way I came to be employed was this : Higginbotham had retained Frank Glendye, a great brick in " damage cases," to bring the suit, and G. had prepared the papers, and got the case on the pleadings, ready for trial. But, while the case was getting ready, Frank was suddenly taken dangerously drunk, a disease to which his constitution was subject. The case had been continued for several terms, and had been set for a particular day of the term then going on, to be disposed of finally and positively when called. It was hoped that the lawyer would recover *his health* in time to prosecute the case; but he had continued the drunken fit with the suit. The morning of the trial came on; and, on going to see his counsel, the client found him utterly prostrate , not a hope remained of his being able to get to the court-house. He was in collapse ; a perfect cholera case. Passing down the street, almost in despair, as my good or evil genius would have it, Higginbotham met Sam Hicks, a tailor, whom I had honored with my patronage (as his books showed) for many years ; and, as one good turn deserves another—a suit for a suit— he, on hearing the predicament H. was in, boldly suggested my name to supply the place of the fallen Glendye; adding certain assurances and encomiums which did infinite credit to his friendship and his imagination.

I gathered from my calumniated client, as well as I could, the facts of the case, and got a young friend to look me up the law of slander, to be ready when it should be put through, if it ever *did* get to the jury.

The defendant was represented by old Cæsar Kasm, a famous man in those days; and well might he be. This venerable limb of the law had long practised at the M—— bar, and been the terror of this generation. He was an old-time lawyer, the race of which is now fortunately extinct, or else the survivors "lag superfluous on the stage." He was about sixty-five years old at the time I am writing of; was of stout build, and something less than six feet in height. He dressed in the old-fashioned fair-top boots and shorts; ruffled shirt, buff vest, and hair, a grizzly gray, roached up flat and stiff in front, and hanging down in a queue behind, tied with an eel-skin and pomatumed. He was close shaven and powdered every morning; and, except a few scattering grains of snuff which fell occasionally between his nose and an old-fashioned gold snuff-box, a speck of dirt was never seen on or about his carefully preserved person. The taking out of his deliciously perfumed handkerchief, scattered incense around like the shaking of a lilac bush in full flower. His face was round, and a sickly florid, interspersed with purple spots, overspread it, as if the natural dye of the old cogniac were maintaining an unequal contest with the decay of the vital energies. His bearing was decidedly soldierly, as it had a right to be, he having served as a captain some eight years before he took to the bar, as being the more pugnacious profession. His features, especially the mouth, turned down at the corners like a bull-dog's or a crescent, and a nose perked up with unutterable scorn and self-conceit, and eyes of a sensual, bluish gray, that seemed to be all light and no heat, were never pleasing to the opposing side. In his way, old Kasm was a very polite man. Whenever he chose, which was when it was his interest, to be polite, and when his blood was cool and he was not trying a law case, he would have made Chesterfield and Beau Brummel ashamed of themselves. He knew all the gymnastics of manners, and all forms and ceremonies of deportment; but there was no more soul or kindness in the manual he went through, than in an iceberg. His politeness, however seemingly deferential, had a frost-bitten air, as if it had lain out over night and got the *rheumatics* before it came in; and really, one felt less at ease under his frozen smiles, than under any body else's frowns.

He was the proudest man I ever saw: he would have made the Warwicks and the Nevilles, not to say the Plantagenets or Mr. Dombey, feel very limber and meek if introduced into their company; and selfish to that extent, that, if by giving up the nutmeg on his noon glass of toddy, he could have christianized the Burmese empire, millennium never would come for him.

How far back he traced his lineage, I do not remember, but he had the best blood of both worlds in his veins; sired high up on the paternal side by some Prince or Duke, and dammed on the mother's by one or two Pocahontases. Of course, from this, he was a Virginian, and the only one I ever knew that did not quote those Eleusinian mysteries, the Resolutions of 1798–99.   He did not.   He was a Federalist, and denounced Jefferson as a low-flung demagogue, and Madison as his tool.   He bragged largely on Virginia, though—he was not eccentric on this point—but it was the Virginia of Washington, the Lees, Henry, &c., of which he boasted.   The old dame may take it as a compliment that he bragged of her at all.

The old Captain had a few negroes, which, with a declining practice, furnished him a support.   His credit, in consequence of his not having paid any thing in the shape of a debt for something less than a quarter of a century, was rather limited.   The property was covered up by a deed or other instrument, drawn up by Kasm himself, with such infernal artifice and diabolical skill, that all the lawyers in the county were not able to decide, by a legal construction of its various clauses, who the negroes belonged to, or whether they belonged to any body at all.

He was an inveterate opponent of new laws, new books, new men.   He would have revolutionized the government if he could, should a law have been passed, curing defects in Indictments.

Yet he was a friend of strong government and strong laws : he might approve of a law making it death for a man to blow his nose in the street, but would be for rebelling if it allowed the indictment to dispense with stating in which hand he held it.

This eminent barrister was brought up at a time when zeal for a client was one of the chief virtues of a lawyer— the client standing in the place of truth, justice and decency, and monopolizing the respect due to all. He, therefore, went into all causes with equal zeal and confidence, and took all points that could be raised with the same earnestness, and belabored them with the same force. He personated the client just as a great actor identifies himself with the character he represents on the stage.

The faculty he chiefly employed was a talent for vituperation which would have gained him distinction on any theatre, from the village partisan press, down to the House of Representatives itself. He had cultivated vituperation as a science, which was like putting guano on the Mississippi bottoms, the natural fertility of his mind for satirical productions was so great. He was as much fitted by temper as by talent for this sort of rhetoric, especially when kept from his dinner or toddy by the trial of a case—then an alligator whose digestion had been disturbed by the horns of a billy-goat taken for lunch, was no mean type of old Sar Kasm (as the wags of the bar called him, by nickname, formed by joining the last syllable of his christian, or rather, heathen name, to his patronymic). After a case began to grow interesting, the old fellow would get fully stirred up. He grew as quarrelsome as a little bull terrier. He snapped at witnesses, kept up a constant snarl at the counsel, and growled, at intervals, at the judge, whom, whoever he was, he considered as *ex officio*, his natural enemy, and so regard-

2

ed every thing got from him as so much wrung from an unwilling witness.

But his great *forte* was in cross-examining a witness. His
countenance was the very expression of sneering incredulity.
Such a look of cold, unsympathizing, scornful penetration
as gleamed from his eyes of ice and face of brass, is not
often seen on the human face divine. Scarcely any eye
could meet unshrinkingly that basilisk gaze : it needed no
translation : the language was plain : " Now you are swear-
ing to a lie, and I'll catch you in it in a minute ; " and then
the look of surprise which greeted each new fact stated, as
if to say, " I expected some lying, but really this exceeds
all my expectations." The meek politeness with which he
would address a witness, was any thing but encouraging ; and
the officious kindness with which he volunteered to remind
him of a real or fictitious embarrassment, by asking him to
take his time and not to suffer himself to be confused, as
far as possible from being a relief ; while the air of triumph
that lit up his face the while, was too provoking for a saint
to endure.

Many a witness broke down under his examination, that
would have stood the fire of a masked battery unmoved, and
many another, voluble and animated enough in the opening
narrative, " slunk his pitch mightily," when old Kasm put
him through on the cross-examination.

His last look at them as they left the box, was an adver-
tisement to come back, " and they would hear something to
their advantage ; " and if they came. they heard it, if hu-
mility is worth buying at such a price.

How it was, that in such a fighting country, old Kasm continued at this dangerous business, can only be understood, by those who know the entire readiness—nay, eagerness of the old gentleman, to do reason to all serious inquirers;—and one or two results which happened some years before the time I am writing of, to say nothing of some traditions in the army, convinced the public, that his practice was as sharp at the small sword as at the cut and thrust of professional digladiation.

Indeed, it was such an evident satisfaction to the old fellow to meet these emergencies, which to him were merely lively episodes breaking the monotony of the profession, that his enemies, out of spite, resolutely refused to gratify him, or answer the sneering challenge stereotyped on his countenance. "Now if you can do any better, suppose you help yourself?" So, by common consent, he was elected free libeller of the bar. But it was very dangerous to repeat after him.

When he argued a case, you would suppose he had bursted his gall-bag—such, not vials but demijohns, of vituperation as he poured out with a fluency only interrupted by a pause to gather, like a tree-frog, the venom sweltering under his tongue into a concentrated essence. He could look more sarcasm than any body else could express; and in his scornful gaze, virtue herself looked like something sneaking and contemptible. He could not arouse the nobler passions or emotions; but he could throw a wet blanket over them. It took Frank Glendye and half a pint of good

French brandy, to warm the court-house after old Kasm was done speaking: but *they* could do it.

My client was a respectable butcher: his opponent a well-to-do farmer. On getting to the court-house, I found the court in session. The clerk was just reading the minutes. My *case*—I can well speak in the singular—was set the first on the docket for that morning. I looked around and saw old Kasm, who somehow had found out I was in the case, with his green bag and half a library of old books on the bar before him. The old fellow gave me a look of malicious pleasure—like that of a hungry tiger from his lair, cast upon an unsuspecting calf browsing near him. I had tried to put on a bold face. I felt that it would be very unprofessional to let on to my client that I was at all scared, though my heart was running down like a jack-screw under a heavy wagon. My conscience—I had not practised it away then—was not quite easy. I couldn't help feeling that it was hardly honest to be leading my client, like Falstaff his men, where he was sure to be peppered. But then it was my only chance; my bread depended on it; and I reflected that the same thing has to happen in every lawyer's practice. I tried to arrange my ideas in form and excogitate a speech: they flitted through my brain in odds and ends. I could neither think nor quit thinking. I would lose myself in the first twenty words of the opening sentence and stop at a particle;—the trail run clean out. I would start it again with no better luck: then I thought a moment of the disgrace of a dead break-down; and then I would commence again with "gentlemen of the jury," &c., and go on as before.

At length the judge signed the minutes and took up the docket: "Special case—Higginbotham *vs.* Swink: Slander. Mr. Glendye for plff.; Mr. Kasm for deft. Is Mr. G. in court? Call him, Sheriff." The sheriff called three times. He might as well have called the dead. No answer of course came. Mr. Kasm rose and told the court that he was sorry his brother was too much (stroking his chin and looking down and pausing) indisposed, or otherwise engaged, to attend the case; but he must insist on its being disposed of, &c.: the court said it would be. I then spoke up (though my voice seemed to me *very* low down and very hard to get up), that I had just been spoken to in the cause: I believed we were ready, if the cause must be then tried; but I should much prefer it to be laid over, if the court would consent, until the next day, or even that evening. Kasm protested vehemently against this; reminded the court of its peremptory order; referred to the former proceedings, and was going on to discuss the whole merits of the case, when he was interrupted by the judge, who, turning himself to me, remarked that he should be happy to oblige me, but that he was precluded by what had happened: he hoped, however, that the counsel on the other side would extend the desired indulgence; to which Kasm immediately rejoined, that this was a case in which he neither asked favors nor meant to give them. So the case had to go on. Several members of the bar had their hats in hand, ready to leave the room when the case

was called up; but seeing that I was in it alone, suffered
their curiosity to get the better of other engagements, and
staid to see it out; a circumstance which did not diminish
my trepidation in the least.

I had the witnesses called up, posted my client behind
me in the bar, and put the case to the jury. The defendant
had pleaded justification and not guilty. I got along pretty
well, I thought, on the proofs. The cross-examination of old
Kasm didn't seem to me to hurt any thing—though he
quibbled, misconstrued, and bullied mightily; objected to
all my questions as leading, and all the witnesses' answers
as irrelevant: but the judge, who was a very clever sort of a
man, and who didn't like Kasm much, helped me along and
over the bad places, occasionally taking the examination
himself when old Kasm had got the statements of the witness in a fog.

I had a strong case; the plaintiff showed a good character : that the lodge of Masons had refused to admit him to
fellowship until he could clear up these charges: that the
Methodist Church, of which he was a class-leader, had required of him to have these charges judicially settled: that
he had offered to satisfy the defendant that they were false,
and proposed to refer it to disinterested men, and to be satisfied—if they decided for him—to receive a written retrac-
tion, in which the defendant should only declare he was mistaken ; that the defendant refused this proffer and reiterated
the charges with increased bitterness and aggravated insult;
that the defendant had suffered in reputation and credit ;
that the defendant declared he meant to run him off and

buy his land at his (defendant's) own price; and that defendant was rich, and often repeated his slanders at public meetings, and once at the church door, and finally *now justified*.

The defendant's testimony was weak : it did not controvert the proof as to the speaking of the words, or the matters of aggravation.   Many witnesses were examined as to the character of the plaintiff; but those against us only referred to what they had heard since the slanders, except one who was unfriendly.   Some witnesses spoke of butchering hogs at night, and hearing them squeal at a late hour at the plaintiff's slaughter house, and of the dead hogs they had seen with various marks, and something of hogs having been stolen in the neighborhood.

This was about all the proof.

The plaintiff laid his damages at $10,000.

I rose to address the jury.   By this time a good deal of the excitement had worn off.   The tremor left, only gave me that sort of feeling which is rather favorable than otherwise to a public speaker.

I might have made a pretty good *out* of it, if I had thrown myself upon the merits of my case, acknowledged modestly my own inexperience, plainly stated the evidence and the law, and let the case go—reserving myself in the conclusion *for a splurge*, if I chose to make one.   But the evil genius that presides over the first bantlings of all lawyerlings, would have it otherwise.   The citizens of the town and those of the country, then in the village, had gathered

in great numbers into the courthouse to hear the speeches,
and I could not miss such an opportunity for display.

Looking over the jury I found them a plain, matter-of-
fact looking set of fellows; but I did not note, or probably
know a fact or two about them, which I found out afterwards.

I started, as I thought, in pretty good style. As I went
on, however, my fancy began to get the better of my judgment. Argument and common sense grew tame. Poetry
and declamation, and, at last, pathos and fiery invective,
took their place. I grew as *quotatious* as Richard Swivel-
ler. Shakspeare suffered. I quoted, among other things
of less value and aptness, " He who steals my purse steals
trash," &c. I spoke of the woful sufferings of my poor
client, almost heart-broken beneath the weight of the terrible
persecutions of his enemy : and, growing bolder, I turned
on old Kasm, and congratulated the jury that the genius of
slander had found an appropriate defender in the genius of
chicane and malignity. I complimented the jury on their
patience—on their intelligence—on their estimate of the
value of character; spoke of the public expectation—of that
feeling outside of the box which would welcome with thundering plaudits the righteous verdict the jury would render;
and wound up by declaring that I had never known a case
of slander so aggravated in the course of my practice at
that bar; and felicitated myself that its grossness and barbarity justified my client in relying upon even the youth and
inexperience of an unpractised advocate, whose poverty of

resources was unaided by opportunities of previous preparation. Much more I said that happily has now escaped me.

When I concluded Sam Hicks and one or two other friends gave a faint sign of applause—but not enough to make any impression.

I observed that old Kasm held his head down when I was speaking. I entertained the hope that I had cowed him! His usual port was that of cynical composure, or bold and brazen defiance. It was a special kindness if he only smiled in covert scorn: that was his most amiable expression in a trial.

But when he raised up his head I saw the very devil was to pay. His face was of a burning red. He seemed almost to choke with rage. His eyes were blood-shot and flamed out fire and fury. His queue stuck out behind, and shook itself stiffly like a buffalo bull's tail when he is about making a fatal plunge. I had struck him between wind and water. There was an audacity in a stripling like me bearding him, which infuriated him. He meant to massacre me —and wanted to be a long time doing it. It was to be a regular *auto da fé*. I was to be the representative of the young bar, and to expiate his malice against all. The court adjourned for dinner. It met again after an hour's recess.

By this time the public interest, and especially that of the bar, grew very great. There was a rush to the privileged seats, and the sheriff had to command order,—the shuffling of feet and the pressure of the crowd forward was so great.

2*

I took my seat within the bar, looked around with an affectation of indifference so belying the perturbation within, that the same power of acting on the stage would have made my fortune on *that* theatre.

Kasm rose—took a glass of water: his hand trembled a little—I could see that; took a pinch of snuff, and led off in a voice slow and measured, but slightly—very slightly—tremulous. By a strong effort he had recovered his composure. The bar was surprised at his calmness. They all knew it was affected; but they wondered that he *could* affect it. Nobody was deceived by it. We felt assured "it was the torrent's smoothness ere it dash below." I thought he would come down on me in a tempest, and flattered myself it would soon be over. But malice is cunning. He had no idea of letting me off so easily.

He commenced by saying that he had been some years in the practice. He would not say he was an old man: that would be in bad taste, perhaps. The young gentleman who had just closed his remarkable speech, harangue, poetic effusion, or rigmarole, or whatever it might be called, if, indeed, any name could be safely given to this motley mixture of incongruous slang—the young gentleman evidently did not think he was an old man; for he could hardly have been guilty of such rank indecency as to have treated age with such disrespect—he would not say with such insufferable impertinence: and yet, " I am," he continued, " of age enough to recollect, if I had charged my memory with so inconsiderable an event, the day of *his* birth, and then I was in full practice in this courthouse. I confess, though, gentlemen, I *am old* enough to remember the period when a youth's first appearance at the bar was not signalized by impertinence towards his seniors; and when public opinion did not think flatulent bombast and florid trash, picked out of fifth-rate romances and namby-pamby rhymes, redeemed by the upstart sauciness of a raw popinjay, towards the experienced members of the profession he disgraced. And yet, to some extent, this ranting youth may be right: I am not old in that sense which disables me from defending myself *here* by words, or *elsewhere*, if need be, by blows: and that, this young gentleman shall right well know before I have done with him. You will bear in mind, gentlemen, that what I say is in self-defence—that I did not begin this quarrel—that it was forced on me; and that I am bound by no restraints of courtesy, or of respect, or of kindness. Let him charge to the account of his own rashness and rudeness, whatever he receives in return therefor.

"Let me retort on this youth that he is a worthy advocate of his butcher client. He fights with the dirty weapons of his barbarous trade, and brings into his speech the reeking odor of his client's slaughter-house.

"Perhaps something of this congeniality commended him to the notice of his worthy client, and to this, his first retainer: and no wonder, for when we heard his vehement roaring, we might have supposed his client had brought his most unruly bull-calf into court to defend him, had not the matter of the roaring soon convinced us the animal was more remarkable for the length of his ears, than even the power of his lungs. Perhaps the young gentleman has taken his retainer, and contracted for butchering my client on the same terms as his client contracts in his line—that is, on the shares. But I think, gentlemen, he will find the contract a more dirty than profitable job. Or, perhaps, it might not be uncharitable to suggest that his client, who seems to be pretty well up to the business *of saving other people's bacon*, may have desired, as far as possible, to save his own; and, therefore turning from members of the bar who would have charged him for their services according to their value, took this occasion of getting off some of his stale wares: for has not Shakspeare said—(the gentleman will allow me to quote Shakspeare, too, while yet his reputation survives *his* barbarous mouthing of the poet's words)—he knew an attorney 'who would defend a cause for a starved hen, or leg of mutton fly-blown.' I trust, however, whatever was the contract, that the gentleman will make his equally worthy client stand up to it; for I should like, that on one occasion it might be said the excellent butcher *was made to pay for his swine.*

"I find it difficult, gentlemen, to reply to any part of the young man's effort, except his argument, which is the smallest part in compass, and, next to his pathos, the most amusing. His figures of speech are some of them quite good, and have been so considered by the best judges for the last thousand years. I must confess, that as to these, I find no other fault than that they were badly applied and ridiculously pronounced; and this further fault, that they have become so common-place by constant use, that, unless some new vamping or felicity of application be given them, they tire nearly as much as his original matter—*videlicet*, that matter which being more ridiculous than we ever heard before, carries internal evidence of its being his own. Indeed,. it was never hard to tell when the gentleman recurred to his own ideas. He is like a cat-bird—the only intolerable discord she makes being her own notes—though she gets on well enough as long as she copies and cobbles the songs of other warblers.

"But, gentlemen, if this young orator's argument was amusing, what shall I say of his pathos? What farce ever equalled the fun of it? The play of 'The Liar' probably approaches nearest to it, not only in the humor, but in the veracious character of the incidents from which the humor comes. Such a face—so woe-begone, so whimpering, as if the short period since he was flogged at school (probably in reference to those eggs falsely charged to the hound puppy) had neither obliterated the remembrance of his juvenile affliction, nor the looks he bore when he endured it.

"There was something exquisite in his picture of the woes, the wasting grief of his disconsolate client, the butcher Higginbotham, mourning—as Rachel mourned for her children—for his character *because it was not*. Gentlemen, look at him! Why he weighs twelve stone *now!* He has three inches of fat on his ribs this minute! He would make as many links of sausage as any hog that ever squealed at

midnight in his slaughter pen, and has lard enough in him
to cook it all.   Look at his face! why, his chops remind a
hungry man of jowls and greens.   If this is a shadow, in
the name of propriety, why didn't he show himself, when in
flesh, at the last Fair, beside the Kentucky ox; that were a
more honest way of making a living than stealing hogs.
But Hig is pining in grief!   I wonder the poetic youth—
his learned connsel—did not quote Shakspeare again.   'He
never told his '—woe—'but let concealment, like the worm
i' the bud, prey on his damask cheek.'   He looked like
Patience on a monument smiling at grief—or beef I should
rather say.   But, gentlemen, probably I am wrong; it may
be that this tender-hearted, sensitive butcher, was lean before, and like Falstaff, throws the blame of his fat on sorrow
and sighing, which 'has puffed him up like a bladder.'
(Here Higginbotham left in disgust.)

   "There, gentlemen, he goes, 'larding the lean earth as
he walks along.'   Well has Doctor Johnson said, 'who kills
fat oxen should himself be fat.'   Poor Hig! stuffed like one
of his own blood-puddings, with a dropsical grief which
nothing short of ten thousand dollars of Swink's money can
cure.   Well, as grief puffs him up, I don't wonder that
nothing but depleting another man can cure him.

   "And now, gentlemen, I come to the blood and thunder
part of this young gentleman's harangue : empty and vapid;
words and nothing else.   If any part of his rigmarole was
windier than any other part, this was it.   He turned himself into a small cascade, making a great deal of noise to

make a great deal of froth; tumbling; roaring; foaming; the shallower it ran all the noisier it seemed. He fretted and knitted his brows; he beat the air and he vociferated, always emphasizing the meaningless words most loudly; he puffed, swelled out and blowed off, until he seemed like a new bellows, all brass and wind. How he mouthed it —as those villainous stage players ranting out fustian in a barn theatre, mimicking—'Who steals my purse, steals trash.' (I don't deny it.) ''Tis something,' (query?) 'nothing,' (exactly.) ''Tis mine; 'twas his, and has been slave to thousands—but he who filches from me my good name, robs me of that which not enricheth him,' (not in the least,) 'but makes me poor indeed;' (just so, but whether any poorer than before he parted with the encumbrance, is another matter.)

But the young gentleman refers to his youth. He ought not to reproach us of maturer age in that indirect way: no one would have suspected it of him, or him of it, if he had not told it: indeed, from hearing him speak, we were prepared to give him credit for almost *any length of ears*. But does not the youth remember that Grotius was only seventeen when he was in full practice, and that he was Attorney General at twenty-two; and what is Grotius to this greater light? Not the burning of my smoke house to the conflagration of Moscow!

" And yet, young Grotius tells us in the next breath, that he never knew such a slander in the course of his practice? Wonderful, indeed! seeing that his practice has all been done within the last six hours.   Why, to hear him talk, you would suppose that he was an old Continental lawyer, grown grey in the service. -H-i-s p-r-a-c-t-i-c-e !   Why he is just in his legal swaddling clothes !   His PRACTICE ! !   But I don't wonder he can't see the absurdity of such talk.   How long does it take one of the canine tribe, after birth, to open his eyes !

   " He talked, too, of *outside* influences; of the *public* expectations, and all that sort of demagoguism.   I observed no evidence of any great popular demonstrations in his favor, unless it be a tailor I saw stamping his feet ; but whether that was because he had sat cross-legged so long he wanted exercise, or was rejoicing because he had got orders for a new suit, *or a prospect of payment for an old one*, the gentleman can possibly tell better than I can.   (Here Hicks left.)   However, if this case *is* to be decided by the populace *here*, the gentleman will allow *me* the benefit of a writ of error to the regimental muster, to be held, next Friday, at Reinhert's Distillery.

   " But, I suppose he meant to frighten *you* into a verdict, by intimating that the mob, frenzied by *his* eloquence, would tear you to pieces if you gave a verdict for defendant ; like the equally eloquent barrister out West, who, concluding a case, said, 'Gentlemen, my client are as innocent of stealing that cotting as the Sun at noonday, and if you give it agin him, his brother, Sam Ketchins, next muster, w'll maul every mother's son of you.'   I hope the Sheriff will see to his duty and keep the crowd from you, gentlemen, if you should give us a verdict !

"But, gentlemen, I am tired of winnowing chaff; I have not had the reward paid by Gratiano for sifting *his* discourse: the two grains of wheat to the bushel. It is all froth—all wind—all bubble."

Kasm left me here for a time, and turned upon my client. Poor Higginbotham caught it thick and heavy. He wooled him, then skinned him, and then took to skinning off the under cuticle. Hig never skinned a beef so thoroughly. He put together all the facts about the witnesses' hearing the hogs squealing at night; the different marks of the hogs; the losses in the neighborhood; perverted the testimony and supplied omissions, until you would suppose, on hearing him, that it had been fully proved that poor Hig had stolen all the meat he had ever sold in the market. He asseverated that this suit was a malicious conspiracy between the Methodists and Masons, to crush his client. But all this I leave out, as not bearing on the main *subject*—myself.

He came back to me with a renewed appetite. He said he would conclude by paying his valedictory respects to his juvenile friend—as this was the last time he ever expected to have the pleasure of meeting him.

"That poetic young gentleman had said, that by your verdict against his client, you would blight for ever his reputation and that of his family—'that you would bend down the spirit of his manly son, and dim the radiance of his blooming daughter's beauty.' Very pretty, upon my word! But, gentlemen, not so fine—not so poetical by half, as a precious morceau of poetry which adorns the columns of the village

newspaper, bearing the initials J. C. R.   As this admirable
production has excited a great deal of applause in the nur-
series and boarding schools, I must beg to read it; not for
the instruction of the gentleman, he has already seen it; but
for the entertainment of the Jury.   It is addressed to R***
B***, a young lady of this place.   Here it goes."

Judge my horror, when, on looking up, I saw him take an
old newspaper from his pocket, and, pulling down his spectacles, begin to read off in a stage-actor style, some verses I
had written for Rose Bell's Album.   Rose had been worrying me for some time, to write her something.   To get rid
of her importunities, I had scribbled off a few lines and copied them in the precious volume.   Rose, the little fool,
took them for something very clever (she never had more
than a thimbleful of brains in her doll-baby head)—and was
so tickled with them, that she got her brother, Bill, then
about fourteen, to copy them off, as well as he could, and
take them to the printing office.   Bill threw them under the
door; the printer, as big a fool as either, not only published
them, but, in his infernal kindness, puffed them in some critical commendations of his own, referring to "the gifted author," as "one of the most promising of the younger members of our bar."

The fun, by this time, grew fast and furious.   The country people, who have about as much sympathy for a young
town lawyer, badgered by an older one, as for a young cub
beset by curs; and who have about as much idea or respect
for poetry, as for witchcraft, joined in the mirth with great

THE CURE OF POETRY

glee. They crowded around old Kasm, and stamped and roared as at a circus. The Judge and Sheriff in vain tried to keep order. Indeed, his honor *smiled out loud once* or twice; and to cover his retreat, pretended to cough, and fined the Sheriff five dollars for not keeping silence in court. Even the old Clerk, whose immemorial pen behind his right ear, had worn the hair from that side of his head, and who had not smiled in court for twenty years, and boasted that Patrick Henry couldn't disturb him in making up a judgment entry, actually turned his chair from the desk and *put down* his pen: afterwards he put his hand to his head three times in search of it; forgetting, in his attention to old Kasm, what he had done with it.

Old Kasm went on reading and commenting by turns. I forget what the ineffable trash was. I wouldn't recollect it if I could. My equanimity will only stand a phrase or two that still lingers in my memory, fixed there by old Kasm's ridicule. I had said something about my "bosom's anguish" —about the passion that was consuming me; and, to illustrate it, or to make the line jingle, put in something about "Egypt's Queen taking the Asp to her bosom"—which, for the sake of rhyme or metre, I called "the venomous worm" —how the confounded thing was brought in, I neither know nor want to know. When old Kasm came to that, he said he fully appreciated what the young bard said—he believed it. He spoke of venomous *worms*. Now, if he (Kasm) might presume to give the young gentleman advice, he would recommend Swain's Patent Vermifuge. He had no doubt that it would effectually cure him of his malady, his love, and last, but not least, of his rhymes—which would be the happiest passage in his eventful history.

I couldn't stand it any longer. I had borne it to the last point of human endurance. When it came only to skinning, I was there; but when he showered down aquafortis on the raw, and then seemed disposed to rub it in, I fled. *Abii, erupi, evasi.* The last thing I heard was old Kasm calling me back, amidst the shouts of the audidence—but no more.

*·   *   *   *   *   *

The next information I received of the case, was in a letter that came to me at Natchez, my new residence, from Hicks, about a month afterwards, telling me that the jury (on which I should have stated old Kasm had got two infidels and four anti-masons) had given in a verdict for defendant: that before the court adjourned, Frank Glendye had got sober, and moved for a new trial, on the ground that the verdict was against evidence, and that the plaintiff had not had justice, *by reason of the incompetency of his counsel, and the abandonment of his cause;* and that he got a new trial (as well he should have done).

I learned through Hicks, some twelve months later, that the case had been tried; that Frank Glendye had made one of his greatest and most eloquent speeches; that Glendye had joined the Temperance Society, and was now one of the soberest and most attentive men to business at the bar, and was at the head of it in practice; that Higginbotham had recovered a verdict of $2000, and had put Swink in for $500 costs, besides.

Hicks' letter gave me, too, the *melancholy* intelligence of old Kasm's death. He had died in an apoplectic fit, in the court house, while abusing an old preacher who had testified against him in a *crim. con.* case. He enclosed the proceedings of a bar meeting, in which " the melancholy dispensation which called our beloved brother hence while in the active discharge of his duties," was much deplored ; but, with a pious resignation, which was greatly to be admired, " they submitted to the will," &c., and, with a confidence old Kasm himself, if alive, might have envied, " *trusted* he had gone to a better and brighter world," &c., &c., which carried the doctrine of Universalism as far as it could well go. They concluded by resolving that the bar would wear crape on the left arm for thirty days. I don't know what the rest did, I didn't. Though not mentioned in his will, he had left me something to remember him by. Bright be the bloom and sweet the fragrance of the thistles on his grave !

Reader! I eschewed *genius* from that day. I took to accounts; did up every species of paper that came into my office with a tape string; had pigeon holes for all the bits of paper about me; walked down the street as if I were just going to bank and it wanted only five minutes to three o'clock; got me a green bag and stuffed it full of old newspapers, carefully folded and labelled; read law, to fit imaginary cases, with great industry; dunned one of the wealthiest men in the city for fifty cents; sold out a widow for a twenty dollar debt, and bought in her things myself, publicly (and gave them back to her secretly, afterwards); associated only with skinflints, brokers and married men, and discussed investments and stocks; soon got into business; looked wise and shook my head when I was consulted, and passed for a "powerful good judge of law;" confirmed the opinion by reading, in court, all the books and papers I could lay my hands on, and clearing out the court-house by hum-drum details, common-place and statistics, whenever I made a speech at the bar— and thus, by this course of things, am able to write from *my sugar plantation*, this memorable history of the fall of *genius* and the rise of solemn humbug !   J. C. R.

THE BENCH AND THE BAR.

In the month of March, A. D., 1836, the writer of these faithful chronicles of law-doings in the South West, duly equipped for forensic warfare, having perused nearly the whole of Sir William Blackstone's Commentaries on the Laws of England, left behind him the red hills of his native village, in the valley of the Shenandoah, to seek his fortune. He turned his horse's head to the setting sun. His loyalty to the Old Dominion extorts the explanation that his was no voluntary expatriation. He went under the compulsion which produced the author's book—" Urged by hunger and request of friends." The gentle momentum of a female slipper, too, it might as well be confessed, added its moral suasion to the more pressing urgencies of breakfast, dinner and supper. To the South West he started because magnificent accounts came from that sunny land of most cheering and exhilarating prospects of fussing, quarrelling, murdering, violation of contracts, and the whole catalogue of *crimen falsi*—in fine, of a flush tide of litigation in all of its departments, civil and criminal. It was extolled as a legal Utopia, peopled by a race of eager litigants, only waiting for the lawyers to come on and divide out to them the shells of a bountiful system of squabbling: a California of Law, whose surface strife only indicated the vast *placers* of legal dispute waiting in untold profusion, the presence of a few craftsmen to bring out the crude suits to some forum, or into chancery for trial or essay.

He resigned prospects of great brilliancy at home. His family connections were numerous, though those of influence were lawyers themselves, which made this fact only contingently beneficial—to wit, the contingency of their dying before him—which was a sort of *remotissima potentia*, seeing they were in the enjoyment of excellent health, the profession being remarkably salubrious in that village; and seeing further, that, after their death, their influence might be gone. Not counting, therefore, too much on this advantage, it was a well-ascertained fact that no man of *real* talent and energy—and, of course, every lawyerling has both at the start—had ever come to that bar, who did not, in the course of five or six years, with any thing like moderate luck, make expenses, and, surviving that short probation on board wages, lay up money, ranging from $250 to $500, according to merit and good fortune, *per annum*. In evidence of the correctness of this calculation, it may be added that seven young gentlemen, all of fine promise, were enjoying *high* life—in upper stories —cultivating the cardinal virtues of Faith and Hope in themselves, and the greater virtue of Charity in their friends— the only briefs as yet known to them being brief of money and brief of credit; their barrenness of fruition in the day time relieved by oriental dreams of fairy clients, with fifteen shilling fees in each hand, and glorious ten dollar contingents in the perspective, beckoning them on to Fame and Fortune. But Poverty, the rugged mother of the *wind-sellers* of all times and countries, as poor Peter Peebles so irreverently calls our honorable craft,—the Necessity which knows no Law, yet teaches so much of it, tore him from scenes and prospects of such allurement : with the heroism of old Regulus, he turned his back upon his country and put *all* to hazard—*videlicet*, a pony valued at $35, a pair of saddle-bags and contents, a new razor not much needed at that early day, and $75 in Virginia bank bills.

Passing leisurely along through East Tennessee, he was struck with the sturdy independence of the natives, of the enervating refinements of artificial society and its concomitants ; not less than with the patriotic encouragement they extended to their own productions and manufactures : the writer frequently saw pretty farmers' daughters working barefooted in the field, and his attention was often drawn to the number of the distilleries and to evident symptoms of a liberal patronage of their products. He stopped at a seat of Justice for half a day, while court was in session, to witness the manner in which the natives did up judicature; but with the exception of a few cases under a statute of universal authority and delicacy, he saw nothing of special interest; and these did not seem to excite much attention beyond the domestic circle.

The transition from East Tennessee to South Western

3

Alabama and East Mississippi was something marked. It was somewhat like a sudden change from "Sleepy Hollow" to the Strand. A man, retailing onions by the dozen in Weathersfield, and the same man suddenly turned into a real estate broker in San Francisco, would realize the contrast between the picayune standard of the one region, and the wild spendthriftism, the impetuous rush and the magnificent scale of operations in the other.

The writer pitched his tabernacle on the thither side of the state line of Alabama, in the charming village of P., one of the loveliest hamlets of the plain, or rather it would be, did it not stand on a hill. Gamblers, then a numerous class, included, the village boasted a population of some five hundred souls; about a third of whom were single gentlemen who had come out on the vague errand of seeking their fortune, or the more definite one of seeking somebody else's; philosophers who mingled the spirit of Anacreon with the enterprise of Astor, and who enjoyed the present as well as laid projects for the future, to be worked out for their own profit upon the safe plan of some other person's risk.

Why he selected this particular spot for his *locus in quo*, is easily told. The capital he had invested in emigration was nearly expended and had not as yet declared any dividend; and, with native pride, he was ambitious to carry money enough with him to excite the hopes of his landlord. Besides, he was willing to try his hand on the practice where competition was not formidable.

The " accommodations " at the " American Hotel " were

not such as were calculated to beguile a spiritual mind to things of sense. The writer has been at the Astor, the Revere and the St. Charles since, and did not note the resemblance. A huge cross-piece, like a gibbet, stood before the door—the usual *inn*-sign of the country; and though a very apt device as typifying death, it was not happy in denoting the specific kind of destruction that menaced the guest. The vigor of his constitution, however, proved sufficient for the trial; though, for a long time, the contest was dubious.

In the fall of the year so scarce were provisions—bull-beef excepted, which seemed to be every where—that we were forced to eat green corn, baked or fried with lard, for bread; and he remembers, when biscuits came again, a mad wag, Jim Cole, shouted out from the table that he should certainly die *now*, for want of a new bolting cloth to his throat.

A shed for an office procured, the next thing was a license; and this a Circuit Judge was authorized to grant, which service was rendered by the Hon. J. F. T. in a manner which shall ever inspire gratitude—he asking not a single legal question; an eloquent silence which can never be appreciated except by those who are unable to stand an examination.

This egotism over, and its purpose of merely introducing the witness accomplished, the narrative will proceed without further mention of him or his fortunes; and if any reader thinks he loses any thing by this abbreviation, perhaps it will be full consolation to him to know that if it proceeded further, the author might lose a great deal more.

Dropping the third for the more convenient first person, he will proceed to give some account of what was done by or to Themis in that part of her noisy domain.

———

Those were jolly times.   Imagine thirty or forty young men collected together in a new country, armed with fresh licenses which they had got gratuitously, and a plentiful stock of brass which they had got in the natural way; and standing ready to supply any distressed citizen who wanted law, with their wares counterfeiting the article.   I must confess it looked to me something like a swindle.   It was doing business on the wooden nutmeg, or rather the patent brass-clock principle.   There was one consolation : the clients were generally as sham as the counsellors.   For the most part, they were either broke or in a rapid decline.   They usually paid us the compliment of retaining us, but they usually retained the fee too, a double retainer we did not much fancy. However, we got as much as we were entitled to and something over, *videlicet*, as much over as we got at all.   The most that we made was experience.   We learned before long, how every possible sort of case could be successfully lost; there was no way of getting out of court that we had not tested.   The last way we learned was *via* a verdict : it was a considerable triumph to get *to* the jury, though it seemed a sufficiently easy matter to get away from one again.   But the perils of the road from the writ to an issue or issues—for there were generally several of them—were great indeed.   The way was infested and ambushed, with all imaginable points of practice, quirks and quibbles, that had strayed off from the litigation of every sort of foreign judicature,—that had been successfully tried in, or been driven out of, regularly organized forums, besides a smart sprinkling of indigenous growth. Nothing was settled. Chaos had come again, or rather, had never gone away. Order, Heaven's first law, seemed unwilling to remain where there was no other law to keep it company. I spoke of the thirty or forty barristers on their first legs— but I omitted to speak of the older members who had had the advantage of several years' practice and precedence. These were the leaders on the Circuit. They had the law— that is the practice and rulings of the courts—and kept it as a close monopoly. The earliest information we got of it was when some precious dogma was drawn out on us with fatal effect. They had conned the statutes for the last fifteen years, which were inaccessible to us, and we occasionally, much to our astonishment, got the benefit of instruction in a clause or two of " the act in such cases made and provided " at a considerable tuition fee to be paid by our clients. Occasionally, too, a repealed statute was revived for our especial benefit. The courts being forbidden to charge except as specially asked, took away from us, in a great measure, the protection of the natural guardians of our ignorant innocence : there could be no prayer for general relief, and we did not— many of us—know how to pray specially, and always ran great risks of prejudicing our cases before the jury, by having instructions refused. It was better to trust to the "uncovenanted mercies " of the jury, and risk a decision on the

honesty of the thing, than blunder along after charges. As
to reserving points except as a bluff or scarecrow, that was a
thing unheard of: the Supreme Court was a perfect *terra incognita :* we had all heard there was such a place, as we had
heard of Heaven's Chancery, to which the Accusing Spirit
took up Uncle Toby's oath, but we as little knew the way there,
and as little expected to go there. Out of one thousand
cases, butchered in cold blood without and with the forms of
law, not one in that first year's practice, ever got to the High
Court of Errors and Appeals; (or, as Prentiss called it, the
Court of High Errors and Appeals.)   No wonder we never
started.   How could we ever get them there ?   If we had to
run a gauntlet of technicalities and quibbles to get a judgment on " a plain note of hand," in the Circuit Court, Tam
O'Shanter's race through the witches, would be nothing to
the journey to and through the Supreme Court !   It would
have been a writ of error indeed—or rather a writ of many
errors.   This is but speculation, however—we never tried it
—the experiment was too much even for our brass.   The
leaders were a good deal but not generally retained.   The
réason was, they wanted the money, or like Falstaff's mercer,
good security ; a most uncomfortable requisition with the
mass of our litigants.   *We*, of the local bar trusted—so did
our clients : it is hard to say which did the wildest credit
business.

The leaders were sharp fellows—keen as briars—*au fait*
in all trap points—quick to discern small errors—perfect in
forms and ceremonies—very pharisees in " anise, mint and

cummin—*but neglecting judgment and the weightier matters of the law.*" They seemed to think that judicature was a tanyard—clients skins to be curried—the court the mill, and the thing " to work on their leather" with—*bark :* the idea that justice had any thing to do with trying causes, or sense had any thing to do with legal principles, never seemed to occur to them once, as a possible conception.

Those were quashing times, and they were the *out quashingest* set of fellows ever known. They moved to quash every thing, from a *venire* to a *subpœna :* indeed, I knew one of them to quash the whole court, on the ground that the Board of Police was bound by law to furnish the building for holding the Court, and there was no proof that the building in which the court was sitting was so furnished. They usually, however, commenced at the *capias*—and kept quashing on until they got to the forthcoming bond which, being set aside, released the security for the debt, and then, generally, it was no use to quash any thing more. In one court, forthcoming bonds, to the amount of some hundred thousands of dollars, were quashed, because the execution was written " State of Mississippi"—instead of " *the* State of Mississippi," the constitution requiring the style of process to be the State of Mississippi : a quashing process which vindicated the constitution at the expense of the foreign creditors in the matter of these bonds, almost as effectively as a subsequent vindication in respect of other bonds, about which more clamor was raised.

Attachments were much resorted to, there being about

that time as the pressure was coming on, a lively stampede to Texas. It became the interest of the debtors and their securities, and of rival creditors, to quash these, and quashed they were, almost without exception. J. H. was sheriff of W., and used to keep a book in which he noted the disposition of the cases called on the docket. Opposite nearly every attachment case, was the brief annotation—"*quashed* for the lack of form." This fatality surprised me at first, as the statute declared the attachment law should be liberally construed, and gave a form, and the act required only the substantial requisites of the form to be observed : but it seems the form given for the bond in the statute, varied materially from the requirements of the statute in other portions of the act : and so the circuit courts held the forms to be a sort of legislative gull trap, by following which, the creditor lost his debt.

This ingenious turn for quibbling derived great assistance and many occasions of exercise from the manner in which business had been done, and the character of the officials who did it, or rather who didn't do it. The justices of the peace, probate judges, and clerks, and sheriffs, were not unfrequently in a state of as unsophisticated ignorance of conventionalities as could be desired by J. J. Rousseau or any other eulogist of the savage state. They were all elected by the people, who neither knew nor cared whether they were qualified or not. If they were "good fellows" and *wanted* the office, that is, were too poor and lazy to support themselves in any other way, that was enough. If poor John Rogers, with nine small children and one at the breast, had been in Mississippi instead of Smithfield, he could have got any office he wanted, that is, if he had quit preaching and taken to treating. The result of these official blunders was, that about every other thing done at all, was done wrong: indeed, the only question was as between *void and voidable.* Even in capital cases, the convictions were worth nothing—the record not showing enough to satisfy the High Court that the prisoner was tried in the county, or at the place required by law or that the grand jury were freeholders, &c., of the county where the offence was committed, or that they had found a bill. They had put an old negro, Cupid, in C—— county, in question for his life, and convicted him three times, but the conviction never would stick. The last time the jury brought him in guilty, he was very composedly eating an apple. The sheriff asked him how he liked the idea of being hung. "Hung," said he—"hung! You don't think they are going to *hang* me, do you? I don't mind these little circuit judges: wait till old *Shurkey* says the word in the High Court, and then it will be time enough to be getting ready."

But if quashing was the general order of the day, it was the special order when the State docket was taken up. Such quashing of indictments! It seemed as by a curious display of skill in missing, the pleader never could get an indictment to hold water. I recollect S., who was prosecuting *pro tem.* for the State, convicted a poor Indian of murder, the Indian having only counsel volunteering on his

3*

arraignment; S. turned around and said with emphatic complacency: " I tell you, gentlemen, there is a fatality attending my indictments." " Yes," rejoined B., " they *are* generally quashed."

It was in criminal trials that the juniors flourished. We went into them with the same feeling of irresponsibility that Allen Fairfield went into the trial of poor Peter Peeble's suit *vs.* Plainstaines, namely—that there was but little danger of hurting the case. Any ordinary jury would have acquitted nine cases out of ten without counsel's instigating them thereto—to say nothing of the hundred avenues of escape through informalities and technical points. In fact, criminals were so unskilfully defended in many instances, that the jury had to acquit in spite of the counsel. Almost any thing made out a case of self-defence—a threat—a quarrel—an insult—going armed, as almost all the wild fellows did—shooting from behind a corner, or out of a store door, in front or from behind—it was all self-defence! The only skill in the matter, was in getting the right sort of a jury, which fact could be easily ascertained, either from the general character of the men, or ·from certain discoveries the defendant had been enabled to make in his mingling among " his friends and the public generally,"—for they were all, or nearly all, let out on bail or without it. Usually, the sheriff, too, was a friendly man, and not inclined to omit a kind service that was likely to be remembered with gratitude at the next election.

The major part of criminal cases, except misdemeanors,

were for killing, or assaults with intent to kill. They were usually defended upon points of chivalry. The iron rules of British law were too tyrannical for free Americans, and too cold and unfeeling for the hot blood of the sunny south. They were denounced accordingly, and practically scouted from Mississippi judicature, on the broad ground that they were unsuited to the genius of American institutions and the American character. There was nothing technical in this, certainly.

But if the case was a hopeless or very dangerous one, there was another way to get rid of it. "The world was all before" the culprit "where to choose." The jails were in such a condition—generally small log pens—that they held the prisoner very little better than did the indictment: for the most part, they held no one but Indians, who had no friend outside who could help them, and no skill inside to prize out. It was a matter of free election for the culprit in a desperate case, whether he would remain in jail or not; and it is astonishing how few exercised their privilege in favor of staying. The pains of exile seemed to present no stronger *bars* to expatriation, than the jail doors or windows.

The inefficiency of the arresting officers, too, was generally such that the malefactor could wind up his affairs and leave before the constable was on his track. If he gave bail, there were the chances of breaking the bond or recognizance, and the assurance against injury, derived from the fact that the recognizors were already broke.

The aforesaid leaders carried it with a high hand over us lawyerlings. If they took nothing by their false clamor, they certainly lost nothing by sleeping on their rights, or by failing to claim all they were entitled to. What they cóuldn't get by asking the court, they got by sneering and brow-beating. It was pleasant to watch the countenances of some of them when one of us made a motion, or took a point, or asked a question of a witness that they disapproved of. They could sneer like Malgroucher, and scold like Madame Caudle, and hector like Bully Ajax.

We had a goodly youth, a little our senior but more their junior, a goodly youth from the Republic of South Carolina, Jim T. by name. The elders had tried his mettle: he wouldn't fag for them, but stood up to them like a man. When he came to the bar, Sam J. made a motion at him on the motion docket, requiring him to produce his original book of entries on the trial or be *non suit*. (He had brought an action of assumpsit on a blacksmith's account.) When the case was called, Sam demanded whether the book was in court. Jim told him " No, and it wouldn't be," and denied his right to call for it; whereupon, Sam let the motion go, and suffered Jim T. to go on and prove the account and get the verdict ; a feat worthy of no little praise. Jim was equal to any of them in law, knowledge and talent, and superior in application and self-confidence, if that last *could* be justly said of mere humanity. He rode over *us* rough-shod, but we forgave him for it in consideration of his worrying the elders, and standing up to the rack. He was the best lawyer of his age I had ever seen. He had accomplished himself in the elegant science of special pleading,—had learned all the arts of confusing a case by all manner of pleas and motions, and took as much interest in enveloping a plain suit in all the cobwebs of technical defence as Vidocq ever took in laying snares for a rogue. He could " entangle justice in such a web of law," that the blind hussey could have never found her way out again if Theseus had been there to give her the clew. His thought by day and his meditation by night, was special pleas. He loved a demurrer as Domine Dobiensis loved a pun—with a solemn affection. He could draw a volume of pleas a night, each one so nearly presenting a regular defence, that there was scarcely any telling whether it hit it or not. If we replied, ten to one he demurred to the replication, and would assign fifteen special causes of demurrer in as many minutes. If we took issue, we ran an imminent risk of either being caught up on the facts, or of having the judgment set aside as rendered on an immaterial issue. It was always dangerous to demur, for the demurrer being overruled, the defendant was entitled to judgment final. Cases were triable at the first term, if the writ had been served twenty days before court. It may be seen, therefore, at a glance, that, with an overwhelming docket, and without books, or time to consult them if at hand, and without previous knowledge, we were not reposing either on a bed of roses or of safety. Jim T. was great on variances, too. If the note was not described properly in the declaration, we were sure to catch it before the jury : and, if any point

could be made on the proofs, he was sure to make it.   How
we trembled when we began to read the note to the jury !
And how ominous seemed the words " I object"—of a most
cruel and untimely end about being put to our case.   How
many cases where, on a full presentment of the legal merits
of them, there was no pretence of a defence, he gained, it is impossible to tell.   But if the ghosts of the murdered victims
could now arise, Macbeth would have had an easy time of it
compared with Jim T. How we admired, envied, feared and
hated him !   With what a bold, self-relying air he took his
points !   With what sarcastic emphasis he replied to our defences and half defences !   We thought that he knew all the
law there was : and when, in a short time, he caught the old
leaders up, we thought if we couldn't be George Washington,
how we should like to be Jim T.

He has risen since that time to merited distinction as a
ripe and finished lawyer ; yet, " in his noon of fame," he never so tasted the luxury of power,—never so knew the bliss
of envied and unapproached preëmenence, as when in the old
log court-houses he was throwing the boys right and left as
fast as they came to him, by pleas dilatory, sham and meri-
torious, demurrers, motions and variances.   So infallible was
his skill in these infernal arts, that it was almost a tempting
of Providence not to employ him.

I never thought Jim acted altogether fairly by squire A.
The squire had come to the bar rather late in life, and though
an excellent justice and a sensible man, was not profoundly
versed in the metaphysics of special pleading.   He was par-

ticularly pleased when he got to a jury on ' a plain note,' and
particularly annoyed when the road was blocked up by pleas
in abatement and demurrers or special pleas in bar.   He
had the most unlimited admiration of Jim.   Indeed, he had
an awful reverence for him.   He looked up to him as Bos-
well looked up to Sam Johnson, or Timothy to Paul.   The
squire had a note he was anxious to get judgment on.   He
had declared with great care and after anxious deliberation.
Not only was the declaration copied from the most approv-
ed precedent, but the common counts were all put in with
all due punctilios, to meet every imaginable phase the case
could assume.   Jim found a variance in the count on the
note : but how to get rid of the common counts was the difficulty.   He put a bold face on the matter, however, went
up to A. in the court-house, and threw himself into a passion.   " Well," said he, with freezing dignity—" I see, sir
you have gone and put the common counts in this declaration—do I understand you to mean them to stand?   I desire
to be informed, sir ? "   " Why, y-e-s, that is, I put 'em there
—but look here, H——, what are you mad at ?   What's
wrong ? "   " What's wrong ? "—a pretty question !   Do you
pretend, sir, that my client ever borrowed any money of
yours—that yours ever paid out money for mine ?   Did your
client ever give you instructions to sue mine for borrowed
money ?   No, sir, you know he didn't.   Is that endorsed on
the writ ?   No, sir.   Don't you know the statute requires
the cause of action to be endorsed on the *capias ad respondendum ?*   I mean to see whether an action for a malicious

suit wouldn't lie for this; and shall move to strike out all these counts as multifarious and incongruous and heterogeneous." "Well, Jim, don't get mad about it, old fellow—I took it from the books." "Yes, from the English books—but didn't you know we don't govern ourselves by the British statute?—if you don't, I'll instruct you." "Now ," said A., " Jim, hold on—all I want is a fair trial—if you will let me go to the jury, I'll strike out these common counts." " Well," said Jim, " *I will this time*, as it is you; but let this be a warning to you, A., how you get to suing my clients on promiscuous, and fictitious, and pretensed causes of action."

Accordingly they joined issue on the count in chief—A. offered to read his note—H. objected—it was voted out, and A. was nonsuited. " Now," said Jim, " that is doing the thing in the regular way. See how pleasant it is to get on with business when the rules are observed ! "

The case of most interest at the fall term of N—e court, 1837, was the State of Mississippi *vs.* Major Foreman, charged with assault with intent to kill one Tommy Peabody, a Yankee schoolmaster in the neighborhood of M—ville. The District Attorney being absent, the court appointed J. T. to prosecute. All the preliminary motions and points of order having been gone through, and having failed of success, the defendant had to go to trial before the jury. The defendant being a warm democrat, selected T. M., the then leader of that party, and Washington B. T., then a rising light of the same political sect, to defend him. The evidence was not very clear or positive. It seemed that an altercation had arisen at the grocery (fashionably called doggery), between a son of the defendant and the schoolmaster, which led to the shooting of the pistol by the younger F. at the aforesaid Thomas, as the said Thomas was making his way with equal regard to speed of transit and safety of conveyance from that locality. As it was Thomas's business to teach the young idea to shoot, he had no idea of putting to hazard " the delightful task " by being shot himself: and by thinking him of " what troubles do environ the man that meddles with cold iron" on the drawing thereof, resolved himself into a committee of safety, and proceeded energetically to the dispatch of the appropriate business of the board. But fast as Thomas travelled, a bevy of mischievous buckshot, as full of devilment as Thomas's scholars just escaped from school, rushed after, and one of them, striking him about two feet above the calf of his right leg, made his seat on the scholastic tripod for a while rather unpleasant to him. In fact, Thomas suffered a good deal in that particular region in which he had been the cause of much suffering in others. Thomas also added to the fun naturally attaching, in the eyes of the mercurial and reckless population of the time, to a Yankee schoolmaster's being shot while running, in so tender a point, by clapping his hands behind at the fire, and bellowing out that the murderer had blown out his brains ! A mistake very pardonable in one who had come fresh from a country where pistols were not known, and who could not be expected, under these distressing circumstances, to estimate, with much precision, the effect of a gun-shot wound.

Young Foreman, immediately after the pistol went off, followed its example. And not being of a curious turn, did not come back to see what the sheriff had done with a document he had for him, though assured that it related to important business. The proof against him—as it usually was against any one who couldn't be hurt by it—was clear enough, but it was not so much so against his father. The Major was there, had participated in the quarrel, and about the time of the firing, a voice the witness took—but wasn't certain—to be the Major's, was heard to cry out, "Shoot! Shoot!" and, shortly after the firing, the Major was heard to halloo to Peabody, "Run—Run, you d—d rascal—run!" This was about the strength of the testimony. The Major was a gentleman of about fifty-five—of ruddy complexion, which he had got out of a jug he kept under his bed of cold nights, without acknowledging his obligations for the loan—about five feet eight inches high and nearly that much broad. Nature or accident had shortened one leg, so that he limped when he walked. His eyes stood out and were streaked like a boy's white alley—and he wore a ruffled shirt; the same, perhaps, which he had worn on training days in Georgia, but which did not match very well with a yellow linsey vest, and a pair of copperas-colored jeans pantaloons he had squeezed in the form of a crescent over his protuberant paunch: on the whole, he was a pretty good live parody on an enormous goggle-eyed sun perch.

He had come from Georgia, where he had been a major in the militia, if that is not tautology; for I believe that every man that ever comes from Georgia *is* a major,—repaying the honor of the commission or title by undeviating fidelity to the democratic ticket. He would almost as soon been convicted as to have been successfully defended by a whig lawyer.

Old F. held up his head for some time—indeed, seemed to enjoy the mirth that was going on during the testimony, very much. But when J. T. began to pour broadside after broadside into him, and bring up fact after fact and appeal after appeal, and the court-house grew still and solemn, the old fellow could stand it no longer. Like the Kentucky militia at New Orleans, he ingloriously fled, sneaking out when no one was looking at him. The sheriff, however, soon missed him, and seeing him crossing the bridge and moving towards the swamp, raised a *posse* and followed after. The trial in the mean time proceeded—as did the Major.

I said he was defended in part by W. B. T.

You didn't know Wash ? Well, you missed a good deal. He would have impressed you. He was about thirty years old at the time I am writing of. He came to N. from East Tennessee, among whose romantic mountains he had "beat the drum ecclesiastic" as a Methodist preacher. He had, however, doffed the cassock, or rather, the shadbelly, for the gown. He had fallen from grace—not a high fall—and having warred against the devil for a time—a quarter or more—Dalgetty-like, he got him a law license, and took arms on the other side. His mind was not cramped, nor his originality fettered by technical rules or other learn-

ing. His voice, had not affectation injured the effect of it,
was remarkably fine, full, musical and sonorous, and of any
degree of compass and strength. He was as fluent of words
as a Frenchman. He was never known to falter for a word,
nd if he ever paused for an idea, he paused in vain. He
practised on his voice as on an organ, and had as many ups
and downs, high keys and low, as many gyrations and wind-
ings as an opera singer or a stage horn. H. G—y used to
say of him that he just shined his eyes, threw up his arms,
twirled his tongue, opened his mouth, and left the consequences to heaven. He practised on the injunction to the apos-
tles, and took no thought what he should say, but spoke
without labor—mental or physical. To add to the charms
of his delivery, he wore a poppaw smile, a sort of sickly-
-sweet expression on his countenance, that worked like Do-
ver's powders on the spectator.

     After J. T. had concluded his opening speech, Washing-
ton rose to open for the defence. The speech was a remarkable specimen of forensic eloquence. It had all the charms
of Counsellor Phillips' most ornate efforts, lacking only the
ideas. Great was the sensation when Wash. turned upon
the prosecutor. "Gentlemen of the jury," said the orator,
"this prosecutor is one of the vilest ingrates that ever
lived since the time of Judas Iscariot; for, gentlemen, did
you not hear from the witnesses, that when this prosecutor
was in the very extremity of his peril, my client, moved by
the tenderest emotions of pity and compassion, shouted out,
'Run! run! you d—d rascal—run!' It is true (lowering

his voice and smiling), gentlemen, he said ' you d—d rascal,' but the honorable court will instruct you that that was mercly *descriptio personæ.*" The effect was prodigious.

After Washington had made an end, old Tallabola rose slowly, as if oppressed by the weight of his subject. Now T. never made a jury speech without telling an anecdote. Whatever else was omitted the anecdote had to come. It is true, the point and application were both sometimes hard to see; and it is also true that as T's stock was by no means extensive, he had to make up in repetition what he lacked in variety. He had, however, one stand-by which never failed him. He might be said to have chartered it. He had told it until it had got to be a necessity of speech. The anecdote was a relation of a Georgia major's prowess in war. It ran thus: The major was very brave when the enemy was at a distance, and exhorted his men to fight to the death;—the enemy came nearer—the major told his soldiers to fight bravely, but to be prudent;—the foe came in sight, their arms gleaming in the sunshine—and the major told the men that, if they could not do better, they ought to retreat; and added he, " being a little lame, I believe *I* will leave now." And so, said T., it was with the prosecutor. At length after a long speech, T. concluded. J. T. rose to reply. He said, before proceeding to the argument, he would pay his respects to his old acquaintance, the anecdote of the Georgia major. He had known it a long while, indeed almost as long as he had known his friend T. It had afforded him amusement for many courts—how many he

couldn't now stop to count.   Knowing the major to have been
drafted into Mr. T's speeches for many a campaign, he had
hoped the war-worn veteran had been discharged from duty
and pensioned off, in consideration of long and hard usage,
or at least, that he was resting on furlough; but it seems he
was still in active service.   His friend had not been very
happy in his anecdote on other occasions, but, he must say,
on this occasion he was most *felicitously unhappy;* for the
DEFENDANT was a major—he was a Georgia major too ; unfortunately, he was a little lame also; and, to complete the
parallel, " in the heat of *this* action, on looking around," said
J. T., " I find he has left ! "   T. jumped up—" No evidence
of that, Mr. H. Confine yourself to the record, if you
please." " Well," said J. T., " gentlemen, my friend is a
little restive. You may look around, and judge for your-
selves."   Tallabola never told that anecdote any more ;—
he had to get another.

The jury having been sufficiently confused as to the law
by which about twenty abstract propositions bearing various,
and some of them no relation to the facts (the legislature,
in its excessive veneration for the sanctity of jury trial having prohibited the judges from charging in an intelligible
way), retired from the bar to consider of their verdict.   In
a few moments they returned into court.   But where was
the prisoner ?   Like Lara, he wouldn't come.   The court refused to receive the verdict in the absence of the defendant.
Finally, after waiting a long while, the Major was brought,
an officer holding on to each arm, and a crowd following at

his heels. (The Major had been caught in the swamp.) When he came in, he thought he was a gone sucker. The court directed the clerk to call over the jury : they were called, and severally answered to their names. The perspiration rolled from the Major's face—his eyes stuck out as if he had been choked. At the end of the call, the judge asked " Are you agreed on your verdict ? " The foreman answered " Yes," and handed to the clerk the indictment on which the verdict was endorsed. The clerk read it slowly. " We—the jury—find the—de—fen—dant (the Major held his breath) *not* guilty." One moment more and he had fainted. He breathed easy, then uttering a sort of relieving groan shortly after, he came to Tallabola—" Tal," said he, blubbering and wiping his nose on his cuff, " I'm going to quit the dimmycratic party and jine the whigs." " Why, Major," said Tal, " what do you mean ? you're one of our chief spokes at your box. Don't you believe in our doctrines ? " " Yes," said the Major, " I do ; but after my disgraceful run I'm not fit to be a dimmycrat any longer— I'd disgrace the party—and am no better than a dratted, blue-bellied, federal whig ! "

HOW THE TIMES SERVED THE VIRGINIANS. VIRGINIANS IN A NEW COUNTRY. THE RISE, DECLINE, AND FALL OF THE RAG EMPIRE.

THE disposition to be proud and vain of one's country, and to boast of it, is a natural feeling, indulged or not in respect to the pride, vanity, and boasting, according to the character of the native: but, with a Virginian, it is a passion. It inheres in him even as the flavor of a York river oyster in that bivalve, and no distance of deportation, and no trimmings of a gracious prosperity, and no pickling in the sharp acids of adversity, can destroy it. It is a part of the Virginia character—just as the flavor is a distinctive part of the oyster—" which cannot, save by annihilating, die." It is no use talking about it—the thing may be right, or wrong :—like Falstaff's victims at Gadshill, it is past praying for : it is a sort of cocoa grass that has got into the soil, and has so matted over it, and so *fibred* through it, as to have become a part of it ; at least, there is no telling which is the grass and which is the soil ; and certainly it is useless labor to try to root it out. You may destroy the soil, but you can't root out the grass.

Patriotism with a Virginian is a noun personal. It is the Virginian himself and something over. He loves Virginia *per se* and *propter se:* he loves her for herself and for himself—because *she is* Virginia and—every thing else beside. He loves to talk about her: out of the abundance of the heart the mouth speaketh. It makes no odds where he goes, he carries Virginia with him; not in the entirety always—but the little spot he came from is Virginia—as Swedenborg says the smallest part of the brain is an abridgment of all of it. "*Cœlum non animum mutant qui trans mare currunt*," was made for a Virginian. He never gets acclimated elsewhere ; he never loses citizenship to the old Home. The right of expatriation is a pure abstraction to him. He may breathe in Alabama, but he lives in Virginia. His treasure is there, and his heart also. If he looks at the Delta of the Mississippi, it reminds him of James River " low grounds ;" if he sees the vast prairies of Texas, it is a memorial of the meadows of the Valley. Richmond is the centre of attraction, the *depot* of all that is grand, great, good and glorious. "It is the Kentucky of a place," which the preacher described Heaven to be to the Kentucky congregation.

Those who came many years ago from the borough towns, especially from the vicinity of Williamsburg, exceed, in attachment to their birthplace, if possible, the *emigrés* from the metropolis. It is refreshing in these costermonger times,

4

to hear them speak of it:—they remember it when the old burg was the seat of fashion, taste, refinement, hospitality, wealth, wit, and all social graces; when genius threw its spell over the public assemblages and illumined the halls of justice, and when beauty brightened the social hour with her unmatched and matchless brilliancy.

Then the spirited and gifted youths of the College of old William and Mary, some of them just giving out the first scintillations of the genius that afterwards shone refulgent in the forum and the senate, added to the attractions of a society gay, cultivated and refined beyond example—*even* in the Old Dominion. A hallowed charm seems to rest upon the venerable city, clothing its very dilapidation in a drapery of romance and of serene and classic interest: as if all the sweet and softened splendor which invests the " Midsummer Night's Dream" were poured in a flood of mellow and poetic radiance over the now quiet and half " deserted village." There is something in the shadow from the old college walls, cast by the moon upon the grass and sleeping on the sward, that throws a like shadow soft, sad and melancholy upon the heart of the returning pilgrim who saunters out to view again, by moonlight, his old *Alma Mater*—the nursing mother of such a list and such a line of statesmen and heroes.

There is nothing presumptuously froward in this Virginianism. The Virginian does not make broad his phylacteries and crow over the poor Carolinian and Tennesseeian. He does not reproach him with his misfortune of birthplace.

No, he thinks the affliction is enough without the triumph. The franchise of having been born in Virginia, and the prerogative founded thereon, are too patent of honor and distinction to be arrogantly pretended. The bare mention is enough. He finds occasion to let the fact be known, and then the fact is fully able to protect and take care of itself. Like a ducal title, there is no need of saying more than to name it: modesty then is a becoming and expected virtue; forbearance to boast is true dignity.

The Virginian is a magnanimous man. He never throws up to a Yankee the fact of his birthplace. He feels on the subject as a man of delicacy feels in alluding to a rope in the presence of a person, one of whose brothers "stood upon nothing and kicked at the U. S.," or to a female indiscretion, where there had been scandal concerning the family. So far do they carry this refinement, that I have known one of my countrymen, on occasion of a Bostonian owning where he was born, generously protest that he had never heard of it before. As if honest confession half obliterated the shame of the fact. Yet he does not lack the grace to acknowledge worth or merit in another, wherever the native place of that other: for it is a common thing to hear them say of a neighbor, "he is a clever fellow, *though* he *did* come from New Jersey or even Connecticut."

In politics the Virginian is learned much beyond what is written—for they have heard a great deal of speaking on that prolific subject, especially by one or two Randolphs and any number of Barbours. They read the same papers here they read in Virginia—the *Richmond Enquirer* and the *Rich mond Whig.* The democrat stoutly asseverates a fact, and gives *the Enquirer* as his authority with an air that means to say, *that* settles it : while the whig quoted Hampden Pleasants with the same confidence. But the faculty of personalizing every thing which the exceeding social turn of a Virginian gives him, rarely allowed a reference to the paper, *eo nomine ;* but made him refer to the editor : as " Ritchie said " so and so, or " Hampden Pleasants said " this or that. When two of opposite politics got together, it was amusing, if you had nothing else to do that day, to hear the discussion. I never knew a debate that did not start *ab urbe condita.* They not only went back to first principles, but also to first times; nor did I ever hear a discussion in which old John Adams and Thomas Jefferson did not figure—as if an interminable dispute had been going on for so many generations between those disputatious personages; as if the quarrel had begun before time, but was not to end with it. But the strangest part of it to me was, that the dispute seemed to be going on without poor Adams having any defence or champion; and never waxed hotter than when both parties agreed in denouncing the man of Braintree as the worst of public sinners and the vilest of political heretics. They both agreed on one thing, and that was to refer the matter to the Resolutions of 1798–99; which said Resolutions, like Goldsmith's "Good Natured Man," arbitrating between Mr. and Mrs. Croaker, seemed so impartial that they agreed with both parties on every occasion.

Nor do I recollect of hearing any question debated that did not resolve itself into a question of constitution—strict construction, &c.,—the constitution being a thing of that curious virtue that its chief excellency consisted in not allowing the government to do any thing; or in being a regular prize fighter that knocked all laws and legislators into a cocked hat, except those of the objector's party.

Frequent reference was reciprocally made to " gorgons, hydras, and chimeras dire," to black cockades, blue lights, Essex juntos, the Reign of Terror, and some other mystic entities—but who or what these monsters were, I never could distinctly learn; and was surprised, on looking into the history of the country, to find that, by some strange oversight, no allusion was made to them.

Great is the Virginian's reverence of great men, that is to say, of great Virginians. This reverence is not Unitarian. He is a Polytheist. He believes in a multitude of Virginia Gods. As the Romans of every province and village had their tutelary or other divinities, besides having divers national gods, so the Virginian of every county has his great man, the like of whom cannot be found in the new country he has exiled himself to. This sentiment of veneration for talent, especially for speaking talent,—this amiable propensity to lionize men, is not peculiar to any class of Virginians among us: it abides in all. I was amused to hear " old Culpepper," as we call him (by nickname derived from the county he came from), declaiming in favor of the Union. " What, gentlemen," said the old man, with a sonorous swell—" what,

burst up this glorious Union ! and who, if *this* Union is torn
up, could write another ?   Nobody except Henry Clay and
J— S. B—, of Culpepper—and may be *they* wouldn't—and
what then would you do for another ? "

The greatest compliment a Virginian can ever pay to a
speaker, is to say that he reminds him of a Col. Broadhorn
or a Captain Smith, who represented some royal-named county some forty years or less in the Virginia House of Dele-
gates ; and of whom, the auditor, of course, has heard, as he
made several speeches in the capitol at Richmond.   But
the force of the compliment is somewhat broken, by a long
narrative, in which the personal reminiscences of the speaker
go back to sundry sketches of the Virginia statesman's efforts,
and recapitulations of his sayings, interspersed *par paren-
these*, with many valuable notes illustrative of his pedigree
and performances ; the whole of which, given with great historical fidelity of detail, leaves nothing to be wished for except the point, or rather, two points, the gist and the period.

It is not to be denied that Virginia is the land of orators,
heroes and statesmen ; and that, directly or indirectly, she
has exerted an influence upon the national councils nearly as
great as all the rest of the States combined.   It is wonderful
that a State of its size and population should have turned out
such an unprecedented quantum of talent, and of talent as
various in kind as prodigious in amount.   She has reason to
be proud ; and the other States so largely in her debt (for,
from Cape May to Puget's Sound she has colonized the other
States and the territories with her surplus talent,) ought to

allow her the harmless privilege of a little bragging. In the showy talent of oratory has she especially shone. To accomplish her in this art the State has been turned into a debating society, and while she has been *talking* for the benefit of the nation, as she thought, the other, and, by nature, less favored States, have been *doing* for their own. Consequently, what she has gained in reputation, she has lost in wealth and *material aids*. Certainly the Virginia character has been less distinguished for its practical than its ornamental traits, and for its business qualities than for its speculative temper. *Cui bono* and utilitarianism, at least until latterly, were not favorite or congenial inquiries and subjects of attention to the Virginia politician. What the Virginian was upon his native soil, that he was abroad; indeed, it may be said that the *amor patriæ*, strengthened by absence, made him more of a conservative abroad than he would have been if he had staid at home; for most of them here would not, had they been consulted, have changed either of the old constitutions.

It is far, however, from my purpose to treat of such themes. I only glance at them to show their influence on the character as it was developed on a new theatre.

Eminently social and hospitable, kind, humane and generous is a Virginian, at home or abroad. They are so by nature and habit. These qualities and their exercise develope and strengthen other virtues. By reason of these social traits, they necessarily become well mannered, honorable, spirited, and careful of reputation, desirous of pleasing, and

skilled in the accomplishments which please. Their insular position and sparse population, mostly rural, and easy
but not affluent fortunes kept them from the artificial refinements and the strong temptations which corrupt so much of
the society of the old world and some portions of the new.
There was no character more attractive than that of a young
Virginian, fifteen years ago, of intelligence, of good family,
education and breeding.

It was of the instinct of a Virginian to seek society : he
belongs to the gregarious, not to the solitary division of
animals ; and society can only be kept up by grub and gab—
something to eat, and, if not something to talk about, talk.
Accordingly they came accomplished already in the knowledge and the talent for these important duties.

A Virginian could always get up a good dinner. He
could also do his share—a full hand's work—in disposing
of one after it was got up. The qualifications for hostman-
ship were signal—the old Udaller himself, assisted by Claud
Halrco, could not do up the thing in better style, or with a
heartier relish, or a more cordial hospitality. In *petite*
manners—the little attentions of the table, the filling up of
the chinks of the conversation with small fugitive observations, the supplying the hooks and eyes that *kept* the discourse
together, the genial good humor, which, like that of the
family of the good Vicar, made up in laughter what was
wanting in wit—in these, and in the science of getting up
and in getting through a picnic or chowder party, or fish fry,
the Virginian, like Eclipse, was first, and there was no sec-

ond.   Great was he too at mixing an apple toddy, or mint
julep, where ice could be got for love or money; and not deficient, by any means when it came to his turn to do honor to
his own fabrics.   It was in this department, that he not
only shone but *out*shone, not merely all others but himself.
Here he was at home indeed.   His elocution, his matter,
his learning, his education, were of the first order.   He could
discourse of every thing around him with an accuracy and a
fulness which would have put Coleridge's or Mrs. Ellis's table talk to the blush.   Every dish was a text, horticulture,
hunting, poultry, fishing—(Isaac Walton or Daniel Webster
would have been charmed and instructed to hear him discourse piscatory-wise,)—a slight divergence in favor of fox-
chasing and a detour towards a horse-race now and then, and
continual parentheses of recommendation of particular dishes
or glasses—Oh ! I tell you if ever there was an interesting
man it was he.   Others might be agreeable, but he was fasci
nating, irresistible, not-to-be-done-without.

     In the fulness of time the new era had set in—the era
of the second great experiment of independence : the experiment, namely, of credit without capital, and enterprise without honesty.   The Age of Brass had succeeded the Arcadi-
an period when men got rich by saving a part of their earn-
ings, and lived at their own cost and in ignorance of the new
plan of making fortunes on the profits of what they owed.
A new theory, not found in the works on political economy,
was broached.   It was found out that the prejudice in favor
of the metals (brass excluded) was an absurd superstition;
                              4*

and that, in reality, any thing else, which the parties interested in giving it currency chose, might serve as a representative of value and medium for exchange of property ; and as gold and silver had served for a great number of years as representatives, the republican doctrine of rotation in office required they should give way.   Accordingly it was decided that Rags, a very familiar character, and very popular and easy of access, should take their place.   Rags belonged to the school of progress.   He was representative of the then Young America.   His administration was not tame.   It was *very* spirited.   It was based on the Bonapartist idea of keeping the imagination of the people excited.   The leading fiscal idea of his system was to *democratize* capital, and to make, for all purposes of trade, credit and enjoyment of wealth, the man that had *no* money a little richer, if any thing, than the man that had a million.   The principle of success and basis of operation, though inexplicable in the hurry of the time, is plain enough now : it was faith.   Let the public believe that a smutted rag is money, it is money : in other words, it was a sort of financial biology, which made, at night, the thing conjured for, the thing that was seen, so far as the patient was concerned, while the fit was on him—except that now a man does not do his trading when under the mesmeric influence : in the flush times he did.

This country was just settling up.   Marvellous accounts had gone forth of the fertility of its virgin lands ; and the productions of the soil were commanding a price remunerating to slave labor as it had never been remunerated before.

Emigrants came flocking in from all quarters of the Union, especially from the slaveholding States. The new country seemed to be a'reservoir, and every road leading to it a vagrant stream of enterprise and adventure. Money, or what passed for money, was the only cheap thing to be had. Every cross-road and every avocation presented an opening,— through which a fortune was seen by the adventurer in near perspective. Credit was a thing of course. To refuse it— if the thing was ever done—were an insult for which a bowie-knife were not a too summary or exemplary a means of redress. The State banks were issuing their bills by the sheet, like a patent steam printing-press *its* issues; and no other showing was asked of the applicant for the loan than an authentication of his great distress for money. Finance, even in its most exclusive quarter, had thus already got, in this wonderful revolution, to work upon the principles of the charity hospital. If an overseer grew tired of supervising a plantation and felt a call to the mercantile life, even if he omitted the compendious method of buying out a merchant wholesale, stock, house and good will, and laying down, at once, his bull-whip for the yard-stick—all he had to do was to go on to New-York, and present himself in Pearl-street with a letter avouching his citizenship, and a clean shirt, and he was regularly given a through ticket to speedy bankruptcy.

Under this stimulating process prices rose like smoke. Lots in obscure villages were held at city prices; lands, bought at the minimum cost of government, were sold at from thirty to forty dollars per acre, and considered dirt cheap at-that. In short, the country had got to be a full ante-type of California, in all except the gold. Society was wholly unorganized: there was no restraining public opinion: the law was well-nigh powerless—and religion scarcely was heard of except as furnishing the oaths and *technics* of profanity. The world saw a fair experiment of what it would have been, if the fiat had never been pronounced which decreed subsistence as the price of labor.

Money, got without work, by those unaccustomed to it, turned the heads of its possessors, and they spent it with a recklessness like that with which they gained it. The pursuits of industry neglected, riot and coarse debauchery filled up the vacant hours. "Where the carcass is, there will the eagles be gathered together;" and the eagles that flocked to the Southwest, were of the same sort as the *black eagles* the Duke of Saxe-Weimar saw on his celebrated journey to the Natural Bridge. " The cankers of a long peace and a calm world "—there were no Mexican wars and filibuster expeditions in those days—gathered in the villages and cities by scores.

Even the little boys caught the taint of the general infection of morals ; and I knew one of them—Jim Ellett by name—to give a man ten dollars to hold him up to bet at the table of a faro-bank. James was a fast youth ; and I sincerely hope he may not fulfil his early promise, and some day be *assisted up still higher*.

The groceries—*vulgice*—doggeries, were in full blast in

those days, no village having less than a half-dozen all busy
all the time: gaming and horse-racing were polite and well
patronized amusements. I knew of a Judge to adjourn two
courts (or court twice) to attend a horse-race, at which he
officiated judicially and ministerially, and with more appro-
priateness than in the judicial chair. Occasionally the scene
was diversified by a murder or two, which though perpetra-
ted from behind a corner, or behind the back of the deceased, whenever the accused *chose* to stand his trial, was always
found to be committed in self-defence, securing the homicide
an honorable acquittal *at the hands of his peers.*

The old rules of business and the calculations of prudence were alike disregarded, and profligacy, in all the departments of the *crimen falsi*, held riotous carnival. Larceny grew not only respectable, but genteel, and ruffled it in
all the pomp of purple and fine linen. Swindling was raised
to the dignity of the fine arts. Felony came forth from its
covert, put on more seemly habiliments, and took its seat
with unabashed front in the upper places of the synagogue.
Before the first circles of the patrons of this brilliant and
dashing villainy, Blunt Honesty felt as abashed as poor Hal-
bert Glendinning by the courtly refinement and supercilious
airs of Sir Piercie Shafton.

Public office represented, by its incumbents, the state of
public morals with some approach to accuracy. Out of six-
ty-six receivers of public money in the new States, sixty-two
were discovered to be defaulters; and the agent, sent to
look into the affairs of a peccant office-holder in the

South-West, reported him *minus* some tens of thousands, but advised the government to retain him, for a reason one of Æsop's fables illustrates : the agent ingeniously surmising that the appointee succeeding would do his stealing without any regard to the proficiency already made by his predecessor; while the present incumbent would probably consider, in mercy to the treasury, that he *had* done *something* of the pious duty of providing for his household.

There was no petit larceny : there was all the difference between stealing by the small and the " operations" manipulated, that there is between a single assassination and an hundred thousand men killed in an opium war. The placeman robbed with the gorgeous magnificence of a Governor-General of Bengal.

The man of straw, not worth the buttons on his shirt, with a sublime audacity, bought lands and negroes, and provided times and terms of payment which a Wall-street capitalist would have to re-cast his arrangements to meet.

Oh, Paul Clifford and Augustus Tomlinson, philosophers of the road, practical and theoretical ! if ye had lived to see those times, how great an improvement on your ruder scheme of distribution would these gentle arts have seemed ; arts whereby, without risk, or loss of character, or the vulgar barbarism of personal violence, the same beneficial results flowed with no greater injury to the superstitions of moral education !

With the change of times and the imagination of wealth easily acquired came a change in the thoughts and habits of the people. " Old times were changed—old manners gone."

Visions of affluence, such as crowded Dr. Samuel Johnson's mind, when advertising a sale of Thrale's Brewery, and casting a soft sheep's eye towards Thrale's widow, thronged upon the popular fancy.　Avarice and hope joined partnership. It was strange how the reptile arts of humanity, as at a faro table, warmed into life beneath their heat.　The *cacoethes accrescendi* became epidemic.　It seized upon the universal community.　The pulpits even were not safe from its insidious invasion.　What men anxiously desire they willingly believe; and all believed a good time was coming—nay, had come.

"Commerce was king"—and Rags, Tag and Bobtail his cabinet council.　Rags was treasurer.　Banks, chartered on a specie basis, did a very flourishing business on the promissory notes of the individual stockholders ingeniously substituted in lieu of cash.　They issued ten for one, the *one* being fictitious.　They generously loaned all the directors could not use themselves, and were not choice whether Bardolph was the endorser for Falstaff, or Falstaff borrowed on his own proper credit, or the funds advanced him by Shallow. The stampede towards the golden temple became general : the delusion prevailed far and wide that this thing was not a burlesque on commerce and finance.　Even the directors of the banks began to have their doubts whether the intended swindle was not a failure.　Like Lord Clive, when reproached for extortion to the extent of some millions in Bengal, they exclaimed, after the bubble burst, "When they thought of what they had got, and what they might have got, they were astounded at their own moderation."

The old capitalists for a while stood out. With the Tory conservatism of cash in hand, worked for, they couldn't reconcile their old notions to the new regime. They looked for the thing's ending, and *then* their time. But the stampede still kept on. Paper fortunes still multiplied—houses and lands changed hands—real estate see-sawed up as morals went down on the other end of the plank—men of straw, corpulent with bank bills, strutted past them on 'Change. They began, too, to think there might be something in this new thing. Peeping cautiously, like hedge-hogs out of their holes, they saw the stream of wealth and adventurers passing by—then, looking carefully around, they inched themselves half way out—then, sallying forth and snatching up a morsel, ran back, until, at last, grown more bold, *they* ran out too with their hoarded store, in full chase with the other unclean beasts of adventure. They never got back again. Jonah's gourd withered one night, and next morning the vermin that had nestled under its broad shade were left unprotected, a prey to the swift retribution that came upon them. They were left naked, or only clothed themselves with cursing (the Specie Circular on the United States Bank) as with a garment. To drop the figure : Shylock himself couldn't live in those times, so reversed was every thing. Shaving paper and loaning money at a usury of fifty per cent, was for the first time since the Jews left Jerusalem, a breaking business to the operator.

The condition of society may be imagined :—vulgarity— ignorance—fussy and arrogant pretension—unmitigated rowdyism—bullying insolence, if they did not rule the hour, *seemed* to wield unchecked dominion. The workings of these choice spirits were patent upon the face of society; and the modest, unobtrusive, retiring men of worth and character (for there were many, perhaps a large majority of such) were almost lost sight of in the hurly-burly of those strange and shifting scenes.

Even in the professions were the same characteristics visible. Men dropped down into their places as from the clouds. Nobody knew who or what they were, except as they claimed, or as a surface view of their characters indicated. Instead of taking to the highway and magnanimously calling upon the wayfarer to stand and deliver, or to the fashionable larceny of credit without prospect or design of paying, some unscrupulous horse-doctor would set up his sign as " Physician and Surgeon," and draw his lancet on you, or fire at random a box of his pills into your bowels, with a vague chance of hitting some disease unknown to him, but with a better prospect of killing the patient, whom or whose administrator he charged some ten dollars a trial for his markmanship.

A superannuated justice or constable in one of the old States was metamorphosed into a lawyer; and though he knew not the distinction between a *fee tail* and a *female*, would undertake to construe, off-hand, a will involving all the subtleties of *uses and trusts*.

But this state of things could not last for ever: society cannot always stand on its head with its heels in the air.

The Jupiter Tonans of the White House saw the monster of a free credit prowling about like a beast of apocalyptic vision, and marked him for his prey. Gathering all his bolts in his sinewy grasp, and standing back on his heels, and waving his wiry arm, he let them all fly, hard and swift upon all the hydra's heads. Then came a crash, as "if the ribs of nature broke," and a scattering, like the bursting of a thousand magazines, and a smell of brimstone, as if Pandemonium had opened a window next to earth for ventilation, —and all was silent. The beast never stirred in his tracks. To get down from the clouds to level ground, the Specie Circular was issued without warning, and the splendid lie of a false credit burst into fragments. It came in the midst of the dance and the frolic—as Tam O'Shanter came to disturb the infernal glee of the warlocks, and to disperse the rioters. Its effect was like that of a general creditor's bill in the chancery court, and a marshalling of all the assets of the trades-people. Gen. Jackson was no fairy; but he did some very pretty fairy work, in converting the bank bills back again into rags and oak-leaves. Men worth a million were insolvent for two millions : promising young cities marched back again into the wilderness. The ambitious town plat was re-annexed to the plantation, like a country girl taken home from the city. The frolic was ended, and what headaches, and feverish limbs the next morning! The retreat from Moscow was performed over again, and "Devil take the hindmost" was the tune to which the soldiers of fortune marched. The only question was as to the means of escape, and the nearest and best route to Texas.   The sheriff was as busy as a militia adjutant on review day ; and the lawyers were mere wreckers, earning salvage.   Where are ye now my ruffling gallants ?   Where now the braw cloths and watch chains and rings and fine horses ?   Alas! for ye—they are glimmering among the things that were—the wonder of an hour !   They live only in memory, as unsubstantial as the promissory notes ye gave for them.   When it came to be tested, the whole matter was found to be hollow and falla-cious.   Like a sum ciphered out through a long column, the first figure an error, the whole, and all the parts were wrong, throughout the entire calculation.

Such is a charcoal sketch of the interesting region—now inferior to none in resources, and the character of its popula-tion—during the FLUSH TIMES ; a period constituting an epi-sode in the commercial history of the world—the reign of humbug, and wholesale insanity, just overthrown in time to save the whole country from ruin.   But while it lasted, many of our countrymen came into the South-West in time to get " a benefit."   The *auri sacra fames* is a catching dis-ease.   Many Virginians had lived too fast for their fortunes, and naturally desired to recuperate : many others, with a competency, longed for wealth ; and others again, with wealth, yearned—the common frailty—for still more.   Perhaps some friend or relative, who had come out, wrote back flat-tering accounts of the El Dorado, and fired with dissatisfac-tion those who were doing well enough at home, by the report of his real or imagined success ; for who that ever moved

off, was not " doing well " in the new country, himself or
friends being chroniclers ?

Superior to many of the settlers in elegance of manners,
and general intelligence, it was the weakness of the Virgini-
a₁ to imagine he was superior too in the essential art of being able to hold his hand and make his way in a new country, and especially *such* a country, and at *such* a time.
What a mistake that was ! The times were out of joint.
It was hard to say whether it were more dangerous to stand
still or to move. If the emigrant stood still, he was consumed, by no slow degrees, by expenses : if he moved, ten
to one he went off in a galloping consumption, by a ruinous
investment. Expenses then—necessary articles about three
times as high, and extra articles still more extra-priced—
were a different thing in the new country from what they
were in the old. In the old country, a jolly Virginian, start-
ting the business of free living on a capital of a plantation,
and fifty or sixty negroes, might reasonably calculate, if no
ill luck befell him, by the aid of a usurer, and the occasional
sale of a negro or two, to hold out without declared insol-
vency, until a green old age. His estate melted like an estate in chancery, under the gradual thaw of expenses ; but
in this fast country, it went by the sheer cost of living—
some *poker* losses included—like the fortune of the confec-
tioner in California, who failed for one hundred thousand dollars in the six months keeping of a candy-shop. But all the
habits of his life, his taste, his associations, his education—
every thing—the trustingness of his disposition—his want

of business qualifications—his sanguine temper—all that was
Virginian in him, made him the prey, if not of imposture,
at least of unfortunate speculations.   Where the keenest
jockey often was bit, what chance had *he ?*   About the same
that the verdant Moses had with the venerable old gentleman, his father's friend, at the fair, when he traded the Vicar's pony for the green spectacles.   But how could he believe it ?   how *could* he believe that that stuttering, gram-
marless Georgian, who had never heard of the resolutions
of '98, could beat him in a land trade ?   " Have no money
dealings with my father," said the friendly Martha to Lord
Nigel, " for, idiot though he seems, he will make an ass of
thee."   What a pity some monitor, equally wise and equally
successful with old Trapbois' daughter, had not been at the
elbow of every Virginian !   " Twad frae monie a blunder
free'd him—an' foolish notion."

If he made a bad bargain, how could he expect to get
rid of it ?   *He* knew nothing of the elaborate machinery of
ingenious chicane,—such as feigning bankruptcy—fraudulent
conveyances—making over to his wife—running property—
and had never heard of such tricks of trade as sending out
coffins to the graveyard, with negroes inside, carried off by
sudden spells of imaginary disease, to be " resurrected," in
due time, grinning, on the banks of the Brazos.

The new philosophy, too, had commended itself to his speculative temper.   He readily caught at the idea of a new
spirit of the age having set in, which rejected the saws of Poor
Richard as being as much out of date as his almanacs.   He

was already, by the great rise of property, compared to his condition under the old-time prices, rich; and what were a few thousands of debt, which two or three crops would pay off, compared to the value of his estate? (He never thought that the value of property might come down, while the debt was a fixed fact.) He lived freely, for it was a liberal time, and liberal fashions were in vogue, and it was not for a Virginian to be behind others in hospitality and liberality. He required credit and security, and, of course, had to stand security in return. When the crash came, and no " accommodations " could be had, except in a few instances, and in those on the most ruinous terms, he fell an easy victim. They broke by neighborhoods. They usually endorsed for each other, and when one fell—like the child's play of putting bricks on end at equal distances, and dropping the first in the line against the second, which fell against the third, and so on to the last—all fell; each got broke as security, and yet few or none were able to pay their own debts! So powerless of protection were they in those times, that the witty H. G. used to say they reminded him of an oyster, both shells torn off, lying on the beach, with the sea-gulls screaming over them; the only question being, *which* should " gobble them up."

There was one consolation—if the Virginian involved himself like a fool, he suffered himself to be sold out like a gentleman. When his card house of visionary projects came tumbling about his ears, the next question was, the one Webster plagiarised—" Where am I to go ? " Those who had fathers, uncles, aunts, or other like dernier resorts, in Virginia, limped back with feathers moulted and crestfallen, to the old stamping ground, carrying the returned Californian's fortune of ten thousand dollars—six bits in money, and the balance in experience.   Those who were in the condition of the prodigal, (barring the father, the calf—the fatted one I mean—and the fiddle,) had to turn their accomplishments to account ; and many of them, having lost all by eating and drinking, sought the retributive justice from meat and drink, which might, at least, support them in poverty.   Accordingly, they kept tavern, and made a barter of hospitality, a business, the only disagreeable part of which was receiving the money, and the only one I know of for which a man can eat and drink himself into qualification.   And while I confess I never knew a Virginian, out of the State, to keep a bad tavern, I never knew one to draw a solvent breath from the time he opened house, until death or the sheriff closed it.

Others again got to be, not exactly overseers, but some nameless thing, the duties of which were nearly analogous, for some more fortunate Virginian, who had escaped the wreck, and who had got his former boon companion to live with him on board, or other wages, in some such relation that the friend was not often found at table at the dinings given to the neighbors, and had got to be called Mr. Flournoy instead of Bob, and slept in an out-house in the yard, and only read the *Enquirer* of nights and Sundays.

Some of the younger scions that had been transplanted early, and stripped of their foliage at a tender age, had been

turned into birches for the corrective discipline of youth.
Yes; many, who had received academical or collegiate edu-
cations, disregarding the allurements of the highway—turning from the gala-day exercise of ditching—scorning the
effeminate relaxation of splitting rails—heroically led the
Forlorn Hope of the battle of life, the corps of pedagogues
of country schools—*academies*, I beg pardon for *not* saying;
for, under the Virginia economy, every cross-road log-cabin,
where boys were flogged from B-a-k-e-r to Constantinople,
grew into the dignity of a sort of runt college; and the
teacher vainly endeavored to hide the meanness of the calling beneath the sonorous *sobriquet* of Professor. "Were
there no wars?" Had *all* the oysters been opened? Where
was the regular army? Could not interest procure service
as a deck-hand on a steamboat? Did no stage-driver, with a
contract for running at night, through the prairies in mid-
winter, want help, at board wages, and sweet lying in the
loft, when off duty; thrown in? What right had the Dutch
Jews to monopolize *all* the peddling? "To such vile uses
may we come at last, Horatio." The subject grows melancholy. I had a friend on whom this catastrophe descended.
Tom Edmundson was a buck of the first head—gay, witty,
dashing, vain, proud, handsome and volatile, and, withal, a
dandy and lady's man to the last intent in particular. He
had graduated at the University, and had just settled with
his guardian, and received his patrimony of ten thousand
dollars in money. Being a young gentleman of enterprise,
he sought the alluring fields of South-Western adventure,

and found them in this State. Before he well knew the
condition of his exchequer, he had made a permanent investment of one-half of his fortune in cigars, Champagne,
trinkets, buggies, horses, and current expenses, including
some small losses at poker, which game he patronized merely
for amusement; and found that it diverted him a good deal,
but diverted his cash much more. He invested the balance,
on private information kindly given him, in " *Choctaw
Floats ;*" a most lucrative investment it would have turned
out, but for the facts : 1. That the Indians never had any
title ; 2. The white men who kindly interposed to act as
guardians for the Indians did not have the Indian title; and
3dly, the land, left subject to entry, if the " Floats" had
been good, was not worth entering. " These imperfections
off its head," I know of no fancy stock I would prefer to a
" Choctaw Float." " Brief, brave and glorious" was " Tom's
young career." When Thomas found, as he did shortly,
that he had bought five thousand dollars' worth of moonshine,
and had no title to it, he honestly informed his landlord of
the state of his " fiscality," and that worthy kindly consented
to take a new buggy, at half price, in payment of the old
balance. The horse, a nick-tailed trotter, Tom had raffled
off ; but omitting to require cash, the process of collection
resulted in his getting the price of one chance—the winner
of the horse magnanimously paying his subscription. The
rest either had gambling offsets, or else were not prepared
just at any one particular, given moment, to pay up, though
always ready, generally and in a general way.

4

Unlike his namesake, Tom and his landlady were not—for a sufficient reason—very gracious; and so, the only common bond, Tom's money, being gone, Tom received "notice to quit" in regular form.

In the hurly-burly of the times, I had lost sight of Tom for a considerable period. One day, as I was travelling over the hills in Greene, by a cross-road, leading me near a country mill, I stopped to get water at a spring at the bottom of a hill. Clambering up the hill, after remounting, on the other side, the summit of it brought me to a view, through the bushes, of a log country school-house, the door being wide open, and who did I see but Tom Edmundson, dressed as fine as ever, sitting back in an arm-chair, one thumb in his waistcoat armhole, the other hand brandishing a long switch, or rather pole. As I approached a little nearer, I heard him speak out : " Sir—Thomas Jefferson, of Virginia, was the author of the Declaration of Independence—mind that. I thought everybody knew that—even the Georgians." Just then he saw me coming through the bushes and entering the path that led by the door. Suddenly he broke from the chair of state, and the door was slammed to, and I heard some one of the boys, as I passed the door, say —" Tell him he can't come in—the master's sick." This is the last I ever saw of Tom. I understand he afterwards moved to Louisiana, where he married a rich French widow, having first, however, to fight a duel with one of her sons, whose opposition couldn't be appeased, until some such expiatory sacrifice to the manes of his worthy father was

THE SCHOOLMASTER ABROAD.

attempted; which failing, he made rather a *lame* apology
for his zealous indiscretion—the poor fellow could make no
other—for Tom had unfortunately fixed him for visiting his
mother on crutches the balance of his life.

One thing I will say for the Virginians—I never knew
one of them, under any pressure, extemporize a profession.
The sentiment of reverence for the mysteries of medicine
and law was too large for a deliberate quackery; as to the
pulpit, a man might as well do his starving without the
hypocrisy.

But others were not so nice. I have known them to rush,
when the wolf was after them, from the counting-house or the
plantation, into a doctor's shop or a law office, as if those
places were the sanctuaries from the avenger; some pretend-
ing to be doctors that did not know a liver from a gizzard,
administering medicine by the guess, without knowing enough
of pharmacy to tell whether the stuff exhibited in the big-
bellied blue, red and green bottles at the show-windows of
the apothecaries' shops, was given by the drop or the half-
pint.

Divers others left, but what became of them, I never
knew any more than they know what becomes of the sora
after frost.

Many were the instances of suffering; of pitiable misfortune, involving and crushing whole families; of pride
abased; of honorable sensibilities wounded; of the provision for old age destroyed; of the hopes of manhood overcast; of independence dissipated, and the poor victim with-

out help, or hope, or sympathy, forced to petty shifts for a
bare subsistence, and a ground-scuffle, for what in happier
days, he threw away. But there were too many examples
of this sort for the expenditure of a useless compassion ;
just as the surgeon after a battle, grows case-hardened, from
an excess of objects of pity.

My memory, however, fixes itself on one honored exception, the noblest of the noble, the best of the good. Old
Major Willis Wormley had come in long before the *new era.*
He belonged to the old school of Virginians. Nothing could
have torn him from the Virginia he loved, as Jacopi Foscari,
Venice, but the marrying of his eldest daughter, Mary, to a
gentleman of Alabama. The Major was something between,
or made of about equal parts, of Uncle Toby and Mr. Pick-
wick, with a slight flavor of Mr. Micawber. He was the
soul of kindness, disinterestedness and hospitality. Love to
every thing that had life in it, burned like a flame in his
large and benignant soul ; it flowed over in his countenance,
and glowed through every feature, and moved every muscle
in the frame it animated. The Major lived freely, was
rather corpulent, and had not a lean thing on his plantations ;
the negroes ; the dogs ; the horses ; the cattle ; the very
chickens, wore an air of corpulent complacency, and bustled
about with a good-humored rotundity. There was more
laughing, singing and whistling at " Hollywood," than would
have set up a dozen Irish fairs. The Major's wife had, from
a long life of affection, and the practice of the same pursuits,
and the indulgence of the same feelings and tastes, got so

much like him, that she seemed a feminine and modest edition
of himself. Four daughters were all that remained in the
family—two had been married off—and they had no son.
The girls ranged from sixteen to twenty-two, fine, hearty,
whole-souled, wholesome, cheerful lasses, with constitutions
to last, and a flow of spirits like mountain springs—not
beauties, but good housewife girls, whose open countenances, and neat figures, and rosy cheeks, and laughing eyes,
and frank and cordial manners, made them, at home, abroad,
on horseback or on foot, at the piano or discoursing on the
old English books, or Washington Irving's Sketch Book, a
favorite in the family ever since it was written, as entertain-
ing and as well calculated to fix solid impressions on the
heart, as any four girls in the country. The only difficulty
was, they were so much alike, that you were put to fault
which to fall in love with.   They were all good housewives,
or women, rather.   But Mrs. Wormley, or Aunt Wormley,
as we called her, was as far ahead of any other woman in that
way, as could be found this side of the Virginia border. If there
was any thing good in the culinary line that she couldn't make,
I should like to know it.   The Major lived on the main stage
road, and if any decently dressed man ever passed the house
after sundown, he escaped by sheer accident. The house
was greatly visited.   The Major knew every body, and everybody near him knew the Major.   The stage coach couldn't stop
long, but in the hot summer days, about noon, as the driver toot-
ed his horn at the top of the red hill, two negro boys stood
opposite the door, with trays of the finest fruit, and a pitcher

of cider for the refreshment of the wayfarers. The Major
himself being on the look-out, with his hands over his eyes,
bowing—as he only could bow—vaguely into the coach, and
looking wistfully, to find among the passengers an acquaintance whom he could prevail upon to get out and stay a week
with him. There wasn't a poor neighbor to whom the Major
had not been as good as an insurer, without premium, for
his stock, or for his crop ; and from the way he rendered
the service, you would think he was the party obliged—as
he was.

This is not, in any country I have ever been in, a money-
making business ; and the Major, though he always made
good crops, must have broke at it long ago, but for the fortunate death of a few Aunts, after whom the girls were
named, who, paying their several debts of nature, left the
Major the means to pay his less serious, but still weighty
obligations.

The Major—for a wonder, being a Virginian—had no
partisan politics. He could not have. His heart could not
hold any thing that implied a warfare upon the thoughts or
feelings of others. He voted all the time for his friend, that
is, the candidate living nearest to him, regretting, generally,
that he did not have another vote for the other man.

It would have done a Camanche Indian's heart good to
see all the family together—grand-children and all—of a
winter evening, with a guest or two, to excite sociability a
little—not company enough to embarrass the manifestations
of affection. Such a concordance—as if all hearts were at-

tuned to the same feeling—the old lady knitting in the corner—the old man smoking his pipe opposite—both of their fine faces radiating in the pauses of the laugh, the jest, or the caress, the infinite satisfaction within.

It was enough to convert an abolitionist, to see the old Major when he came home from a long journey of two days to the county town ; the negroes running in a string to the buggy ; this one to hold the horse, that one to help the old man out, and the others to inquire how he was ; and to observe the benignity with which—the kissing of the girls and the old lady hardly over—he distributed a piece of calico here, a plug of tobacco there, or a card of *town* ginger-bread to the little snow-balls that grinned around him ; what was given being but a small part of the gift, divested of the kind, cheerful, rollicking way the old fellow had of giving it.

The Major had given out his autograph (as had almost every body else) as endorser on three several bills of exchange, of even tenor and date, and all maturing at or about the same time. His friend's friend failed to pay as he or his firm agreed, the friend himself did no better, and the Major, before he knew any thing at all of his danger, found a writ served upon him, and was told by his friend that he was dead broke, and all he could give him was his sympathy ; the which, the Major as gratefully received as if it was a legal tender and would pay the debt. The Major's friends advised him he could get clear of it ; that notice of protest not having been sent to the Major's post-office, released him; but the Major wouldn't hear of such a defence; he said *his* understanding was, that he was to pay the debt if his friend didn't ; and to slip out of it by a quibble, was little better than pleading the gambling act.   Besides, what would the lawyers say ?   And what would be said by his old friends in Virginia, when it reached their ears, that he had plead want of notice, to get clear of a debt, when every body knew it was the same thing as if he had got notice.   And if this defence were good at law, it would not be in equity ; and if they took it into chancery, it mattered not what became of the case, the property would all go, and he never could expect to see the last of it.   No, no; he would pay it, and had as well set about it at once.

The rumor of the Major's condition spread far and wide. It reached old N. D., " an angel," whom the Major had " entertained," and one of the few that ever travelled that road.   He came, post haste, to see into the affair ; saw the creditor ; made him, upon threat of defence, agree to take half the amount, and discharge the Major ; advanced the money, and took the Major's negroes—except the house-servants—and put them on his Mississippi plantation to work out the debt.

The Major's heart pained him at the thought of the negroes going off; he couldn't witness it ; though he consoled himself with the idea of the discipline and exercise being good for the health of sundry of them who had contracted sedentary diseases.

The Major turned his house into a tavern—that is,

changed its name—put up a sign, and three weeks afterwards, you couldn't have told that any thing had happened. The family were as happy as ever—the Major never having put on airs of arrogance in prosperity, felt no humiliation in adversity; the girls were as cheerful, as bustling, and as light-hearted as ever, and seemed to think of the duties of hostesses as mere bagatelles, to enliven the time. The old Major was as profluent of anecdotes as ever, and never grew tired of telling the same ones to every new guest; and yet, the Major's anecdotes were all of Virginia growth, and not one of them under the legal age of twenty-one. If the Major had worked his negroes as he had those anecdotes, he would have been able to pay off the bills of exchange without any difficulty.

The old lady and the girls laughed at the anecdotes, though they must have heard them at least a thousand times, and knew them by heart; for the Major told them without the variations; and the other friends of the Major laughed too; indeed, with such an air of thorough benevolence, and in such a truly social spirit did the old fellow proceed " the tale to unfold," that a Cassius like rascal that wouldn't laugh, whether he saw any thing to laugh at or not, ought to have been sent to the Penitentiary for life—half of the time to be spent in solitary confinement.

5*

ASSAULT AND BATTERY.

A trial came off not precisely in our bailiwick, but in the neighborhood, of great comic interest. It was really a case of a good deal of aggravation, and the defendants, fearing the result, employed four of the ablest lawyers practising at the M. bar, to defend them. The offence charged was only assault and battery; but the evidence showed a conspiracy to inflict great violence on the person of the prosecutor, who had done nothing to provoke it, and that the attempt to effect it was followed by severe injury to him. The prosecutor was an original. He had been an old-field schoolmaster, and was as conceited and pedantic a fellow as could be found in a summer's day, even in that profession. It was thought the policy of the defence to make as light of the case as possible, and to cast as much ridicule on the affair as they could. J. E. and W. M. led the defence, and, although the talents of the former were rather adapted to grave discussion than pleasantry, he agreed to doff his heavy armor for the lighter weapons of wit and ridicule. M. was in his element. He was at all times and on all occasions at home when fun was to be raised : the difficulty with him was rather to restrain than to create mirth and laughter. The case was called and put to the jury. The witness, one Burwell Shines, was called for the prosecution. A broad grin was upon the faces of the counsel for the defence as he came forward. It was increased when the clerk said, " *Burrell* Shines come to the book ;" and the witness, with deliberate emphasis, remarked—" My christian name is not *Burrell*, but *Burwell*—though I am vulgarly denominated by the former epithet." " Well," said said the clerk, " Bur-*well* Shines come to the book and be sworn." He *was* sworn and directed to take the stand. He was a picture !

He was dressed with care. His toilet was elaborate and befitting the magnitude and dignity of the occasion, the part he was to fill and the high presence into which he had come. He was evidently favorably impressed with his own personal pulchritude ; yet, with an air of modest deprecation, as if he said by his manner, " after all, what *is* beauty that man should be proud of it, and what are fine clothes, that the wearers should put themselves above the unfortunate mortals who have them not ?"

He advanced with deliberate gravity to the stand. There he stood, his large bell-crowned hat with nankeen-colored nap an inch long in his hand ; which hat he carefully handed over the bar to the clerk, to hold until he should get through his testimony. He wore a blue single-breasted coat with new brass buttons ; a vest of bluish calico ; nankeen pants that struggled to make both ends meet, but failed, by

a few inches, in the legs, yet made up for it by fitting a little
better than the skin every where else; his head stood upon
a shirt collar that held it up by the ears, and a cravat something smaller than a table-cloth, bandaged his throat : his
face was narrow, long and grave, with an indescribable air of
ponderous wisdom, which, as Fox said of Thurlow, " proved
him *necessarily* a hypocrite; as it was *impossible* for *any*
man to be as wise as *he* looked." Gravity and decorum marked every lineament of his countenance, and every line of his
body. All the wit of Hudibras could not have moved a muscle of his face. His conscience would have smitten him for
a laugh almost as soon as for an oath. His hair was roached up, and stood as erect and upright as his body ; and his
voice was slow, deep, in " linked sweetness long drawn out,"
and modulated according to the camp-meeting standard of
elocution. Three such men at a country frolic, would have
turned an old Virginia Reel into a Dead March. He was
one of Carlyle's earnest men. Cromwell would have made
him Ensign of the Ironsides, and ex-officio chaplain at first
sight. He took out his pocket hankerchief, slowly unfolded
it from the shape in which it came from the washerwoman's,
and awaited the interrogation. As he waited, he spat on the
floor and nicely wiped it out with his foot. The solicitor told
him to tell about the difficulty in hand. He gazed around
on the court—then on the bar—then on the jury—then on
the crowd—addressing each respectively as he turned :
" May it please your honor—Gentlemen of the bar—Gentlemen of the jury—Audience. Before proceeding to give my

testimonial observations, I must premise that I am a member of the Methodist Episcopal, otherwise called Wesleyan persuasion of Christian individuals   One bright Sabbath morning in May, the 15th day of the month, the past year, while the birds were singing their matutinal songs from the trees, I sallied forth from the dormitory of my Seminary, to enjoy the reflections so well suited to that auspicious occasion.   I had not proceeded far, before my ears were accosted with certain Bacchanalian sounds of revelry, which proceeded from one of those haunts of vicious depravity, located at the Cross Roads, near the place of my boyhood, and fashionably denominated a doggery.   No sooner had I passed beyond the precincts of this diabolical rendezvous of rioting debauchees, than I heard behind me the sounds of approaching footsteps as if in pursuit.   Having heard previously, sundry menaces, which had been made by these proposterous and incarnadine individuals of hell, now on trial in prospect of condign punishment, fulminated against the longer continuance of my corporeal salubrity, for no better reason than that I reprobated their criminal orgies, and not wishing my reflections to be disturbed, I hurried my steps with a gradual accelerated motion.   Hearing, however, their continued advance, and the repeated shoutings, articulating the murderous accents, " Kill him !   Kill Shadbelly with his praying clothes on ! " (which was a profane designation of myself and my religious profession ;) and casting my head over my left shoulder in a manner somehow reluctantly thus, (throwing his head to one side,) and perceiving their near approximation, I augmented my speed into what might be denominated a gentle slope—and subsequently augmented the same into a species of dog-trot. But all would not do. Gentlemen, the destroyer came. As I reached the fence and was about propelling my body over the same, felicitating myself on my prospect of escape from my remorseless pursuers, they arrived, and James William Jones, called, by nickname, Buck Jones, that red-headed character now at the bar of this honorable court, seized a fence rail, grasped it in both hands, and standing on tip-toe, hurled the same, with mighty emphasis, against my cerebellum : which blow felled me to the earth. Straightway, like ignoble curs upon a disabled lion, these bandit ruffians and incarnadine assassins leaped upon me, some pelting, some bruising, some gouging—" every thing by turns, and nothing long," as the poet hath it ; and one of them, which one unknown to me—having no eyes behind—inflicted with his teeth, a grievous wound upon my person—where, I need not specify. At length, when thus prostrate on the ground, one of those bright ideas, common to minds of men of genius, struck me : I forthwith sprang to my feet—drew forth my cutto—circulated the same with much vivacity among their several and respective corporeal systems, and every time I circulated the same I felt their iron-grasp relax. As cowardly recreants, even to their own guilty friendships, two of these miscreants, though but slightly perforated by my cutto, fled, leaving the other two, whom I had disabled by the vigor and energy of my incisions, prostrate and in my power : these lustily called for quarter, shouting out "enough!" or, in their barbarous dialect, being as corrupt in language as in morals, "nuff;" which quarter I magnanimously extended them, as unworthy of my farther vengeance, and fit only as subject of penal infliction, at the hands of the offended laws of their country; to which laws I do now consign them: hoping such mercy for them as their crimes will permit; which, in my judgment, (having read the code,) is not much. This is my statement on oath, fully and truly, nothing extenuating and naught setting down in malice; and, if I have omitted any thing, in form or substance, I stand ready to supply the omission; and if I have stated any thing amiss, I will cheerfully correct the same, limiting the averment, with appropriate modifications, provisions and re-strictions. The learned counsel may now proceed more particularly to interrogate me of and respecting the premises."

After this oration, Burwell wiped the perspiration from his brow, and the counsel for the State took him. Few questions were asked him, however, by that official; he con-fining himself to a recapitulation in simple terms, of what the witness had declared, and procuring Burwell's assent to his translation. Long and searching was the cross-examination by the defendants' counsel; but it elicited nothing favorable to the defence, and nothing shaking, but much to confirm Burwell's statement.

After some other evidence, the examination closed, and the argument to the jury commenced. The solicitor very briefly adverted to the leading facts, deprecated any attempt to turn the case into ridicule—admitted that the witness was a man of eccentricity and pedantry, but harmless and inoffensive—a man evidently of conscientiousness and respectability ; that he had shown himself to be a peaceable man, but when occasion demanded, a brave man ; that there was a conspiracy to assassinate him upon no cause except an independence, which was honorable to him, and an attempt to execute the purpose, in pursuance of previous threats and severe injury by several confederates on a single person, and this on the Sabbath, and when he was seeking to avoid them.

W. M. rose to reply. All Screamersville turned out to hear him. William was a great favorite—the most popular speaker in the country—had the versatility of a mocking-bird, an aptitude for burlesque that would have given him celebrity as a dramatist, and a power of acting that would have made his fortune on the boards of a theatre. A rich treat was expected, but it didn't come. The witness had taken all the wind out of William's sails. He had rendered burlesque impossible. The thing as acted was more ludicrous than it could be as described. The crowd had laughed themselves hoarse already ; and even M.'s comic powers seemed and were felt by himself to be humble imitations of a greater master. For once in his life, M. dragged his subject heavily along—the matter began to grow serious—fun failed to come when M. called it up. M. closed between a lame argument, a timid deprecation, and some only tolerable humor. He was followed by E., in a discursive, argumentative, sarcastic, drag-net sort of speech, which did all that could be done for the defence. The solicitor briefly closed —seriously and confidently confining himself to a repetition of the matters first insisted, and answering some of the points of the counsel.

It was an ominous fact that a juror, before the jury retired under leave of the court, recalled a witness for the purpose of putting a question to him—the question was, how much the defendants were worth ; the answer was, about two thousand dollars.

The jury shortly after returned into court with a verdict which " sized their pile."

SIMON SUGGS, JR., ESQ.

A Legal Biography.

CORRESPONDENCE.

OFFICE OF THE JURIST-MAKER, ⎱
CITY OF GOT-HIM, NOV. 18, 1852. ⎰

COL. SIMON SUGGS, JR.

My Dear Sir,—Having established, at great expense, and from motives purely patriotic and disinterested, a monthly periodical for the purpose of supplying a desideratum in American Literature, namely, the commemoration and perpetuation of the names, characters, and personal and professional traits and histories of American lawyers and jurists, I have taken the liberty of soliciting *your* consent to be made the subject of one of the memoirs, which shall adorn the columns of this Journal. This suggestion is made from my knowledge, shared by the intelligence of the whole country, of your distinguished standing and merits in our noble profession; and it is seconded by the wishes and requests of many of the most prominent gentlemen in public and private life, who have the honor of your acquaintance.

The advantages of a work of this sort, in its more public and general bearing, are so *patent*, that it would be useless for me to refer to them. The effect of the publication upon the fame of the individual commemorated is, if not equally apparent, at least, equally decided. The fame of an American lawyer, like that of an actor, though sufficiently marked and cognizable within the region of his practice, and by the witnesses of his performances, is nevertheless, for the want of an organ for its national dissemination, or of an enduring memorial for its preservation, apt to be ephemeral, or, at most, to survive among succeeding generations, only in the form of unauthentic and vague traditions. What do we know of Henry or of Grundy as lawyers, except that they were eloquent and successful advocates. But what they did was to acquire reputation, and, of course, the true value of it, is left to conjecture'; or, as in the case of the former, especially, to posthumous invention or embellishment.

It was the observation of the great Pinkney, that the lawyer's distinction was preferable to all others, since it was impossible to acquire in our profession, a false or fraudulent reputation. How true this aphorism is, the pages of this L.w M......e will abundantly illustrate.

The value, and, indeed, the fact of distinction, consists in its uncommonness. In a whole nation of giants, the Welsh monster in Barnum's Museum would be undistin-- guished. Therefore, *we*—excuse the editorial plural—strive to collect the histories only of the most eminent of the profession in the several States.; the aggregate of whom reaches

some two or three hundred names. You have undoubtedly
seen some of the numbers of our work, which will better illustrate our plan, and the mode of its past, as well as the
intended mode of its future, execution.

It would be affectation, my dear sir, to deny that what
mainly consoles us under a sense of the hazardous nature of
such an enterprise to our *personal* fortunes—pardon the pun,
if you please—and amidst the anxieties of so laborious an
undertaking, is the expectation, that, through our labors,
the reputation of distinguished men of the country, constituting its moral treasure, may be preserved for the admiration
and direction of mankind, not for a day, but for all time.
And it has occurred to me, that such true merit as yours
might find a motive for your enrolment among the known sages
and profound intellects of the land, not less in the natural desire of a just perpetuation of renown, than in the patriotism
which desires the improvement of the race of lawyers who
are to come after you, and the adding to the accredited standards of public taste and professional attainment and genius.

We know from experience, that the characteristic diffidence of the profession, in many instances, shrinks from the
seeming, though falsely seeming, indelicacy of an egotistical
parade of one's own talents and accomplishments, and from
walking into a niche of the Pantheon of American genius we
have opened, and over the entrance to which, " FOR THE
GREAT " is inscribed. But the facility with which this difficulty has been surmounted by some, of whose success we had
reason to entertain apprehensions, adds but further evidence

of the capacity which the noble profession of the law gives
for the most arduous exploits. Besides, sir, although the
facts are expected to be furnished by the subject, yet the
first person is but seldom used in the memoir—some complaisant friend, or some friend's name being employed as editor of the work; the subject sometimes, indeed, having nothing to do except to revise it and transmit it to this office.

You may remember, my dear Colonel, the exclamatory
line of the poet—

> ————————"How hard it is to climb
> The steep where fame's proud temple shines afar."

And so it used to be : but in this wonderfully progress-
ive age it is no longer so. It is the pride of your humble
correspondent to have constructed a plan, by means of his
journal, whereby a gentleman of genius may, with the assistance of a single friend, or even without it, wind himself, up
from the vale below, as by a windlass, up to the very cupola
of the temple.

May we rely upon your sending us the necessary papers,
viz., a sketch of your life, genius, exploits, successes, accomplishments, virtues, family antecedents, personal pulchri-
tudes, professional habitudes, and whatever else you may
deem interesting. You can see from former numbers of our
work, that nothing will be irrelevant or out of place. The
sketch may be from ten to sixty pages in length.

Please send also a good daguerreotype likeness of yourself,
from which an engraving may be executed, to accompany the

sketch. *The daguerreotype had better be taken with reference to the engraving to accompany the memoir*—the hair
combed or brushed from the brow, so as to show a high fore-
head—the expression meditative—a book in the hand, &c.

Hoping soon to hear favorably from you, I am, with
great respect and esteem,

                                        THE EDITOR.

P. S. It is possible that sketches of one or two distinguished gentlemen, not lawyers, may be given. If there is
any exception of class made, we hope to be able to give you
a sketch and engraving of the enterprising Mr. Barnum.

                              RACKINSACK, Dec. 1, 1852.

To MR. EDITOR.

Dear Sir—I got your letter dated 18 Nov., asking me
to send you my life and karackter for your Journal. Im
obleeged to you for your perlite say so, and so forth.   I got
a friend to rite it—my own ritin being mostly perfeshunal.
He done it—but he rites such a cussed bad hand I cant rede
it : I reckon its all korrect tho'.

As to my doggerrytype I cant send it there aint any dog-
gerytype man about here now.   There never was but won,
and he tried his mershine on Jemmy O. a lawyer here, and
Jem was so mortal ugly it bust his mershine all to pieces
trying to git him down, and liked to killed the man that in-
gineered the wurks.

You can take father's picter on Jonce Hooper's book—

take off the bend in the back, and about twenty years of age off en it and make it a leetle likelier and it 'll suit me but dress it up gentele in store close.

Respectfully till death,

Simon Suggs, Jr.

P. S.—I rite from here where I am winding up my fust wife's estate which theyve filed a bill in chancery.   S. S. Jr.

———

City of Got-him, Dec. 11, 1852.

Col. Simon Suggs, Jr.

My Dear Sir—The very interesting sketch of your life requested by us, reached here accompanied by your favor of the 1st inst., for which please receive our thanks.

We were very much pleased with the sketch, and think it throws light on a new phase of character, and supplies a desideratum in the branch of literature we are engaged in—the description of a lawyer distinguished in the out-door labors of the profession, and directing great energies to the preparation of proof.

We fear, however, the suggestion you made of the use of the engraving of your distinguished father will not avail; as the author, Mr. Hooper, has copyrighted his work, and we should be exposing ourselves to a prosecution by trespassing on his patent.   Besides, the execution of such a work by no better standard, would not be creditable either to our artist, yourself, or our Journal.   We hope you will conclude to send on your daguerreotype to be appended to the lively and instructive sketch you furnish; and we entertain no doubt that the contemplated publication will redound greatly to your honor, and establish yours among the classical names of the American bar.

With profound respect, &c.,

THE EDITOR.

P. S.—Our delicacy caused us to omit, in our former letter, to mention what we suppose was generally understood, viz., the fact that the cost to us of preparing engravings, &c., &c., for the sketches or memoirs, is one hundred and fifty dollars, which sum it is expected, of course, the gentleman who is perpetuated in our work, will forward to us before the insertion of his biography. We merely allude to this trifling circumstance, lest, in the pressure of important business and engagements with which your mind is charged, it might be forgotten.

Again, very truly, &c.,

ED. JURIST-MAKER.

———

RACKINSACK, Dec. 25, 1852.

Dear Mr. Editor—In your p. s. which seems to be the creem of your correspondents you say I can't get in your book without paying one hundred and fifty dollars—pretty tall entrants fee! I suppose though children and niggers half price—I believe I will pass. I'll enter a nolly prossy q. O-n-e-h-u-n-d-r-e-d dollars and fifty better! Je-whelli-kens!

I just begin to see the pint of many things which was very vague and ondefinit before.   Put Barnum in first—one hundred and fifty dollars!

That's the consideratum you talk of is it.

☞ I REMAIN   Respy

                                          SIMON SUGGS, JR.

Therefore wont go in.

P. S.—Suppose you rite to the old man!!   May be he'd go in with BARNUM!!!   May be he'd like to take TWO chances?   HE's young—never seen MUCH!!   Lives in a new country!!!   AINT SMART!!   I SAY a hundred and fifty dollars!!!

SIMON SUGGS, JR., ESQ.,

OF

RACKINSACK—ARKANSAW.

This distinguished lawyer, unlike the majority of those favored subjects of the biographical muse, whom a patriotic ambition to add to the moral treasures of the country, has prevailed on, over the instincts of a native and professional modesty, to supply subjects for the pens and pencils of their friends, was not quite, either in a literal or metaphorical sense, a self-made man.   He had ancestors.   They were, moreover, men of distinction ; and, on the father's side, in the first and second degrees of ascent, known to fame.   The

6

father of this distinguished barrister was, and, happily, is Capt. Simon Suggs, of the Tallapoosa volunteers, and celebrated not less for his financial skill and abilities, than for his martial exploits.   His grandfather, the Rev. Jedediah Suggs, was a noted divine of the Anti-Missionary or Hardshell Baptist persuasion in Georgia.   For further information respecting these celebrities, the ignorant reader—the well-informed already know them—is referred to the work of Johnson Hooper, Esq., one of the most authentic of modern biographers.

The question of the propagability of mo al and intellectual qualities is a somewhat mooted point, into the metaphysics of which we do not propose to enter ; but that there are instances of moral and intellectual as well as physical likenesses in families, is an undisputed fact, of which the subject of this memoir is a new and striking illustration.

In the month of July, Anno Domini, 1810, on the ever memorable fourth day of the month, in the county of Carroll, and State of Georgia, Simon Suggs, Jr., first saw the light, mingling the first noise he made in the world with the patriotic explosions and rejoicings going on in honor of the day. We have endeavored in vain to ascertain, whether the auspicious period of the birth of young Simon was a matter of accident, or of human calculation, and sharp foresight, for which his immediate ancestor on the paternal side was so eminently distinguished ; but, beyond a knowing wink, and a characteristic laudation of his ability to accomplish wonderful things, and to keep the run of the cards, on the part of the veteran captain, we have obtained no reliable information on this interesting subject. It is something, however, to be remarked upon, that the natal day of his country and of Simon were the same.

Very early in life, our hero—for Peace hath her victories, and, of course, her heroes, as well as war—gave a promise of the hereditary genius of the Suggs's; but as the incidents in proof of this rest on the authority, merely, of family tradition, we shall not violate the sanctity of the domestic fireside, by relating them. In the ninth year of his age he was sent to the public school in the neighborhood. Here he displayed that rare vivacity and enterprise, and that shrewdness and invention, which subsequently distinguished his riper age. Like his father, his study was less of books than of men. Indeed, it required a considerable expenditure of birch, and much wear and tear of patience, to overcome his constitutional aversion to letters sufficiently to enable him to master the alphabet. Not that he was too lazy to learn; on the contrary, it was his extreme industry in other and more congenial pursuits that stood in the way of the sedentary business of instruction. It was not difficult to see that the mantle of the Captain had fallen upon his favorite son ; at any rate, the breeches in which young Simon's lower proportions were encased, bore a wonderful resemblance to the old cloak that the Captain had sported on so many occasions.

Simon's course at school was marked by many of the traits which distinguished him in after life ; so true is the aphorism

which the great Englishman enounced, that the boy is father
to the man.   His genius was eminently commercial, and he
was by no means deficient in practical arithmetic.   This peculiar turn of mind displayed itself in his barterings for the
small wares of schoolboy merchandise—tops, apples, and
marbles, sometimes rising to the dignity of a pen-knife.   In
these exercises of infantile enterprise, it was observable that
Simon always got the advantage in the trade ; and in that
sense of charity which conceals defects, he may be said to
have always displayed that virtue to a considerable degree.
The same love of enterprise early led him into games of
hazard, such as push-pin. marbles, chuck-a-luck, heads and
tails, and other like boyish pastimes, in which his ingenuity
was rewarded by marked success.   The vivacious and eager
spirit of this gifted urchin sometimes evolved and put in
practice, even in the presence of the master, expedients of
such sort as served to enliven the proverbial monotony of
scholastic confinement and study : such, for example, were
the traps set for the unwary and heedless scholar, made by
thrusting a string through the eye of a needle and passing it
through holes in the school bench—one end of the string
being attached to the machinist's leg, and so fixed, that by
pulling the string, the needle would protrude through the
further hole and into the person of the urchin sitting over it,
to the great divertisement of the spectators of this innocent
pastime.   The holes being filled with soft putty, the needle
was easily replaced, and the point concealed, so that when
the outcry of the victim was heard, Simon was diligently

perusing his book, and the only consequence was a dismissal of the complaint, and the amercement of the complainant by the master, *pro falso clamore.* Beginning to be a little more boldly enterprising, the usual fortune of those who " conquer or excel mankind" befell our hero, and he was made the scape-goat. of the school ; all vagrant offences that could not be proved against any one else being visited upon him ; a summary procedure, which, as Simon remarked, brought down genius to the level of blundering mediocrity, and made of no avail the most ingenious arts of deception and concealment. The master of the old field school was one of the regular faculty, who had great faith in the old medicine for the eradication of moral diseases—the cutaneous tonic, as he called it—and repelled, with great scorn, the modern quackeries of kind encouragement and moral suasion. Accordingly, the flagellations and cuffings which Simon received, were such and so many as to give him a high opinion of the powers of endurance, the recuperative energies, and the immense vitality of the human system. Simon tried, on one occasion, the experiment of fits ; but Dominie Dobbs was inexorable ; and as the fainting posture only exposed to the Dominie new and fresher points of attack, Simon was fain to unroll his eyes, draw up again his lower jaw, and come too. Simon, remarking in his moralizing way upon the virtue of perseverance, has been heard to declare that he " lost that ·game" by being unable to keep from scratching during a space of three minutes and a half ; which he would have accomplished, but for the Dominie's touching him on the raw, caused by riding a race bare-backed the Sunday before. " Upon what slender threads hang the greatest events !" Doubtless these experiences of young Suggs were not without effect upon so observing and saga-cious an intellect. To them we may trace that strong re-publican bias and those fervid expressions in favor of Dem-ocratic principles, which, all through life, and in the ranks of whatever party he might be found, he ever exhibited and made ; and probably to the unfeeling, and sometimes unjust inflictions of Dominie Dobbs, was he indebted for his devo-tion to that principle of criminal justice he so pertinaciously upheld, which requires full proof of guilt before it awards punishment.

We must pass over a few years in the life of Simon, who continued at school, growing in size and wisdom ; and not more instructed by what he learned there, than by the valu-able information which his reverend father gave him in the shape of his sage counsels and sharp experiences of the world and its ways and wiles. An event occurred in Simon's fifteenth year, which dissolved the tie that bound him to his rustic *Alma Mater*, the only institution of letters which can boast of his connection with it. Dominie Dobbs, one Friday evening, shortly after the close of the labors of the scholastic week, was quietly taking from a handkerchief in which he had placed it, a flask of powder ; as he pressed the knot of the handkerchief, *it* pressed upon the slide of the flask, which as it revolved, bore upon a lucifer match that ignited the powder ; the explosion tore the handkerchief to pieces, and also one ear and three fingers of the Dominie's right hand—those fingers that had wielded the birch upon young Simon with such effect.   Suspicion fell on Simon, notwithstanding he was the first boy to leave the school that evening.   This suspicion derived some corrobo- ration from other facts; but the evidence was wholly cir- cumstantial.   No positive proof whatever connected Simon with this remarkable accident; but the characteristic pru- dence of the elder Suggs suggested the expediency of Si- mon's leaving for a time a part of the country where char- acter was held in so little esteem.   Accordingly the influ- ence of his father procured for Simon a situation in the neighboring county of Randolph, in the State of Alabama, near the gold mines, as clerk or assistant in a store for re- tailing spirituous liquors, which the owner, one Dixon Tripes, had set up for refreshment of the public, without troubling the County Court for a license.   Here Simon was early initiated into a knowledge of men, in such situations as to present their characters nearly naked to the eye.   The neighbors were in the habit of assembling at the grocery, almost every day, in considerable numbers, urged thereto by the attractions of the society, and the beverage there abounding; and games of various sorts added to the charms of conversation and social intercourse.   It was the general rendezvous of the fast young gentlemen for ten miles around; and horse-racing, shooting-matches, quoit-pitching, cock- fighting, and card-playing filled up the vacant hours between drinks.

In such choice society it may well be supposed that so sprightly a temper and so inquisitive a mind as Simon's found congenial and delightful employment; and it was not long before his acquirements ranked him among the foremost in that select and spirited community. Although good at all the games mentioned, card-playing constituted his favorite amusement, not less for the excitement it afforded him, than for the rare opportunity it gave him of studying the human character.

The skill he attained in measuring distances, was equal to that displayed in his youth, by his venerated father, insomuch that in any disputed question in pitching or shooting, to allow him to measure was to give him the match; while his proficiency " in arranging the papers "—vulgarly called stocking a pack—was nearly equal to sleight of hand. Having been appointed judge of a quarter race on one occasion, he decided in favor of one of the parties by three inches and a half; and such was the sense of the winner of Simon's judicial expertness and impartiality, that immediately after the decision was made, he took Simon behind the grocery and divided the purse with him.   By means of the accumulation of his wonderful industry, Simon went forth with a somewhat heterogeneous assortment of plunder, to set up a traffic on his own account: naturally desiring a wider theatre, which he found in the city of Columbus in his native State.   He returned to the paternal roof with an increased store of goods and experience from his sojourn in Alabama.   Among other property, he brought with him a

TURNING THE JACK. p. 129.

small race mare, which excited the acquisitiveness of his
father, who, desiring an easier mode of acquisition than by
purchase, proposed to stake a horse he had (the same he
had swapped for, on the road to Montgomery, with the land
speculator,) against Simon's mare, upon the issue of a game
of *seven up*.   Since the game of chess between Mr. Jefferson and the French Minister, which lasted three years, perhaps there never has been a more closely contested match
than that between these keen, sagacious and practised sportsmen.   It was played with all advantages; all the lights of
science were shed upon that game.   The old gentleman had
the advantage of experience—the young of genius : it was
the old fogy against young America.   For a long time the
result was dubious ; as if Dame Fortune was unable or unwilling to decide between her favorites.   The game stood
six and six, and young Simon had the deal.   Just as the
deal commenced, after one of the most brilliant shuffles the
senior had ever made, Simon carelessly laid down his tor-
toise-shell snuff-box on the table ; and the father, affecting
nonchalance, and inclining his head towards the box, in
order to peep under as the cards were being dealt, took a
pinch of snuff; the titillating restorative was strongly adul-
terated with cayenne pepper ; the old fogy was compelled to
sneeze ; and just as he recovered from the concussion, the
first object that met his eye was a Jack turning in Simon's
hand.   A struggle seemed to be going on in the old man's
breast between a feeling of pride in his son and a sense of
his individual loss.   It soon ceased, however.   The father

congratulated his son upon his success, and swore that he was wasting his genius in a retail business of " shykeenry " when nature had designed him for the bar.

To follow Simon through the eventful and checkered scenes of his nascent manhood, would be to enlarge this sketch to a volume. We must be content to state briefly, that such was the proficiency he made in the polite accomplishments of the day, and such the reputation he acquired in all those arts which win success in legal practice, when thereto energetically applied, that many sagacious men predicted that *the law would yet elevate Simon to a prominent place in the public view.* In his twenty-first year, Simon, starting out with a single mare to trade in horses in the adjoining State of Alabama, returned, such was his success, with a drove of six horses and a mule, and among them the very mare he started with. These, with the exception of the mare, he converted into money; he had found her invincible in all trials of speed, and determined to keep her. Trying his fortune once more in Alabama, where he had been so eminently successful, Simon went to the city of Wetumpka, where he found the races about coming off. As his mare had too much reputation to get bets upon her, an ingenious idea struck Simon—it was to take bets, through an agent, *against* her, in favor of a long-legged horse, entered for the races. It was very plain to see that Simon's mare was bound to win if he let her. He backed his own mare openly, and got some trifling bets on her; and his agent was fortunate enough to pick up a green-looking

Georgia sucker, who bet with him the full amount left of Simon's " pile." The stakes were deposited in due form to the amount of some two thousand dollars. Simon was to ride his own mare—wild Kate, as he called her—and he had determined to hold her back, so that the other horse should win. But the Georgian, having by accident overheard the conversation between Simon and his agent, before the race, cut the reins of Simon's bridle nearly through, but in so ingenious a manner, that the incision did not appear. The race came off as it had been arranged; and as Simon was carefully holding back his emulous filly, at the same time giving her whip and spur, as though he would have her do her best, the bridle broke under the strain ; and the mare, released from check, flew to and past the goal like the wind, some three hundred yards ahead of the horse, upon the success of which Simon had " piled " up so largely.

A shout of laughter like that which pursued Mazeppa, arose from the crowd (to whom the Georgian had communicated the facts), as Simon swept by, the involuntary winner of the race ; and in that laugh, Simon heard the announcement of the discovery of his ingenious contrivance. He did not return.

Old Simon, when he heard of this counter-mine, fell into paroxysms of grief, which could not find consolation in less than a quart of red-eye. Heart-stricken, the old patriarch exclaimed—" Oh! Simon! my son Simon! to be overcome in that way !—a Suggs to be humbugged! His own Jack to be taken outen his hand and turned on him! Oh! that I should ha' lived to see this day ! "

Proceeding to Montgomery, Simon found an opening on the thither side of a faro table ; and having disposed of the race mare for three hundred dollars, banked on this capital, but with small success. Mr. Suggs' opinion of the people of Montgomery was not high; they were fashioned on a very diminutive scale, he used to say, and degraded the national amusement, by wagers, which an enterprising boy would scorn to hazard at push-pin. One Sam Boggs, a young lawyer " of that ilk," having been cleaned out of his entire stake of ten dollars, wished to continue the game on credit, and Simon gratified him, taking his law license in pawn for two dollars and a half ; which pawn the aforesaid Samuel failed to redeem. Our prudent and careful adventurer filed away the sheepskin, thinking that sometime or other, he might be able to put it to good use.

The losses Simon had met with, and the unpromising prospects of gentlemen who lived on their wits, now that the hard times had set in, produced an awakening influence upon his conscience. He determined to abandon the nomadic life he had led, and to settle himself down to some regular business. He had long felt a call to the law, and he now resolved to " locate," and apply himself to the duties of that learned profession. Simon was not long in deciding upon a location. The spirited manner in which the State of Arkansas had repudiated a public debt of some five hundred thousand dollars gave him a favorable opinion of that people as a community of litigants, while the accounts which came teeming from that bright land, of murders and felonies innumerable, suggested the value of the criminal practice. He wended his way into that State, nor did he tarry until he reached the neighborhood of Fort Smith, a promising border town in the very *Ultima Thule of civilization*, such as it was, just on the confines of the Choctaw nation. It was in this region, in the village of Rackensack, that he put up his sign, and offered himself for practice. I shall not attempt to describe the population. It is indescribable. I shall only say that the Indians and half-breeds across the border complained of it mightily.

The motive for Simon's seeking so remote a location was that he might get in advance of his reputation—being laudably ambitious to acquire forensic distinction, he wished his fame as a lawyer to be independent of all extraneous and adventitious assistance. His first act in the practice was under the statute of *Jeo Fails*. It consisted of an amendment of the license he had got from Boggs, as before related; which amendment, was ingeniously effected by a careful erasure of the name of that gentleman, and the insertion of his own in the place of it. Having accomplished this feat, he presented it to the court, then in session, and was duly admitted an attorney and counsellor at law and solicitor in chancery.

There is a tone and spirit of morality attaching to the profession of the law so elevating and pervasive in its influence, as to work an almost instantaneous reformation in the character and habits of its disciples. If this be not so, it was certainly a most singular coincidence that, just at the time of his adoption of this vocation, Simon abandoned the favorite pastimes of his youth, and the irregularities of his earlier years. Indeed, he has been heard to declare that any lawyer, fulfilling conscientiously the duties of his profession, will find enough to employ all his resources of art, stratagem and dexterity, without resorting to other and more equivocal methods for their exercise.

It was not long before Simon's genius began to find occasions and opportunities of exhibition. When he first came to the bar, there were but seven suits on the docket, two of those being appeals from a justice's court. In the course of six months, so indefatigable was he in instructing clients, as to their rights, the number of suits grew to forty. Simon —or as he is now called—*Colonel* Suggs, determined on winning reputation in a most effective branch of practice— one that he shrewdly perceived was too much neglected by the profession—the branch of preparing cases *out of court* for trial. While other lawyers were busy in getting up the law of their cases, the Colonel was no less busy in getting up the facts of his.

One of the most successful of Col. Suggs' efforts, was in behalf of his landlady, in whom he felt a warm and decided interest. She had been living for many years in ignorant contentedness, with an indolent, easy natured man, her husband, who was not managing her separate estate, consisting of a plantation and about twenty negroes, and some town property, with much thrift. The lady was buxom and gay; and the union of the couple was unblessed with children.

By the most insinuating manners, Col. Suggs at length succeeded in opening the lady's eyes to a true sense of her hapless condition, and the danger in which her property was placed, from the improvident habits of her spouse ; and, having ingeniously deceived the unsuspecting husband into some suspicious appearances, which were duly observed by a witness or two provided for the purpose, he soon prevailed upon his fair hostess to file a bill of divorce ; which she readily procured under the Colonel's auspices. Under the pretence of protecting her property from the claims of her husband's creditors, the Colonel was kind enough to take a conveyance of it to himself ; and, shortly afterwards, the fair libellant ; by which means he secured himself from those distracting cares which beset the young legal practitioner, who stands in immediate need of the wherewithal.

Col. Suggs' prospects now greatly improved, and he saw before him an extended field of usefulness. The whole community felt the effects of his activity. Long dormant claims came to light; and rights, of the very existence of which, suitors were not before aware, were brought into practical assertion. From restlessness and inactivity, the population became excited, inquisitive and intelligent, as to the laws of their country ; and the ruinous effects of servile acquiescence in wrong and oppression, were averted.

The fault of lawyers in preparing their cases was too generally a dilatoriness of movement, which sometimes deferred until it was too late, the creating of the proper impression upon the minds of the jury. This was not the fault of Col. Suggs ; he always took time by the forelock. Instead of waiting to create prejudices in the minds of the jury, until they were in the box, or deferring until then the arts of persuasion, he waited upon them before they were empannelled; and he always succeeded better at that time, as they had not then received an improper bias from the testimony. In a case of any importance, he always managed to have his friends in the court room, so that when any of the jurors were challenged, he might have their places filled by good men and true ; and, although this increased his expenses considerably, by a large annual bill at the grocery, he never regretted any expense, either of time, labor or mo- ney, necessary to success in his business. Such was his zeal for his clients !

He was in the habit, too, of free correspondence with the opposite party, which enabled him at once to conduct his case with better advantage, and to supply any omissions or chasms in the proof : and so far did he carry the habit of testifying in his own cases, that his clients were always assured that in employing him, they were procuring counsel and witness at the same time, and by the same retainer. By a very easy process, he secured a large debt barred by the statute of limitations, and completely circumvented a fraudulent defendant who was about to avail himself of that mendacious defence. He ante-dated the writ, and thus brought the case clear of the statute.

One of the most harassing annoyances that were inflicted upon the emigrant community around him, was the revival of old claims contracted in the State from which they came, and which the Shylocks holding them, although they well knew that the pretended debtors had, expressly in consideration of getting rid of them, put themselves to the pains of exile and to the losses and discomforts of leaving their old homes and settling in a new country, in fraudulent violation of this object, were ruinously seeking to enforce, even to the deprivation of the property of the citizen. In one instance, a cashier of a Bank in Alabama brought on claims against some of the best citizens of the country, to a large amount, and instituted suits on them. Col. Suggs was retained to defend them. The cashier, a venerable-looking old gentleman, who had extorted promises of payment, or at least had heard from the debtors promises of payment, which their necessitous circumstances had extorted, but to which he well knew they did not attach much importance, was waiting to become a witness against them. Col. Suggs so concerted operations, as to have some half-dozen of the most worthless of the population follow the old gentleman about whenever he went out of doors, and to be seen with him on various occasions ; and busying himself in circulating through the community, divers reports disparaging the reputation of the witness, got the cases ready for trial. It was agreed that *one* verdict should settle all the cases. The defendant pleaded the statute of limitations; and to do away with the effect of it, the plaintiff offered the cashier as a witness. Not a single question was asked on cross-examination; but a smile of derision, which was accompanied by a foreordained titter behind the bar, was visible on the faces of Simon and his client, as he testified. The defendant then offered a dozen or more witnesses, who, much to the surprise of the venerable cashier, discredited him; and the jury, without leaving the box, found a verdict for the defendant. The cashier was about moving for a new trial, when, it being intimated to him that a warrant was about to be issued for his apprehension on a charge of perjury, he concluded not to see the result of such a process, and indignantly left the country.

The criminal practice, especially, fascinated the regards and engaged the attention of Col. Suggs, as a department of his profession and energies. He soon became acquainted with all the arts and contrivances by which public justice is circumvented. Indictments that could not be quashed, were sometimes mysteriously out of the way; and the clerk had occasion to reproach his carelessness in not filing them in the proper places, when, some days after cases had been dismissed for the want of them, they were discovered by him in some old file, or among the executions. He was requested, or rather he volunteered in one capital case, to draw a recognizance for a committing magistrate, as he (Suggs) was idly looking on, not being concerned in the trial, and so felicitously did he happen to introduce the negative particle in the condition of the bond, that he bound the defendant, under a heavy penalty, " *not* " to appear at court and answer to the charge; which appearance, doubtless, much against his will, and merely to save his sureties, the defendant proceeded faithfully not to make.

Col. Suggs also extricated a client and his sureties from a forfeited recognizance, by having the defaulting defendant's obituary notice somewhat prematurely inserted in the newspapers; the solicitor, seeing which, discontinued proceedings; for which service, the deceased, immediately after the adjournment of court, returned to the officer his personal acknowledgments: "not that," as he expressed it, "it mattered any thing to him personally, but because it *would have aggravated the feelings* of his friends he had left behind him, to of let the thing rip arter he was defunck."

The most difficult case Col. Suggs ever had to manage, was to extricate a client from jail, after sentence of death had been passed upon him. But difficulties, so far from discouraging him, only had the effect of stimulating his energies. He procured the aid of a young physician in the premises—the prisoner was suddenly taken ill—the physician pronounced the disease small pox. The wife of the prisoner, with true womanly devotion, attended on him. The prisoner, after a few a days, was reported dead, and the doctor gave out that it would be dangerous to approach the corpse. A coffin was brought into the jail, and the wife was put into it by the physician—she being enveloped in her husband's clothes. The coffin was put in a cart and driven off—the husband, habited in the woman's apparel, following after, mourning piteously, until, getting out of the village, he disappeared in the thicket, where he found a horse prepared for him. The wife obstinately refused to be buried in the husband's place when she got to the grave; but the mistake was discovered too late for the recapture of the prisoner.

The tact and address of Col. Suggs opposed such obstacles to the enforcement of the criminal law in that part of the country, that, following the example of the English government, when Irish patriotism begins to create annoyances, the State naturally felt anxious to engage his services in its behalf. Accordingly, at the meeting of the Arkansas legislature, at its session of 184–, so soon as the matter of the killing a member on the floor of the house, by the speaker, with a Bowie knife, was disposed of by a resolution of mild censure, for imprudent precipitancy, Simon Suggs, Jr., Esquire, was elected solicitor for the Rackensack district. Col. Suggs brought to the discharge of the duties of his office energies as unimpaired and vigorous as in the days of his first practice; and entered upon it with a mind free from the vexations of domestic cares, having procured a divorce from his wife on the ground of infidelity, but magnanimously giving her one of the negroes, and a horse, saddle and bridle.

The business of the State now flourished beyond all precedent. Indictments multiplied : and though many of them were not tried—the solicitor discovering, after the finding of them, as he honestly confessed to the court, that the evidence would not support them : yet, the Colonel could well say, with an eminent English barrister, that if he tried fewer cases in court, he settled more cases out of court than any other counsel.

The marriage of Col. Suggs, some three years after his appointment of solicitor, with the lovely and accomplished Che-wee-na-tubbe, daughter of a distinguished prophet and warrior, and head-man of the neighboring territory of the Choctaw Indians, induced his removal into that beautiful and improving country. His talents and connections at once raised him to the councils of that interesting people; and he received the appointment of agent for the settlement of claims on the part of that tribe, and particular individuals of it, upon the treasury of the United States. This responsible and lucrative office now engages the time and talents of Col. Suggs, who may be seen every winter at Washington, faithfully and laboriously engaged with members of Congress and in the departments, urging the matters of his misssion upon the dull sense of the Janitors of the Federal Treasury.

May his shadow never grow less; and may the Indians live to get their dividends of the arrears paid to their agent.

SQUIRE A. AND THE FRITTERS.

Now, in the times we write of, the flourishing village of
M. was in its infancy.   She had not dreamed of the great
things in store for her when she should have reached her teens,
and railroad cars crowded with visitors, should make her the
belle-village of all the surrounding country. A few log houses
hastily erected and overcrowded with inmates, alone were to be
seen; nor did the inn, either in the order or style of its architec-
ture, or in the beauty or comfort of its interior arrangements
and accommodations, differ from the other and less public ed-
ifices about her.   In sober truth, it must be confessed that,
like the great man after whom she was named, the promise
of her youth was by no means equal to the respectability of
her more advanced age.   It was the season of the year most
unpropitious to the development of the resources of the
landlord and the skill of the cook.   Fall had set in, and flour
made cakes were not set out.   Wheat was not then an article of home growth, and supplies of flour were only to be got
from Mobile, and not from thence, unless when the Tom-
bigbee river was up ; so, for a long time, the boarders and
guests of the tavern had to rough it on *corn dodger*, as it

was called, greatly to their discontent. At length the joyful tidings were proclaimed, that a barrel of flour had come from Mobile. Much excitement prevailed. An animated discussion arose as to the form in which the new aliment should be served up; and on the motion of A., who eloquently seconded his own resolution, it was determined that *Fritters* should be had for supper that night. Supper time dragged its slow length along: it came, however, at last.

There were a good many boarders at the Inn—some wenty or more—and but one negro waiter, except a servant of J. T., whom he kept about him, and who waited at table. Now, if Squire A. had any particular weakness, it was in favor of fritters. Fritters were a great favorite, even *per se;* but in the dearth of edibles, they were most especially so. He had a way of eating them with molasses, which gave them a rare and delectable relish. Accordingly, seating himself the first at the table, and taking a position next the door nearest to the kitchen, he prepared himself for the onslaught. He ordered a soup-plate and filled it half full of molasses— tucked up his sleeves—brought the public towel from the roller in the porch, and fixed it before him at the neck, so as to protect his whole bust—and stood as ready as the jolly Abbot over the haunch of venison, at the widow Glendinning's, to do full justice to the provant, when announced.

Now, A. had a distinguished reputation and immense skill in the art and mystery of fritter eating. How many he could eat at a meal I forget, if I ever heard him say, but *I* should say—making allowances for exaggeration in such things—from

the various estimates I have heard, well on to the matter
of a bushel— possibly a half a peck or so, more or less.
When right brown and reeking with fresh fat, it would take as
many persons to feed him as a carding-machine.　Sam Hark-
ness used to say, that if a wick were run down his throat after a fritter dinner, and lit, it would burn a week—but I don't
believe that.

He used no implement in eating but a fork.　He passed
the fork through the fritter in such a way as to break its
back, and double it up in the form of the letter W, and pressing it through and closing up the lines, would flourish it
around in the molasses two or three times, and then convey
it, whole, to his mouth—drawing the fork out with a sort of
c-h-u-g.

If A. ever intended to have his daguerreotype taken—
that was the time—for a more hopeful, complacent, benevo-
lent cast of countenance, I never saw than his, when the
door being left a little ajar, the cook could be seen in the
kitchen, making time about the skillet, and the fat was heard
cheerfully spitting and spattering in the pan.

" But pleasures are like poppies spread," and so forth.
As when some guileless cock-robin is innocently regaling
himself in the chase of a rainbow spangled butterfly, pois-
ing himself on wing, and in the very act of conveying the
gay insect to his expectant spouse for domestic use, some ill-
omened vulture, seated in solitary state on a tree hard by,
unfurls his wing, and swoops in fell destruction upon the
hapless warbler, leaving nothing of this scene of peace and

innocence but a smothered cry and a string of feathers. So did J. T. look upon this scene of Squire A.'s expectant and hopeful countenance with a like and kindred malignity and fell purpose.   In plain prose,—confederating and conspiring with three other masterful fritter eaters and Sandy, the amateur waiter at the Inn, it was agreed that Sandy should station himself at the door, and, as the waiting-girl came in with the fritters, he should receive the plate, and convey the same to the other confederates for their special behoof, to the entire neglect of the claim of Squire A. in the premises.

Accordingly the girl brought in the first plate—which was received by Sandy—Sandy brought the plate on with stately step close by Squire A.—the Squire's fork was raised to transfix at least six of the smoking cakes with a contingency of sweeping the whole platter; but the wary Sandy raised the plate high in air, nor heeded he the Squire's cajoling tones—" Here, Sandy, here, this way, Sandy." Again the plate went and came, but with no better success to the Squire.   Sandy came past a third time—" I say, Sandy, this way—this way—come Sandy—come now—do—I'll remember you;"—but Sandy walked on like the Queen of the West unheeding; the Squire threw himself back in his chair and looked in the puddle of molasses in his plate sourly enough to have fermented it.   Again—again—again and yet again —the plate passed on—the fritters getting browner and browner, and distance lending enchantment to the view: but the Squire couldn't get a showing.   The Squire began to be

7

peremptory, and threatened Sandy with all sorts of extermination for his contumacy; but the intrepid servitor passed along as if he had been deaf and dumb, and his only business to carry fritters to the other end of the table. At length Sandy came back with an empty plate, and reported that the fritters were all out. The Squire could contain himself no longer—unharnessing himself of the towel and striking his fist on the table, upsetting thereby about a pint of molasses from his plate, he exclaimed in tones of thunder, "I'll quit this dratted house: I'll be eternally and constitutionally dad blamed, if I stand such infernal partiality!" and rushed out of the house into the porch, where he met J. T., who, coolly picking his teeth, asked the Squire how he "liked the fritters?" We need not give the reply —as all *that* matter was afterwards honourably settled by a board of honor.

JONATHAN AND THE CONSTABLE.

Now, brother Jonathan was a distinguished member of the fraternity, and had maintained a leading position in the profession for many years, ever since, indeed, he had migrated from the land of steady habits. His masculine sense, acuteness and shrewdness, were relieved and mellowed by fine social habits and an original and genial humor, more grateful because coming from an exterior something rigid and inflexible. He had—and we hope we may be able to say so for thirty years yet—a remarkably acute and quick sense of the ridiculous, and is not fonder than other humorists of exposing a full front to the batteries of others than turning them on his friends. Some fifty-five years has passed over his head, but he is one of those evergreen or never-green plants upon which time makes but little impression. He has his whims and prejudices, and being an elder of the Presbyterian church, he is especially annoyed by a drunken man.

It so happened that a certain Ned Ellett was pretty high, as well in office as in liquor, one drizzly winter evening—during the session of the S. Circuit Court. He had taken

in charge one Nash, a horse-thief, and also a tickler of rye
whiskey; and this double duty coming upon him somewhat unexpectedly, was more than he could well sustain
himself under.   The task of discharging the prisoner over,
Ned was sitting by the fire in the hall of the Choctaw
House, in deep meditation upon the mutations in human affairs, when he received a summons from Jonathan, to come
to his room, for the purpose of receiving a letter to be carried to a client in the part of the county in which Ned resided.   It was about ten o'clock at night.   Jonathan and I
occupied the same room and bed on the ground-floor of the
building, and I had retired for the night.

Presently Ned came in, and took his seat by the fire.
The spirits, by this time, began to produce their usual effects.
Ned was habited in a green blanket over-coat, into which the
rain had soaked, and the action of the fire on it raised a considerable fog.   Ned was a raw-boned, rough-looking customer, about six feet high and weighing about two hundred
net—clothes, liquor, beard and all, about three hundred.
After Jonathan had given him the letter, and Ned had criti-
cally examined the superscription, remarking something
about the handwriting, which, sooth to say, was not copy-
plate—he put it in his hat, and Jonathan asked him some
question about his errand to L.

" Why, Squire," said Ned, " you see I had to take Nash
—Nash had been stealing of hosses, and I had a warrant
for him and took him.—Blass, Nash is the smartest feller
you ever see.   He knows about most every thing and every

body. He knows all the lawyers, Blass—I tell you he does, and no mistake. He was the merriest, jovialest feller you ever see, and can sing more chronicle songs than one of these show fellers that comes round with the suckus. He didn't seem to mind bein took than a pet sheep. I tell you he didn't, Blass—and when I tell you a thing, Blass, you better had believe it, you· had. Blass, did you ever hear of my telling a lie? No, not by a jug-full. Blass, aint I an hones' man? (Yes, said B., I guess you are.)—" Guess— Guess—*I* say guess. Well, as I was a saying, about Nash —I asked Nash, what he was doin perusin about the country, and Nash said he was just perusin about the country to see the climit? But I know'd Harvey Thompson wouldn't like me to be bringin a prisner in loose, so I put the strings on Nash, and then his feathers drapped, and then Blass, he got to crying—and, Blass, he told me—(blubbering) he told me about his——old mother in Tennessee, and how her heart would be broke, and all that—and, Blass, I'm a hard man and my feelins aint easy teched—but (here Ned boohood right out,) Blass, I'll be —— if I can bar to see a man ex- hausted."

Ned drew his coat-sleeve over his eyes, blew his nose, and snapped his fingers over the fire and proceeded : " Blass, he asked about you and Lewis Scott, and what for a lawyer you was, and I'll tell you jest what I told him, Blass, says I, old Blass, when it comes to hard law, Nash, knows about all the law they is—but whether he kin norate it from the stump or not, that's the question. Blass, show me down some of these pairs of stairs. [They were on the ground-floor, but Ned, no doubt, was entitled to think himself high.]—B. showed him out.

All this time I was possuming sleep in the bed as inno-cent as a lamb. Blass came to the bedside and looked in-quisitively on for a moment, and went to disrobing himself. All I could hear was a short soliloquy—" Well, doesn't that beat all ? It's one comfort, J. didn't hear that—I never would have heard the last of it. It's most too good to be lost. I believe I'll lay it on him."

I got up in the morning, and as I was drawing on my left boot, muttered as if to myself, " but whither he kin nor-ate it from the stump—*that's* the question." B. turned his head so suddenly—he was shaving, sitting on a trunk—that he came near cutting his nose off.

" You doosn't mean to say you eaves-dropped and heard that drunken fool—do you ? Remember, young man, that what you hear said to a lawyer in conference is confidential, and don't get to making an ass of yourself, by blabbing this thing all over town." I told him " I thought I should have to norate it a little."

SHARP FINANCIERING.

In the times of 1836, there dwelt in the pleasant town of T. a smooth oily-mannered gentleman, who diversified a commonplace pursuit by some exciting episodes of finance—dealing occasionally in exchange, buying and selling uncurrent money, &c. We will suppose this gentleman's name to be Thompson. It happened that a Mr. Ripley of North Carolina, was in T., having some $1200, in North Carolina money, and desiring to return to the old North State with his funds, not wishing to encounter the risk of robbery through the Creek country, in which there were rumors of hostilities between the whites and the Indians, he bethought him of buying exchange on Raleigh, as the safest mode of transmitting his money. On inquiry he was referred to Mr. Thompson, as the only person dealing in exchange in that place. He called on Mr. T. and made known his wishes. With his characteristic politeness, Mr. Thompson agreed to accommodate him with a sight bill on his correspondent in Raleigh, charging him the moderate premium of five per cent. for it. Mr. Thompson retired into his counting-room, and

in a rew minutes returned with the bill and a letter, which
he delivered to Mr. Ripley, at the same time receiving the
money from that gentleman plus the exchange. As the in-
terlocutors were exchanging valedictory compliments, it occurred to Mr. Thompson that it would be a favor to him if
Mr. Ripley would be so kind as to convey to Mr. T.'s correspondent a package he was desirous of sending, which request
Mr. Ripley assured Mr. T. it would afford him great pleasure
to comply with. Mr. Thompson then handed Mr. Ripley a
package, strongly enveloped and sealed, addressed to the
Raleigh Banker, after which the gentlemen parted with many
polite expressions of regard and civility.

Arriving without any accident or hindrance at Raleigh, Mr.
Ripley's first care was to call on the Banker and present his
documents. He found him at his office, presented the bill
and letter to him, and requested payment of the former. That,
said the Banker, will depend a good deal upon the contents
of the package. Opening which, Mr. Ripley found the iden-
tical bills, minus the premium, he had paid Mr. T. for his
bill : and which the Banker paid over to that gentleman,
who was not a little surprised to find that the expert Mr.
Thompson had charged him five per cent. for carrying his
own money to Raleigh, to avoid the risk and trouble of which
he had bought the exchange.

T. used to remark that that was the safest operation, all
around, he ever knew. He had got his exchange—the buyer
had got his bill and the money, too,—and the drawee was
fully protected ! There was profit without outlay or risk.

CAVE BURTON, ESQ., OF KENTUCKY.

PROMINENT among the lawyers that had gathered into the new country, was Cave Burton. Cave was a man of mark : not very profoundly versed in the black letter, but adapting, or, more properly, applying his talents to the slang-whanging departments of the profession. He went in for gab. A court he could not see the use of—the jury was the thing for him. And he was for *"jurying"* every thing, and allowing the jury—the apostolic twelve as he was wont to call them —a very free exercise of their privileges, uncramped by any impertinent interference of the court. Cave thought the judge an aristocratic institution, but the jury was republicanism in action. He liked a free swing at them. He had no idea of being interrupted on presumed misstatements, or out-of-the-record revelations : he liked to be communicative when he was speaking to them, and was not stingy with any little scraps of gossip, or hearsay, or neighborhood reports, which he had been able to pick up concerning the matter in hand or the parties. He was fond, too, of giving his private experiences—as if he were at a love-feast—and was profuse

7*

of personal assurances and solemn asseverations of personal belief or knowledge of fact and of law. He claimed Kentucky for his native State, and for a reason that will suggest itself at once, was called by the bar THE BLOWING CAVE. Cave had evidently invoiced himself very high when he came out, thinking rather of the specific than the *ad valorem* standard. He had, to hear him tell it, renounced so many advantages, and made such sacrifices, for the happy privilege of getting to the backwoods, that the people, out of sheer gratitude, should have set great store by so rare an article brought out at such cost :—but they didn't do it. He had brought his wares to the wrong market. The market was glutted with brass. And although that metal was indispensable, yet it was valuable only for plating. Burton was the pure metal all through. He might have been moulded at a brass foundry. He had not much intellect, but what he had he kept going with a wonderful clatter. Indeed, with his habits and ignorance, it were better not to have had more, unless he had a great deal ; for his chief capital was an unconsciousness of how ridiculous he was making himself, and a total blindness as to the merits of his case, which protected him, as a somnambulist is protected from falling by being unconscious of danger. He was just as good on a bad cause as on a good one, and just as bad on a good side as on a bad one. The first intimation he had of how a case ought to go, was on seeing how it had gone. Discrimination was not his forte. Indeed, accuracy of any kind was not his forte. He lumbered away lustily, very well content if he were in the neighborhood of a fact or proposition, without seeming to expect to be *at* the precise point. He had a good deal of that sort of wit which comes of a bold, dashing audacity, without fear or care ; such wit as a man has who lets his tongue swing free of all control of judgment, memory, or taste, or conscience. He scattered like an old shot-gun, and occasionally, as he was always firing, some of the shot would hit.

A large, red-faced, burly fellow, good-natured and unscrupulous, with a good run of anecdote and natural humor, and some power of narrative, was Cave,—a monstrous demagogue withal, and a free and easy sort of creature, who lived as if he expected to-day were all the time he had to live in : and who considered the business of the day over when he had got his three meals with intermediate drinks.

I cannot say Burton was a liar. I never knew him to fabricate a lie " out and out"—outside of the bar ;—his invention was hardly sufficient for that. In one sense, his regard for truth was considerable—indeed, so great that he spent most of his conversation in embellishing it. It was a sponging habit he had of building on other men's foundations; but having got a start in this way, it is wonderful how he laid on his own work.

Cave, like almost every other demagogue I ever knew, was " considerable " in all animal appetites : he could dispose of the provant in a way Capt. Dalgetty would have admired, and, like the Captain, he was not very nice as to the kind or quality of the viands; or, rather, he had a happy faculty of making up in quantity what was lacking in quality. I don't think he ever rose from a table satisfied, though he often rose surfeited. You might founder him before you could subdue his appetite. He was as good in liquids as in solids. He never refused a drink : the parable of neglected invitations would have had no application to him if he had lived in those times. You might wake him up at midnight to take something hot or cold, edible or liquor, and he would take his full allowance, and smack his lips for more. He could scent out a frolic like a raven a carcass—by a separate instinct. He always fell in just in time. He was not a sponge. He would as soon treat as be treated, if he had any thing—as under the credit system he had—to treat with ; but the main thing was the provant, and loafing was one of his auxiliaries. He had a clamorous garrison in his bowels that seemed to be always in a state of siege, and boisterous for supplies. Cave's idea of money was connected inseparably with bread and meat and " sperits :" money was not the representative of value in his political economy, but the representative of breakfast, dinner, supper and liquor. He was never really pathetic, though always trying it, until he came to describing, in defending against a pro- missory note, the horrors of want, that is, of hunger—then he really *was* touching, for he was earnest, and he shed tears like a watering pot. He reckoned every calamity by the standard of the stomach. If a man lost money, he con- sidered it a diversion of so much from the natural aliment. If he lost his health, so much was discounted from life, that is, from good living : if he died, death had stopped his rations. Cave had a mean idea of war, and never voted for a military man in his life. It wasted too much of the fruits of the earth. An account of a campaign never excited his horror, until the fasting of the soldiers and the burning of the supplies was treated of—then he felt it like a nightmare. Cave had a small opinion of clothes; they were but a shallow, surface mode of treating the great problem, man. He went deeper; he was for providing for the inner man— though his idea of human nature never went beyond the entrails. Studying human nature with him was anatomy and physic, and testing the capacity of the body for feats of the knife and fork. A great man with him was not so much shown by what he could do, as by what he could hold; not by what he left, but by what he consumed.

Cave's mind was in some doubt as to things in which the majority of men are agreed. For example, he was not satisfied that Esau made as foolish a bargain with his brother Jacob as some think. Before committing himself, he should like to taste the pottage, and see some estimate of the net value of the birthright in the beef and venison market. If the birthright were a mere matter of pride and precedence, Cave was not sure that Esau had not " sold " the father of Israel.

If Cave had a hundred thousand dollars, he would have laid it all out in provisions; for *non constat* there might be no more made; at any rate, he would have enough to answer all the ends and aims of life, which are to eat and drink as much as possible.

Cave attended the Episcopal church every Sunday when there was service—i. e. once a month, and, though his attention was a little drowsy during most of the services, yet he brightened up mightily when the preacher read the prayer against famine, and for preserving the kindly fruits of the earth to be enjoyed in due season.

Cave was some forty-five years of age at the time I am writing of :—so long had he warred on the pantry.

He was an active man, indeed some part of him was always going—jaws, tongue, hands or legs, and to a more limited extent, brains. He never was idle. Indeed, taking in such fuel, he couldn't well help going. Even in sleep he was not quiet. Such fighting with unknown enemies—probably the ghosts of the animals he had consumed;—such awful contortions of countenance, and screams—and, when most quiet, such snorings (he once set a passenger running down stairs with his trunk, thinking it was the steamboat coming), you, possibly, never heard. I slept with him one night (I blush to tell it) on the circuit, and he seemed to be in spasms, going off at last into a suppressed rattle in the throat : I thought he was dying, and after some trouble, woke him. He opened his eyes, and rolled them around, like a goose egg on an axle. " Cave," said I, " Cave—can I do any thing for you ? "

" Yes," was his answer. " Look in my saddle-bags, and get me a black bottle of ' red-eye.' "

I got it ; he drank almost a half pint, and went to sleep like a child that has just received its nourishment.

Burton had largely stored his memory with all manner of slang-phrases and odd expressions, whereby he gave his speech a relish of variety somewhat at the expense of classic purity.   Indeed, his mind seemed to be a sort of water-gate, which caught and retained the foam and trash, but let the main stream pass through.

But, as honest Bunyan hath it, we detain the reader too long in the porch.

In the Christmas week of the year of Grace, 1838, some of us were preparing to celebrate that jovial time by a social gathering at Dick Bowling's office.   There were about a dozen of us, as fun-loving ' *youth*,' as since the old frolics at Cheapside or the Boar's Head, ever met together, the judge and the State's attorney among them.   The boats had just got up, on their first trip, from Mobile, and had brought, on a special order Dick had given, three barrels of oysters, a demijohn of Irish whiskey, and a box of lemons.   Those were not the days of invitations : a lawyer's office, night or day, was as public a place as the court-house, and, among the members of the bar at that early period, there were no priv- ileged seats at a frolic any more than in the pit of a theatre. All came who chose.   Old Judge Sawbridge, who could tell from smelling a cork the very region whence the liquor came, and could, by looking into the neck of the bottle, tell the age as well as a jockey could the age of a horse by looking into his mouth, was there before the bells had rung for the tavern supper.   Several of the rest were in before long. Burton had not come yet.   The old Judge suggested a trick, which was to get Burton to telling one of his Kentucky yarns, and, as he was in the agony of it, to withdraw, one by one, and eat up all the oysters. We agreed to try it, but doubted very much the success of the experiment; although the Judge seemed to be sanguine.

Dropping in, one by one, at last all came, filling the room pretty well. Among them was Cave. That domestic bereavement which had kept him from such a gathering, were a sad one. He entered the room in high feather. He was in fine spirits, ardent and animal. If he had been going, twenty years before, to a trysting-place, he could not have been in a gayer frame of mind. He came prepared. He had ravished himself from the supper table, scarcely eating any thing —three or four cups of coffee, emptying the cream-pitcher of its sky-blue milk, a card of spare-ribs and one or two feet of stuffed sausages, or some such matter; a light condiment of "cracklin bread," and a half pint of hog-brains thrown in just by way of parenthesis. He merely took in these trifles by way of sandwich, to provoke his appetite for the main exercises of the evening. When he came in the fire was booming and crackling—a half cord of hickory having been piled upon the broad hearth. The night was cold, clear, and frosty.

The back room adjoining was as busy as a barracks, in the culinary preparations. The oysters, like our clients, were being forced, with characteristic reluctance, to shell out. And as the knife went tip, tip, tip, on the shells, Cave's mouth watered like the bivalve's, as he caught the sound— more delicious music to his ears than Jenny Lind and the

whole Italian troupe could give out.   His spirits rose in this
congenial atmosphere like the spirits in a barometer.   He
was soon in a gale, as if he had been taking laughing gas.
Now Cave was as fond of oysters as a seal.   A regiment of
such men on the sea-shore, or near the oyster banks, would
have exterminated the species in a season.   The act against
the destruction of the oyster ought to have embraced Cave
in a special clause of interdiction from their use.   He used
to boast that he and D. L. had never failed to break an oyster cellar in Tuscaloosa whenever they made a run on it.

Judge Sawbridge made a pass at him as soon almost as
he was seated.   He commenced by inquiring after some
Kentucky celebrities—Crittenden, Hardin, Wickliffe, &c.,
whom he found intimate friends of Cave; and then he asked
Cave to tell him the anecdote he had heard repeated, but not
in its particulars, of the Earthquake-story.   He led up to
Cave's strong suit: for if there was one thing that Cave liked
better than every thing else, eating and drinking excepted, it
was telling a story; and if he liked telling any one story better than any other, it was the Earthquake-story.   This story
was, like Frank Plummer's speech on the Wiscasset collector-
ship, interminable ; and, like Frank's speech, the principal
part of it bore no imaginable relation to the ostensible subject.   No mortal man had ever heard the end of this story :
like Coleridge's soliloquies, it branched out with innumerable
suggestions, each in its turn the parent of others, and these
again breeding a new spawn, so that the further he travelled
the less he went on.   Like Kit Kunker's dog howling after

the singing master and getting tangled up in the tune, the *denouement* was lost in the episodes. What the story was originally, could not be conjectured; for Cave had gone over the ground so often, that the first and many subsequent traces were rubbed out by later footprints. Cave, however, refreshing himself with about a pint of hot-stuff, rose, turned his back to the fire, and, parting his coat-tail, and squatting two or three times as was his wont when in the act of speaking, began

The Earthquake-story.

We can only give it in *our* way, and only such parts as we can remember, leaving out most of the episodes, the casual explanations and the slang; which is almost the play of Hamlet with the Prince of Denmark omitted. But, thus emasculated, and Cave's gas let off, here goes a report about as faithful as a Congressman's report of his spoken eloquence when nobody was listening in the House.

*   *   *   *   *   *   *   *   *

" Well, Judge, the thing happened in 1834, in Steubenville, Kentucky, where I was raised. I and Ben Hardin were prosecuting the great suit, which probably you have heard of, *Susan Beeler* vs. *Samuel Whistler*, for breach of promise of marriage. The trial came on, and the court-house was crowded. Every body turned out, men, women, and children; for it was understood I was to close the argument in reply to Tom Marshall and Bob Wickliffe. I had been speaking about three hours and· a half, and had just got to my full speed—the genius licks were falling pretty heavy. It was an aggravated case. Susan, her mother and three sisters were crying like babies ; her old father, the preacher, was taking on too, pretty solemn ; and the women generally were going it pretty strong on the briny line. The court-house was as solemn as a camp-meeting when they are calling up the mourners. I had been giving them a rousing, soul-searching appeal on the moral question, and had been stirring up their consciences with a long pole. I had touched them a little on the feelings —' affections ' —' broken-hearts ' —' pining away '—' patience on a monument,' and so forth ; but I hadn't probed them deep on these tender points. It isn't the right way to throw them into spasms of emotion : reaction is apt to come. Ben Hardin cautioned me against this. Says Ben, ' Cave, tap them gently and milk them of their brine easy. Let the pathetics sink into 'em like a spring shower.' I saw the sense of it and took the hint. I led them gently along, not drawing more than a tear a minute or so : and when I saw their mouths opening with mine, as I went on, and their eyes following mine, and winking as I winked, I would put it down a little stronger by way of a clincher. [Hello, Dick, ain't they nearly all opened ? I believe I would take a few raw by way of relish."]

" No," Dick said : " they would be ready after a while." Here Cave took another drink of the punch and proceeded.

"I say—old Van Tromp Ramkat was Judge. You knew old Ramkat, Judge—didn't you ? No ? Well, *you* ought to have known him. He was the bloodiest tyrant alive. I reckon the old cuss has fined me not less than $500."

Sawbridge.—" What for, Cave ? "

" Why, for contempt at ten dollars a clip—that was old Ramkat's tariff; and if every other man had been fined the same for *contempt* of Van Tromp, the fines would pay off the national debt. Old Ram had a crazy fit for fining persons. He thought he owed it to the people to pay off all the expenses of the judicial system by fines. He was at it all the time. His fines against the sheriff and clerk amounted to not less than ten per cent. on their salaries. If a court passed without fining somebody for contempt, he thought it was a failure of court, and he called a special term. Every thing was a contempt : a lawyer couldn't go out of court without asking leave; and the lawyers proposed, at a bar-meeting, to get a shingle and write on one side of it " In," and on the other " Out," like an old-field school. He fined Tid Stiffness for refusing to testify in a gambling case $10 ; and then asked him again in the politest and most obsequious tones—if he hadn't better testify ? Tid, thinking it a matter of choice, said ' No.' Old Ram nodded to the clerk, who set Tid down for another five. Ram got still more polite, and suggested the question again—and kept on till *he bid him up to* $250 ; and then told him what he had done, and then adjourned the case over, with Tid in custody, till next morning. Tid came into measures when the case was called, and agreed to testify, and wanted old Van to let him off with the fines; but Ram wouldn't hear to it. The clerk, however, suggested that, on looking over the tallies, he found he had scored him down twice on one bid. Ram remarked that, as there seemed to be some question about it, and as Tid had been a good customer, he would split the difference with him and deduct a V; and then, in order to make the change even, he fined old Taxcross, the clerk, five dollars for not making up the entry right; but to let it come light on him, as he had a large family, allowed him to make it off of Tid by making separate entries of the fines—thus swelling his fees.

" Oh, I tell you, old Ramkat was the bloodiest tyrant this side of France. I reckon that old cuss has cheated my clients out of half a million of dollars, by arbitrarily and officiously interfering to tell the juries the law, when I had got them all with me on the facts. There was no doing any thing with him. He would lay the law down so positive, that he could instruct a jury out of a stock,—a little, bald-headed, high-heel-booted, hen-pecked son of thunder! Fining and sending to the penitentiary were the chief delights of his insignificant life. Did not the little villain once say, in open court, that the finding of a bill of indictment was a half conviction, and it ought to be law that the defendant ought to be convicted if he couldnt get a unanimous verdict from the petty jury? Why, Judge, he convicted a client of mine for stealing a calf. I proved that the fellow was poor and had nothing to eat, and stole it in self defence of his life. 'Twouldn't do: he convicted him, or made the jury do it.

And old Ram told the fellow he should sentence him for
five years.   I plead with him to reduce the time.   The boy's
father was in court, and was weeping : I wept :—even old
Ramkat boohoo'd outright.   I thought I had him this time ;
but what did he do ?   Says he, ' Young man, your vile conduct has done so much wrong, given your worthy father so
much pain, and given your eloquent counsel so much pain,
and this court so much pain—I really must ENLARGE your
time to TEN years.'   And for stealing a calf !   Egad, if *I*
was starving, *I'd* steal a calf—yes, if I had been in Noah's
ark and the critter was the seed calf of the world !   [I say,
where is Dick Bowling ?   Them oysters certainly must be
ready by this time;—it seems to me I've smelt them for the
last half hour."]

    " No," the judge told him ; " the oysters were not ready—
they were stewing a big tureen full at once."

    Cave called for crackers and butter, and, through the
course of the evening, just in a coquetting way, disposed of
about half a tray full of dough, and half a pound of Goshen
butter.

    The reader will understand that during the progress of
this oration, though at different times, the members withdrew to the back room and ' oystered.'

    " Well, but," said Tom Cottle—" about the earthquake ? "

    " Yes—true—exactly—just so—my mind is so disturbed
by the idea that those oysters will be stewed out of all flavor,
that I ramble.   Where was I ?   Yes, I recollect now.   I
was commenting on Tom Marshall's attack on Molly Mug-

gin's testimony. Moll was our main witness. She was an Irish servant girl, and had peeped through the key-hole of the parlor door, and seen the breach of promise going on upon the sofa. Well, I was speaking of Ireland, Emmet, Curran and so on, and I had my arm stretched out, and the jury were agape—old Ramkat leaning over the bench—and the crowd as still as death. When, what *should* happen? Such a clatter and noise above stairs, as if the whole building were tumbling down. It seems that a jury was hung, up stairs, in the second story—six and six—a dead lock, on a case of Jim Snipes *vs.* Jerry Legg for a bull yearling; all Nubbin Fork was in excitement about it;—forty witnesses on a side, not including impeaching and sustaining witnesses. The sheriff had just summoned the witnesses from the muster-roll at random; fourteen swore one way, and twenty-four the other, as to identity and ownership; and it turned out the calf belonged to neither; there was more perjury than would pale the lower regions to white heat to hear it. One witness swore"—

Sawbridge.—" But, Cave, about the case *you* were trying."

Cave.—" Yes—about that. Well, the jury wanted to hear *my* speech, and the sheriff wouldn't let them out. He locked the door and came down. One of them, Sim Coley, kicked at the door so hard that the jar broke the stove-pipe off from the wires in the Mason's Lodge-room above, and about forty yards of stove-pipe, about as thick round as a barrel, came lumbering over the banisters, and fell, with a crash like thunder, in the grand jury-room below, and then came rolling down stairs, four steps at a leap, bouncing like a rock from a mountain side."

Here Sam Watson inquired how such a long pipe could get down a " pair of stairs," and how much broader a stair-case of a Kentucky court-house was than a turnpike road.

Cave.—" Of course, I meant that it onjointed, and one or more of the joints rolled down. A loose, gangling fellow like you, Sam, ought to see no great difficulty *in any thing* being onjointed. I could just unscrew you"—

" Order! Order!" interposed Judge Sawbridge. " No interruption of the speaker ; Mr. Burton has the floor."

" Well," continued Cave, " I had prepared the minds of the audience for a catastrophe, and this, coming as it did, had a fearful effect ; but the hung jury coming down stairs on the other side of the building from the lodge, and by the opposite stairway, hearing the noise, started to running down like so many wild buffalo. A general hubbub arose below—old Ramkat rose in his place, with a smile at the prospect of so much good fining. ' Sheriff,' said he, ' bring before me the authors of that confusion.' Just then the plaster of the ceiling of the court room began to fall, and the women raised a shriek. Old Ramkat bellowed up— ' Sheriff, consider the whole audience fined ten dollars a piece, and mind and collect the fees at the door before they depart. Clerk, consider the whole court house fined—wo-men and children half price—and take down their names. Sheriff, see to the doors being closed.' But just then ano-

ther section of the stove-pipe came thundering down, and
about the eighth of an acre of plastering fell, knocking down
sixty or seventy men and women ; and the people in the
galleries came rushing down, some jumping over into the
crowd below ; and a sheet of plastering, about as large as a
tray, came down from above the chandelier, and struck old
Ramkat over the head, and knocked him out of the judge's
stand into the clerk's box ; and he struck old Taxcross on
the shoulders, and turned over about a gallon of ink on the
records.   Then Pug Williams, the bailiff, shouted out,
' *Earthquake!—Earthquake!*' and all the women went
into hysterics ; and Pug, not knowing what to do, caught
the bell-rope, and began furiously to ring the bell.   Such
shouts of ' murder ! fire ! fire !' you never heard.   There
was a rush to the doors, but the day being cold they were
closed, and of course on the inside, and the crowd pressed
in such a mass and mess against them, that, I suppose, there
was a hundred tons' pressure on them, and they could not be
got open.   I was standing before the jury, and just behind
them was a window, but it was down : I leaped over the
jury, carried them before me"—

Watson.—" The first time you ever carried them,
Cave."

Cave.—" Not by a jug full.   I bowed my neck and
jumped leap-frog through the window, carried the sash out
on my neck, and landed safe in the yard, cutting a jugular
vein or two half through, and picked myself up and ran, with
the sash on my neck, up street, bleeding like a butcher, and

8

shouting murder at every jump. I verily thought I never should see supper time.

" In the mean time the very devil was to pay in the court-house. Old Ramkat, half stunned, ran up the steps to the judge's platform, near which was a window, hoisted it and jumped, like a flying mullet, over on to the green, thirty feet below, sprained his ankle and fell. Frank Duer, once the most eloquent man at the bar, but who had fattened himself out of his eloquence—weighing three hundred and ninety, and so fat that he could only wheeze out his figures of speech, and broke down from exhaustion of wind in fifteen minutes—followed suit, just squeezing himself through the same window, muttering a prayer for his soul that was just about leaving such comfortable lodgings, came thundering down on the ground, jarring it like a real earthquake, and bounced a foot, and fell senseless on Ramkat. Ramkat, feeling the jar, and mashed under Frank, thought the earth-quake had shook down the gable end of the court-house and it had fell on him.   So he thought fining time was over with him.   He hollered out in a smothered cry, ' Excavate the Court !—Excavate the Court !'   But nobody would do it, but let him sweat and smother for four hours.

" Then Luke Casey, a little, short, bilious, collecting attorney, as pert and active as if he was made out of watch-springs and gum-elastic, and who always carried a green bag with old newspapers and brickbats in it, and combed his hair over his face to look savage, so as to get up a reputation for being a good hand at dirty work—Luke

was ciphering the interest on a little grocery account of
fifteen dollars ; he had appealed from a justice's court, and
had a big deposition, taken in the case, all the way from
New-York, in his hand ; he sprung over three benches of
the bar at a leap, and grabbed his hand on Girard Moseley's
head to make another leap towards a window—going as if
there was a prospect of a fee ahead, and the client was
about leaving town.   He leaped clear over, but carried Girard's wig with him.   Now Girard was a widower, in a
remarkable state of preservation, and of fine constitution,
having survived three aggravated attacks of matrimony.   He
pretended to practise law ; but his real business was marrying for money.   He had got well off at it, though he never
got more than four thousand dollars with any one wife.   He
did business on the principle of 'quick returns and short
profits.'   He pretended to be thirty and the rise, but was,
at the least, fifty.   He prided himself on his hair, a rich, light
sorrel, sleek and glossy, and greased over with peppermint, cin-
namon, and all sorts of sweet smells.   He smelt like a barber's
shop; and such a polite, nice, easy fellow, *to* BE sure, was
Girard.   Butter wouldn't melt in his mouth, and yet let him
get hold of a dime, and he griped it so hard you might hear
the eagle squall.   He only courted rich old maids in infirm
health, and was too stingy ever to raise a family.   He was
very sweet on old Miss Julia Pritcher, a *girl* of about thirty-
five, who was lank, hysterical, and, the boys said, fitified ;
and who had just got about five thousand dollars from her
aunt, whom she had served about fifteen years as upper ser-

vant, but who was now gone the old road.   Nobody ever
thought of Girard's wearing a wig.   He pretended it was
Jayne's Hair Elixir that brought it out.   Fudge!   But
Luke caught him by the top-knot, and peeled his head like
a white onion.   He left him as bald as a billiard-ball—not
a hair between his scalp and heaven.   Luke took the wig,
and hastily, without thinking what he was doing, filed it in
the deposition.   Mosely had brought Jule Pritcher there,
and she was painted up like a doll : her withered old face
streaked like a June apple.   She needn't have put herself to
that trouble for Girard ; he would have married her in her
winding-sheet, if she had been as ugly as original sin, and
only had enough breath in her to say yes to the preacher.

"And now the fury began to grow outside.   The smoke,
rushing out of the window of the lodge-room, and the cry
of fire brought out the fire-engines and companies, and the
rag, tag and bob-tail boys and negroes that follow on shouting, with great glee, 'fire! fire! fire!' along the streets.
Ting-a-ling came on the engines—there were two of them—
until they brought up in the court-house yard ; one of them
in front, the other at the side or gable end.   It was some
time before the hose could be fixed right ; every fellow acting as captain, and *all* being in the way of *the rest*.   Wood
Chuck, a tanner's journeyman—a long, slim, yellow-breeched
fellow, undertook to act as engineer of engine No. 1.
'Play in at the windows!' cried the crowd outside, 'there's
fire *there*'—and play it was.   They worked the arms of the
thing lustily—no two pulling or letting down at the same

time, until at last, the water came. Wood guided pretty well for a first trial, first slinging the pipe around and scattering the crowd. But, just as they came pouring out of the window, thick as bees, he got his aim, and he sent the water in a sluice into the window; the engine had a squirt like all blazes; and as Chuck levelled the pipe and drew a bead on them, and as it shot into the faces of the crowd—vip, vip, vip—they fell back shouting murder, as if they had been shot from the window-sill. Old Girard had got hold of Jule and brought her to, and was bringing her, she clinging with great maidenly timidity to him, and he hugging her pretty tight, and they, coming to the window—the rest falling back—Chuck had a fair fire at them. He played on old Girard to some purpose—his bald head was a fair mark, and the water splashed and scattered from it like the foam on a figure head. The old fellow's ears rang like a conch shell for two years afterwards. Chuck gave Jule one swipe on one side of her head that drove a bunch of curls through the window opoosite, and which washed all the complexion off that cheek, and the paint ran down the gullies and seams like blood; the other side was still rosy. The only safe place was to get down on the floor and let the water fly over. Old Girard never got over the tic-doloreux and rheumatism he got that day.   The other engine played in the other window; and the more they played, the more the people inside shouted and hollered; and the more they did that, the more Chuck and Bill Jones, the engineer of No. 2, *came to their relief.* It was estimated that at least a thousand hogsheads of water were played into that court-house: indeed, I believe several small boys were drowned.

"Some one shouted out for an axe to cut through the front door. One was brought. A big buck negro struck with all his might, with the back of the axe, to knock it off its hinges; but there were at least twenty heads pushed up against the door, and these were knocked as dead by the blow as ever you saw a fish under the ice."

Sawbridge.—"Were they all killed?"

Cave.—"All? No—not all. Most of them came to, after a while. Indeed, I believe there was only three that were buried—and a tinner's boy, Tom Tyson, had his skull fractured; but they put silver plate in the cracks, and he got over it—a few brains spilt out, or something of the sort—but his appetite was restored.

"By the way, we had some fun when the trial of Luke Casey's little case came on. Moseley was on the other side, and came into court with his head tied up in a bandanna handkerchief. He smiled when some of Luke's proof was offered, and Luke, a little nettled, drew out the deposition, and with an air of triumph said, 'Perhaps, Mr. Moseley, you will laugh at this,' opening the deposition· as he opened it the wig fell out, and, every body recognizing it as Moseley's. a laugh arose which was only stopped by old Ramkat's fining all around the table. Squire Moseley vamosed and left Luke to get a judgment, and the credit of a joke, of which he was innocent as Girard's head was of the hair.

" Well, boys, I reckon you would all like to know what became of my case.   You see "—

Here Dick Bowling, smacking his lips, remarked that the oysters were very fine.

" Oysters ! " said Cave.   " Have you been eating the oysters ? "

Dick said he had.

Cave jumped to the back door at one bound, and called to the servant—" Jo, I say, Jo—get mine ready this minute —a few dozen raw—a half bushel roasted, and all the balance stewed—with plenty of soup ; I'll season them myself ; and put on plenty of crackers, butter and pickles.   Be quick, Jo, old fel."

Jo made his appearance, hat in hand, and answered : " Why, Mas Cave, dey's all gone dis hour past ; de gem'men eat ebery one up."

" The devil they have ! " said Cave.   " Gentlemen," he continued, turning to the crowd, " is this true ? "

" Yes," replied the Judge.   " Cave, I thought you were so interested telling the story, that you would prefer not to be interrupted."

The exclamatory imprecation which Cave lavished upon his soul, his eyes, and the particular persons present, and humanity generally, would not be befitting these chaste pages.   He left without any valedictory salutations of a complimentary or courteous tenor.   And he did not recover his composure until he removed a tray full of blood-puddings, sweetbread, kidneys and the like soporific viands, which had once graced the landlord's larder.

Speaking of the entertainment afterwards, Cave said he did not care a *dern* for the oysters, but it pained him to think that men he took to be his friends, should have done him a secret injury.

JUSTIFICATION AFTER VERDICT.

THE Fall assizes of the year 184—, came on in the East
Riding, and my friend, Paul Beechim, found himself duly
indicted before Judge C., for an assault and battery committed on the body of one Phillip Cousins, in the peace of the
State then and there being.　I felt more than ordinary interest in the case; the aforesaid Paul being a particular
friend of mine, and, moreover, the case presenting some singular and mysterious features.　The defendant was one of the
best-natured and most peaceable citizens of the county, and,
until recently, before this *ex parte* fighting, had been on
terms of intimacy and friendship with the gentleman upon
whom the assault was made.　The assault was of a ferocious
character; no one knew the cause of it; though every one
knew, from the character of Beechim, that some extraordina-
ry provocation had been given him: it was impossible to guess
what it was.　I was no better informed than the rest.　When
Beechim came to employ me in the case, I tried to possess
myself of the facts.　To all inquiries he only replied, that he
had acted as he had done for good and sufficient reasons—

8*

but that he did not choose to say more.   I told him that it was impossible for me to defend him unless he would place me in possession of the facts, and assured him that whatever he communicated should be held in strict professional and personal confidence.   But nothing I could say produced any change in his determination.   I was about abandoning his case, remarking to him that if he felt no confidence in his counsel, or not enough to induce him to tell him the facts, he might be assured that it was no less his interest than my wish, that he should go where he would be better suited. But he persisted that it was from no want of confidence in me that he refused, and that he regarded me with the same feelings of friendship he had always felt for me, and concluded by telling me that if I refused to take his case he should employ no other lawyer, but would let the matter proceed without defence.   I told him I did not see any hope of his escaping severe punishment as the case stood; to which he replied that he expected it, but that he hoped I would, if it were possible, prevent his being sent to jail.   The case came up in the regular course of things and was tried.   The facts were brought out plainly enough.   The assault was made in public, on the square; the weapon a large cane, with which the defendant had given Cousins an awful beating, gashing his head and causing the blood to flow very freely over his clothes.   The only words said by Beechim in the course of the affair were, " How, d—n you, how do you like *that* pine-apple sop ? " spoken just as he was leaving the prostrate Cousins.   Of course on such testimony, the jury found the defendant guilty : and the court retained Beechim in custody until some leisure was given it to fix the punishment, which, by the statute, the court was bound to impose.

Judge C. was something of a martinet in his line.   He was a pretty good disciplinarian and kept the police business of the court in good order.   There had been of late many violations of the law and a growing disposition was felt by the people and the courts to put down these excesses; but Beechim was so popular, and withal, so kind-hearted and gentlemanly a fellow, that a great deal of sympathy was felt for him, and a general wish that he might in some way get out of the scrape.

Among the peculiarities of Judge C. was an itching curiosity.   He was always peeping under the curtain of a case to see if he could not find something behind ; and felt not a little disappointed and vexed when the examination stopped short of bringing out all the facts and incidents, the relations of the parties and the like.

He had been struck with the expression used by Beechim—" pine-apple sop," and was evidently uneasy in mind in his present state of inability to unravel it.   The first pause in the cause he was next trying gave him an opportunity of calling me to him : I came of course : Said he, "B— what did that fellow mean by 'pine-apple sop ?' "   I told him there was a mystery about it which I could not explain. " A mystery, ha ! Well, now, here, B—, in confidence—just tell me ; it shan't go any farther—of course, you know—just give me an item of it."   I told him I really was ignorant of it—as was every one else; but I felt sure that it was something that would place my client's conduct in a better light, though he obstinately refused to tell it to me. The judge then assured me I had better see my client, and get him to state it to the court; that he would give all proper weight to it in fixing the punishment, but that as the case stood, he should have to make an example of him. I took Paul aside and told him what the judge had said, and added my own counsel to his Honor's, but with no effect. He still mildly but resolutely refused to make any explanation. I felt a good deal vexed at this, as it seemed to me, most unreasonable conduct. Revolving the thing in my mind, I got more and more bothered the more I thought about it. I began to look at the circumstances more narrowly ; that it was no sham or trick was very evident; no man would have taken such a beating for fun : that the provocation did not touch any domestic relations which the defendant might have desired to keep from being exposed, was apparent from the fact that my client had no relatives in the country, and the only girl he ever went to see was Cousins's sister. There were two facts I made sure of : the first that this meeting was immediately after Cousins's return from New Orleans, which occurred a few days after Beechim himself had arrived from that city ; the second, that Cousins had kept out of the way and had received a note shortly before court from Beechim. I made up my mind that the quarrel originated in something that had occurred between the parties in New Orleans. I happened to know, too, that Samuel Roberts, Esq., one of the 'cutest chaps we had about town, and ' up to trap ' in whatever was stirring wherever he happened to be, was in New Orleans at the time these young gentlemen were there ; and I determined to get the facts out of him if I could. Shortly after breakfast, on the next day after the verdict,— the judgment still delayed, partly by my request and partly by the judge's curiosity being yet unappeased—I sallied out with a package in my hand as if going to the post office. Sam was on the street. I knew if there was any thing to be concealed by him, the only way to get it was by a *coup d' etat*. So half-passing him, I turned suddenly on him, and putting my hand on his shoulder, and looking him in the eye, broke into a laugh, saying, " Well, Sam, that quarrel between Beechim and Cousins in New Orleans, and the—thing it grew out of—didn't it beat any thing you ever heard of ?— Wasn't it the queerest affair that ever happened ? I am defending Beechim, and, would you believe it ?—he never told me up to last night what was the cause of the fight ? Don't the whole thing look curious ? " I said this very flippantly with a knowing air, as if I knew all about it. Sam's eyes twinkled as he answered, " Well, B—, isn't it the blamedest piece of business *you* ever heard of ? " " Yes," said I, " it is ; and we must get Paul out of this scrape—the judge is viperish, and, if we don't do something, six months in jail is the very lowest time we can get Paul off with. Now, Sam, just step here—tell me the particulars of the matter in New Orleans as *you* understand them ; for you know any discrepancy between Paul's statement and yours might hurt things.

mightily, and I want to know exactly how the case stands."
"No," said Sam, "I can't do it. I promised Paul, on
honor, that I wouldn't mention it to a soul, and I won't do it
unless I am compelled. So you needn't ask me unless you
bring a note from Paul relieving me from the pledge." I
saw he was determined, and it was useless to press the point.
I had a vague idea that a woman was mixed up in the
matter, and was afraid of some exposure of that sort; so I
let out blind to find out : "Well, well, Sam, if you stand on
points of honor, of course that ends it ;—but just explain
this thing—how did *the girl* behave under the circumstances ?
you know it was calculated to be a little trying, and the
thing being so sudden and the parties being strangers, too,—
you understand ? " and I looked several volumes, and searched narrowly for some answer. Sam merely replied, "Why,
as to *the girl* opposite, if you mean her, she behaved very
well. She laughed a little at first, but when Paul showed
how it hurt him, she seemed to feel for him, and let the rest
take all the laugh." I felt better satisfied with this explanation, and determined on my course.

The judge, in the mean time, was on thorns of anxiety.
He had been conversing with the clerk, and sheriff, and
State's attorney, but to no purpose ; they only inflamed his
curiosity the more ; the mystery seemed inscrutable. He
came to my room twice that night—but I was out—to see
me on the subject. Early in the morning, as I was taking a
comfortable snooze, his Honor came into my room, and woke
me up. "Get up, B—, get up—why do you sleep so late in

the morning ?—it's a bad habit." (The judge was in the habit of sleeping until a late breakfast. I got up, and before I could get on my pantaloons, he opened the conversation, " B.," said he, " this thing about young Beechim distresses me a great deal. I feel really concerned about his case ; and if you will tell me now how that difficulty originated, I—I—I—shall feel better about it. My mind would—yes, my mind *would* be relieved. Of course, B., *you* know all about the matter, and I assure you it will be to the interest of your client to reveal the whole affair—de-ci-ded-ly his interest. What is it ?" I told him I really did not know, and could not find out as yet; but I thought I had got the clue to the mystery, and, if he would aid me, it could all be brought to light ; I was convinced, that if it did come out, it would make decidedly for the benefit of Paul, whom I knew to be incapable of making a wanton assault upon any one, especially upon Cousins. The judge told me I might rely on him, and he would see if any one dared to hold back any thing which it was proper to bring out. He was so com-municative as to assure me that, generally speaking, he was a man of but little curiosity : indeed, he sometimes reproached himself, and his wife often reproached him, for not knowing things ;—that is, he said, he meant by " not knowing things" —personal matters, gossip, and so forth—and that he never got any thing but what was played like a trapball all over town ; but, in this case, as a mere matter of speculation, he confessed he *did* feel desirous of unravelling the riddle ; in fact, it preyed on his mind ; he couldn't rest last night ; he even dreamed of a fellow funnelling *him* and pouring down *his* throat a bottle of spirits of turpentine, and asking him as he left him gagged, how *he* liked "*that* pine-apple sop." His Honor then went into many ingenious theories and surmises in elucidation of the mystery; but I felt assured that his explication was more fanciful than true.

Finding a great indisposition still, to reveal any thing, on the part of Beechim, and fearing that, if he were present, he would interpose objections to the presentation of the proof as to the provocation, I arranged it so that the sheriff should detain Paul from the court-house until I could get the testimony in.

In order to a more perfect understanding of the matter, I had as well state here, that Beechim was a young gentleman who had some two or three years before "located" in the county, and was doing a general land agency and collecting business, surveying lands, &c., having before been engaged as principal in an academy. He had graduated at the college at Knoxville, Tennessee, and cherished sentiments of great reverence for his venerable *alma mater*, which showed a very lively condition of the moral sensibilities. He thought very highly of the respectable society of that somewhat secluded village, and conceived a magnified idea of the burgh as a most populous, wealthy and flourishing metropolis. I verily believe he considered Knoxville at once the Athens and Paris of America, abounding in all the refinements, and shining with the polish of a rare and exquisite civilization—the seat of learning, the home of luxury,

and the mart of commerce. Letters, and arts, and great
men, and refined modes, and cultivated manners, and women
of a type that they never before had been moulded into, there
abounded, in his partial fancy prodigal of such generous appreciation. The magnificent self-delusion of dear old Captain Jackson, immortalized by Elia, scarcely equalled the
hallucination of Paul *quoad* the sights and scenes, the little
short of celestial glory of and about the *city* of Knoxville, as
he would persist in calling that out-of-the-way, not-to-be-
gotten-to, Sleepy-Hollow town, fifty miles from the Virginia
line, and a thousand miles from any where else. I speak
of it in pre-railroad times. Paul had been assiduous in the
cultivation of manners. His model was, of course, *that* he
found at Knoxville. He had a great penchant for fashionable life, and fashionable life was the life of the coteries, the
upper-tens of Knoxville. Rusticity and vulgarity were
abominations to him. To go back to Knoxville and get to
the tip of the ton there, was the extreme top-notch of Paul's
ambition. Apart from this high-church Knoxvillism, Paul
was an excellent fellow, somewhat vain, sensitive to a fault,
and thin-skinned ; somewhat pretentious as to fashion, style
and manners ; indeed, the girls had got to regard him as a
sort of village Beau Brummell, " the glass of fashion and
the mould of form"—a character on which he plumed himself not a little, and, I am sorry to say it, he did not bear
his blushing honors as meekly as could have been hoped for
under the circumstances. He had written back to the
friends of his youth (as Mr. Macawber hath it), in Knox-

ville, that he was growing more reconciled to his fate; his mind was calmer, he said, though his exile had, at first, gone very hard with him; but the manners of the natives were evidently, he was pleased to think, under his missionary labor, improving, and he must say for these natives, that they had evinced docility—which gave him hopes of further civilization.

That there could be any thing beyond the pitch of refinement to which Knoxville had gone, Paul could not believe on less than ocular evidence.

I got out a subpœna and sent the sheriff after Roberts, with orders for immediate attendance. The court was in session, and I proposed taking up this matter of Beechim's before the usual business of the day was gone into.

Samuel came into the court somewhat discomposed, but on observing that Beechim was not present, became reassured. His Honor drew from his pouch a fresh quid of tobacco, deposited it in his right cheek, wiped his mouth neatly with his handkerchief, seated himself comfortably in his chair, cleared his throat, blew his nose, and spread out his countenance into a pleasant and encouraging "skew," and directed me to proceed with the witness—commencing at the beginning and telling the witness to take his time.

Roberts took the stand. He testified to this effect : indeed, this is nearly a literal transcript of my notes, taken at the time. "Witness knows the parties—has known them for three years—is intimately acquainted with Beechim being a Tennesseean and having been at one time at Knoxville—knows that Beechim and Cousins were on good terms ; indeed quite friendly until May last. In company with witness they went together to New Orleans; went by way of Jackson and the Mississippi river ; arrived there the 13th of the month—conversed together a good deal—conversation of a friendly character—quite sociable ; Beechim talked a great deal of Knoxville, the girls, fashions and society : Cousins listened attentively : *knows* the parties *must* have been friendly. Arrived in New Orleans on the 18th, about 10 A. M., Monday ; intended to remain until Thursday ; no boat going up until Tuesday night.' B. expressed himself gratified by the zeal of the porters and hackmen to serve him ; said, however, that it marred the enjoyment somewhat to think that probably these attentions might be mercenary. It was well not to be too credulous. Took lodgings at the St. Charles Hotel. Heard a conversation going on between the two—subject, *the mode :* Cousins had been in the city and the hotel, frequently, so he said—knew the rules and the etiquette ; Beechim had been at the best hotels in Knoxville, knew *their* rules, but had been from Knoxville a good while, *therefore* was rusty—was not certain but that he might make some awkward blunder—might be fatal to his character : Cousins offered to act as cicerone—said B. might rely on him, ' to put him through ;' told him to take an item from him—Beechim thanked him kindly. At three the gong rang for dinner—parties were in the gentlemen's sitting room. B. started—thought at first that the steam engine that worked the cooking stove in the kitchen had burst its boiler. C.

told him it was the gong : B. asked him if it were not a *new* thing—long as he had been in Knoxville had never heard of such a thing—asked C. if he could believe it. Went to dinner—bill of fare was handed; B. wished to know if there was any *lincister* to translate the French dishes—said there was in Knoxville; got along pretty well until just as B. had taken a piece of pine-apple on his plate, the waiter came along and put a green-colored bowl before every guest's plate with water and a small slice of lemon in it. Beechim asked Cousins what *that* was. C. replied, ' Sop for the pine-apple.' B. said he thought so. " That's the way it used to be served up at ' The Traveller's Rest ' in Knoxville." Beechim took the bowl and put it in his plate, and then put the pine-apple in the bowl, and commenced cutting up the apple, stirred it around in the fluid with his fork, and ate it, piece after piece. B. kept his eyes on the bowl—did not observe what was passing about him. Many persons at table—five hundred at least—ladies, dandies, foreigners, moustached fellows; began to be an uproar on the other side of the table; every body got to looking down at Beechim—eye-glasses put up—a double-barrelled spy-glass (as witness supposed) levelled at him by a man at the head of the table, who stood up to draw a bead on him—loud laughing—women putting hand-kerchiefs, or napkins, (witness is not certain which,) to their mouths. B. got through with the pine-apple. Cousins had been laughing with the rest—composed himself now, and asked B. " how he liked the pine-apple ? " B. answered in these words : ' I think the pine-apple very good, but don't

you think the sauce is rather insipid ? '—Spoke the words
pretty loud—heard at some distance—great sensation—im-
moderate laughter– women screaming—men calling for wine
—the French consul's clerk drank to the English consul's clerk
' Ze shentleman from ze interiore, may he leeve to a *green*
ole aige,'—drank with all the honors.   Beechim seeing the
fuss, turned to an old man next him and asked what was the
matter—any news of an exciting character ?   The old man,
a cotton broker—an Englishman—replied that he, B., ' had
been making an ass of himself—he had been eating out of
the finger-bowl.'   B.'s face grew as red as a beet—then pale ;
he jumped back—tried to creep out by bending his head
down below the chairs—rushed on and knocked over the
waiter with the coffee—spilt it on a young lady—staggered
back and fell against a Frenchman—tore his ruffles—knocked him, head striking head, over against an Irishman—quarrel—two duels next morning — Frenchman killed.   Gen.
Sacré Frogleggé rose and proposed three cheers for the gentleman of *retiring* habits ; *encored :* wine all around the
board—uproarious doings : Tom Placide called on to rehearse
the scene—done—applause terriffic : Beechim got out—forgot where his hat was—ran bare-headed to the bar (?)—called for his bill—never got his clothes—ran to the steamboat—
shut himself up in the state room for two days ;—thing out
in the Picayune next morning—no names given.   B. came
home—saw Cousins when *he* came up—licked him within an
inch of his life with a hickory stick.   Witness further saith
not."

" Yes " said the judge, " and served him right.   Justification complete !   So enter it, clerk."

During the delivery of this testimony, you may be sure that the crowd were not very serious ; but knowing how sensitive Beechim was on the subject, I was congratulating myself that he was not present.   Turning from the witness as he finished, I was pained to see Beechim—he had come in after the trial began,—poor Paul ! sitting on the bench weeping piteously.   I tried to console him—I told him not to mind it—it was a mere *bagatelle;* but he only squeezed my hand, and brokenly said, " B., thank you ; you are my friend : I shall never forget you ; you meant it for the best :—you have saved my body but you have ruined my character. Good-bye, I leave this morning.   Roberts will settle your fee.   But, B., as a friend—one request ; if—you—can—help—it—don't—let—this—thing—get—back— to— Knox ville."

" Et dulces moriens reminiscitur Argos."

Accordingly Paul left—for good and all.   What became of him I don't know.   I *did* hear of one Paul Beechim in California ; but whether the same one or not, I can't say. He was named in the papers as a manager of the first San Francisco ball of 22d February, 1849.

His Honor made a solemn and affecting charge to the audience, generally, commending the moderation of young Beechim.   " See," said his Honor, " the way that this thing works.   Most men would have seized their gun, or bowie, on such terrible aggravation, and taken the life of the culprit; but this young gentleman has set an example which older heads might well copy: he has contented himself with taking a club and giving him a good, sound, constitutional, conservative licking; and you see, gentlemen, the milder remedy has answered every good purpose! The Court adjourns for refreshment."

AN AFFAIR OF HONOR.

In the pleasant village of Patton's-Hill, in the *Flush Times*, there were several resorts for the refreshment of the weary traveller, and for the allaying of the chronic thirst of more than one of the inhabitants of the place and the country adjacent.   They are closed now, as are the gaping portals of those who were wont in the wild days, to "indulge" in exciting beverages.   A staid, quiet, moral and intelligent community have supplied the place of many of the early settlers "who left their country for their country's good;" and churches, school-houses and Lodges now are prominent where the "doggery" made wild work with "the peace and dignity of the State," and the respectability and decency of particular individuals.

In the old times there came into the village of a Saturday evening, a company more promiscuous than select, who gathered, like bees at the mouth of a hive, around the doors of the grocery.   On one of these occasions a scene occurred, which I think worthy of commemoration; and it may be relied upon as authentic, in the main, as it came regularly before the Court as a part of the proceedings of a trial in a State case.

Jonas Sykes was a very valiant man when in liquor. But Jonas, like a good many other valiant men, was more valiant in peace than in war. He was a very Samson in fight—but, like Samson, he liked to do battle with that description of weapon which so scattered the Philistine hosts —*that* jaw-bone—one of which Nature had furnished Jonas with. Jonas was prodigal in the jaw-work and wind-work of a fight, and he could outswear "our army in Flanders." He had method in his madness, too, as he showed in selecting his enemies. He always knew, or thought he knew, how much a man would stand before he commenced "abusing" him, and his wrath grew the fiercer according as the patience of his enemy grew greater, and he was more fierce—like a bull-dog chained—as he was the more held off.

Jonas had picked a quarrel with a quiet, demure fellow of the name of Samuel Mooney, and lavished upon that gentleman's liver, soul and eyes, many expressions much more fervid than polite or kind. Sam stood it for some time, but at length, like a terrapin with coals on his back, even his sluggish spirit could stand it no longer. He began to retort on Jonas some of the inverted compliments with which Jonas had besprinkled him. Whereupon Jonas felt his chivalry so moved thereat, that he challenged him to mortal combat.

Now, Jonas, as most bullies did at that time, went armed. Samuel had no *weepins*, as he called those dangerous imple-

ments, and gave that fact as an apology for not accepting
Jonas's kind invitation.   But Jonas would not "hear to"
any such paltry excuse ; he denounced Sam, for a white-
livered poltroon, who would insult a gentleman (thereby
meaning himself), and then refuse him satisfaction, and swore
he would post him up all over town ; regretting that he did
not have the chance of blowing a hole through his carcass with
his " Derringer " that " a bull-bat could fly through without
tetching airy wing," and giving him his solemn word of
honor that if he, (Sam,) would only fight him, (Jonas,) he,
(Jonas,) wouldn't hit him, (Sam,) an inch above his hip-
bone—which certainly was encouraging.

Sam still protested he was weaponless.   " Well," said
Jonas, " you shan't have that excuse any longer.   I've got
two as good pistols as ever was bought at Or*leens*, and you
may have choice."   And pulling one out of either side
pocket, he produced two pistols very much alike, and, ad-
vancing to Sam, put his hands behind him and shuffled them
from hand to hand a moment or two, and then held them
forward—one rather in advance of the other—towards Sam,
telling him to take which he chose.   Sam took the one nearest to him, and Jonas called out to Bob Dobbs, who stood
by, " to put them through in a fair duel," and called the
crowd to witness " that he done it to the —— rascal accord-
in' to law."   Bob willingly accepted the honorable position
assigned him; commanded order ; made the crowd stand
back ;—measured off the ground—ten paces—and stationed
the combatants sidewise in duelling position.   Bob then

armed himself with a scythe blade, and flourishing it in the air, swore death and destruction to all who should interfere by word, look, or sign.

Bob took his position at a right angle between two, and gave out in a loud and sonorous voice the programme of proceedings. " Gentlemen," said he, " the rules are as follows : the parties are to be asked—' Gentlemen are you ready '—answering Yes, I, as mutual second, will then pronounce the words slowly, ' Fire : one—two—three ; ' the parties to fire as they choose between the words *Fire* and *three*, and if either fires before or after the time, I shall proceed to put him to death without quarter, bail or main prize." Micajah F., a lawyer present, suggested, " or benefit of clergy." " Yes," said Bob, " or the benefit of a clergyman."

Bob then proceeded to give the words out. At the word *two* Jonas's pistol snapped, but Sam's went off, the ball striking a button on Jonas's drawers and cutting off a little of the skin. Jonas fell—his legs flying up in the air, and shouting, " Murder ! Murder ! he's knocked off all the lower part of my ab*do*men. Send for a doctor ! quick ! quick ! Oh ! Lordy ! oh ! Lordy ! I'm a dead man : the other fellow got the—wrong—pistol ! " (And so he had ; for on examining Jonas's pistol, it was found to have had no load in it. Jonas, by mistake in shuffling, having given the *loaded* one to Sam and kept the empty one himself.)

The testimony in the case was related with such comic humor by one of the witnesses, that the jury were thrown into convulsions of laughter; and the case being submitted without argument, the verdict was a fine of one cent only against the combatants.

Jonas immediately retired from the bullying business after that time, and as soon as he could get his affairs wound up, like "the star of Empire," "westward took his way."

HON. S. S. PRENTISS.

THE character of the bar, in the older portions of the State of Mississippi, was very different from that of the bar in the new districts. Especially was this the case with the counties on and near the Mississippi river. In its front ranks stood Prentiss, Holt, Boyd, Quitman, Wilkinson, Winchester, Foote, Henderson, and others.

It was at the period first mentioned by me, in 1837, that Sargeant S. Prentiss was in the flower of his forensic fame. He had not, at that time, mingled largely in federal politics. He had made but few enemies; and had not " staled his presence," but was in all the freshness of his unmatched faculties. At this day it is difficult for any one to appreciate the enthusiasm which greeted this gifted man, the admiration which was felt for him, and the affection which followed him. He was to Mississippi, in her youth, what Jenny Lind is to the musical world, or what Charles Fox, whom he resembled in many things, was to the whig party of England in his day. Why he was so, it is not difficult to see. He was a type of his times, a representative of the qualities of the people, or rather of the better qualities of the wilder and more impetuous part of them. The proportion of young men—as in all new countries—was great, and the proportion of wild young men was, unfortunately, still greater.

He had all those qualities which make us charitable to the character of Prince Hal, as it is painted by Shakspeare, even when our approval is not fully bestowed. Generous as a prince of the royal blood, brave and chivalrous as a knight templar, of a spirit that scorned every thing mean, underhanded or servile, he was prodigal to improvidence, instant in resentment, and bitter in his animosities, yet magnanimous to forgive when reparation had been made, or misconstruction explained away. There was no littleness about him. Even towards an avowed enemy he was open and manly, and bore himself with a sort of antique courtesy and knightly hostility, in which self-respect mingled with respect for his foe, except when contempt was mixed with hatred; then no words can convey any sense of the intensity of his scorn, the depth of his loathing. When he thus outlawed a man from his courtesy and respect, language could scarce supply words to express his disgust and detestation.

Fear seemed to be a stranger to his nature. He never hesitated to meet, nor did he wait for, "responsibility," but he went in quest of it. To denounce meanness or villainy, in any and all forms, when it came in his way, was, with him, a matter of duty, from which he never shrunk; and so to denounce it as to bring himself in direct collision with the perpetrator or perpetrators—for he took them in crowds as well as singly—was a task for which he was instant in season or out of season.

Even in the vices of Prentiss, there were magnificence and brilliancy imposing in a high degree. When he treated, it was a mass entertainment. On one occasion he chartered the theatre for the special gratification of his friends, —the public generally. He bet thousands on the turn of a card, and witnessed the success or failure of the wager with the *nonchalance* of a Mexican monte-player, or, as was most usual, with the light humor of a Spanish muleteer. He broke a faro-bank by the nerve with which he laid his large bets, and by exciting the passion of the veteran dealer, or awed him into honesty by the glance of his strong and steady eye.

Attachment to his friends was a passion. It was a part of the loyalty to the honorable and chivalric, which formed the sub-soil of his strange and wayward nature. He never deserted a friend. His confidence knew no bounds. It scorned all restraints and considerations of prudence or policy. He made his friends' quarrels his own, and was as guardful of their reputations as of his own. He would put his name on the back of their paper, without looking at the face of it, and give his *carte blanche*, if needed, by the quire. He was above the littleness of jealousy or rivalry; and his love of truth, his fidelity and frankness, were formed on the antique models of the chevaliers. But in social qualities he knew no rival. These made him the delight of every circle; they were adapted to all, and were exercised on all. The same

histrionic and dramatic talent that gave to his oratory so irresistible a charm, and adapted him to all grades and sorts
of people, fitted him, in conversation, to delight all men. He
never staled and never flagged. Even if the fund of acquired capital could have run out, his originality was such, that
his supply from the perennial fountain within was inexhausti-
ble.

His humor was as various as profound—from the most
delicate wit to the broadest farce, from irony to caricature,
from classical allusion to the verge—and sometimes beyond
the verge—of coarse jest and Falstaff extravagance; and no
one knew in which department he most excelled. His animal spirits flowed over like an artesian well, ever gushing
out in a deep, bright, and sparkling current.

He never seemed to despond or droop for a moment: the
cares and anxieties of life were mere bagatelles to him. Sent
to jail for fighting in the court-house, he made the walls of
the prison resound with unaccustomed shouts of merriment
and revelry. Starting to fight a duel, he laid down his hand
at poker, to resume it with a smile when he returned, and
went on the field laughing with his friends, as to a pic-nic.
Yet no one knew better the proprieties of life than himself
—when to put off levity, and treat grave subjects and persons with proper respect; and no one could assume and pre-
serve more gracefully a dignified and sober demeanor.

His early reading and education had been extensive and
deep. Probably no man of his age, in the State, was so well
read in the ancient and modern classics, in the current

literature of the day, and—what may seem stranger—
in the sacred scriptures. His speeches drew some of their
grandest images, strongest expressions, and aptest illustrations from the inspired writings.

The *personnel* of this remarkable man was well calculated to rivet the interest his character inspired. Though he
was low of stature, and deformed in one leg, his frame was
uncommonly athletic and muscular ; his arms and chest were
well formed, the latter deep and broad; his head large, and
a model of classical proportions and noble contour. A handsome face, compact brow, massive and expanded, and eyes of
dark hazel, full and clear, were fitted for the expression of
every passion and flitting shade of feeling and sentiment. His
complexion partook of the bilious rather than the sanguine
temperament. The skin was smooth and bloodless—no excitement or stimulus heightened its color ; nor did the writer ever
see any evidence in his face of irregularity of habit. In repose,
his countenance was serious and rather melancholy—certainly
somewhat soft and quiet in expression, but evidencing
strength and power, and the masculine rather than the
light and flexible qualities which characterized him in his
convivial moments. There was nothing affected or the-
atrical in his manner, though some parts of his printed
speeches would seem to indicate this. He was frank and
artless as a child ; and nothing could have been more winning
than his familiar intercourse with the bar, with whom he was
always a favorite, and without a rival in their affection.

I come now to speak of him as a lawyer.

9*

He was more widely known as a politician than a lawyer, as an advocate than a jurist. This was because politics form a wider and more conspicuous theatre than the bar, and because the mass of men are better judges of oratory than of law. That he was a man of wonderful versatility and varied accomplishments, is most true; that he was a popular orator of the first class is also true; and that all of his faculties did not often, if ever, find employment in his profession, may be true likewise. So far he appeared to better advantage in a deliberative assembly, or before the people, because there he had a wider range and subjects of a more general interest, and was not fettered by rules and precedents; his genius expanded over a larger area, and exercised his powers in greater variety and number. Moreover, a stump speech is rarely made chiefly for conviction and persuasion, but to gratify and delight the auditors, and to raise the character of the speaker. Imagery, anecdote, ornament, eloquence and elocution, are in better taste than in a speech at the bar, where the chief and only legitimate aim is to convince and instruct.

It will always be a mooted point among Prentiss's admirers, as to where his strength chiefly lay. My own opinion is that it was as a jurist that he mostly excelled; that it consisted in *knowing and being able to show to others what was the law*. I state the opinion with some diffidence, and, did it rest on my own judgment alone, should not hazard it at all. But the eminent chief-justice of the high court of errors and appeals of Mississippi thought that

Prentiss appeared to most advantage before that court; and a distinguished judge of the Supreme Court of Alabama, who had heard him before the chancellor of Mississippi, expressed to me the opinion that his talents shone most conspicuously in that forum. These were men who could be led from a fair judgment of a legal argument by mere oratory, about as readily as old Playfair could be turned from a true criticism upon a mathematical treatise, by its being burnished over with extracts from fourth-of-July harangues. Had brilliant declamation been his only or chief faculty, there were plenty of his competitors at the bar, who, by their learning and powers of argument, would have knocked the spangles off him, and sent his cases whirling out of court, to the astonishment of hapless clients who had trusted to such fragile help in time of *trial*.

It may be asked how is this possible ? How is it consistent with the jealous demands which the law makes of the ceaseless and persevering attention of her followers as the condition of her favors ? The question needs an answer. It is to be found somewhere else than in the unaided resources of even such an intellect as that of Sergeant Prentiss. In some form or other, Prentiss *always was* a student. Probably the most largely developed of all his faculties was his memory. He gathered information with marvellous rapidity. The sun-stroke that makes its impression upon the medicated plate is not more rapid in transcribing, or more faithful in fixing its image, than was his perception in taking cognizance of facts and principles, or his ability to retain them. Once fixed, the impression was there for ever. It is true, as Mr. Wirt observed, that genius must have materials to work on. No man, how magnificently soever endowed, can possibly be a safe, much less a great lawyer, who does not understand the facts and law of his case. But some men may understand them much more readily than others. There are labor-saving minds, as well as labor-saving machines, and that of Mr. Prentiss was one of them. In youth he had devoted himself with intense application to legal studies, and had mastered, as few men have done, the elements of the law and much of its textbook learning. So acute and retentive an observer must too—especially in the freshness and novelty of his first years of practice—"have absorbed" no little law as it floated through the court-house, or was distilled from the bench and bar.

But more especially, it should be noted that Mr. Prentiss, until the fruition of his fame, was a laborious man, even in the tapestring sense. While the world was spreading the wild tales of his youth, his deviations, though conspicuous enough while they lasted, were only occasional, and at long intervals, the intervening time being occupied in abstemious application to his studies. Doubtless, too, the supposed obstacles in the way of his success were greatly exaggerated, the vulgar having a great proneness to magnify the frailties of great men, and to lionize genius by making it independent, for its splendid achievements, of all external aids.

With these allowances, however, truth requires the admission that Mr. Prentiss did, when at the seat of government, occupy the hours, usually allotted by the diligent practitioner to books or clients, in amusements not well suited to prepare him for those great efforts which have indissolubly associated his name with the judicial history of the State.

As an advocate, Mr. Prentiss attained a wider celebrity than as a jurist. Indeed, he was more formidable in this than in any other department of his profession. Before the Supreme, or Chancery, or Circuit Court, upon the law of the case, inferior abilities might set off, against greater native powers, superior application and research; or the precedents might overpower him ; or the learning or judgment of the bench might come in aid of the right, even when more feebly defended than assailed. But what protection had mediocrity, or even second-rate talent, against the influences of excitement and fascination, let loose upon a mercurial jury, at least as easily impressed through their passions as their reason? The boldness of his attacks, his iron nerve, his adroitness, his power of debate, the overpowering fire—broadside after broadside—which he poured into the assailable points of his adversary, his facility and plainness of illustration, and his talent of adapting himself to every mind and character he addressed, rendered him, on all debatable issues, next to irresistible. To give him the conclusion was nearly the same thing as to give him the verdict.

In the examination of witnesses, he was thought particu-

larly to excel.   He wasted no time by irrelevant questions.
He seemed to weigh every question before he put it, and see
clearly its bearing upon every part of the case.   The facts
were brought out in natural and simple order.   He examined as few witnesses, and elicited as few facts as he could
safely get along with.   In this way he avoided the danger of
discrepancy, and kept his mind undiverted from the control-
ling points in the case.   The jury were left unwearied and
unconfused, and saw, before the argument, the bearing of the
testimony.

He avoided, too, the miserable error into which so many
lawyers fall, of making every possible point in a case,
and pressing all with equal force and confidence, thereby
prejudicing the mind of the court, and making the jury
believe that the trial of a cause is but running a jockey
race.

In arguing a cause of much public interest, he got all
the benefit of the sympathy and feeling of the by-standers.
He would sometimes turn towards them in an impassioned
appeal, as if looking for a larger audience than court and
jury ; and the excitement of the outsiders, especially in
criminal cases, was thrown with great effect into the jury-
box.

Mr. Prentiss was never thrown off his guard, or seemingly taken by surprise.   He kept his temper ; or, if he got
furious, there was " method in his madness. "

He had a faculty in speaking I never knew possesed by
any other person.   He seemed to speak without any effort

of the will. There seemed to be no governing or guiding power to the particular faculty called into exercise. It worked on, and its treasures flowed spontaneously. There was no air of thought, no elevation, frowning or knitting of the brow—no fixing up of the countenance—no pauses to collect or arrange his thoughts. All seemed natural and unpremeditated. No one ever felt uneasy lest he might fall; in his most brilliant flights " the empyrean heights" into which he soared seemed to be his natural element—as the upper air the eagle's.

Among the most powerful of his jury efforts, were his speeches against Bird, for the murder of Cameron; and against Phelps, the notorious highway robber and murderer. Both were convicted. The former owed his conviction, as General Foote, who defended him with great zeal and ability, thought, to the transcendent eloquence of Prentiss. He was justly convicted, however, as his confession, afterwards made, proved. Phelps was one of the most daring and desperate of ruffians. He fronted his prosecutor and the court, not only with composure, but with scornful and malignant defiance. When Prentiss rose to speak, and for some time afterwards, the criminal scowled upon him a look of hate and insolence. But when the orator, kindling with his subject, turned upon him, and poured down a stream of burning invective, like lava, upon his head; when he depicted the villainy and barbarity of his bloody atrocities; when he pictured, in dark and dismal colors, the fate which awaited him, and the awful judgment, to be pronounced at another bar, upon his crimes, when he should be confronted with his innocent victims : when he fixed his gaze of concentrated power upon him, the strong man's face relaxed ; his eyes faltered and fell ; until at length, unable to bear up longer, self-convicted, he hid his head beneath the bar, and exhibited a picture of ruffian-audacity cowed beneath the spell of true courage and triumphant genius. Though convicted, he was not hung. He broke jail, and resisted recapture so desperately, that although he was encumbered with his fetters, his pursuers had to kill him in self-defence, or permit his escape.

In his defence of criminals, in that large class of cases in which something of elevation or bravery in some sort, redeemed the lawlessness of the act, where murder was committed under a sense of outrage, or upon sudden resentment, and in fair combat, his chivalrous spirit upheld the the public sentiment, which, if it did not justify that sort of " wild justice," could not be brought to punish it ignominiously. His appeals fell like flames on those

"Souls made of fire, and children of the sun,
    With whom revenge was virtue."

I have never heard of but one client of his who was convicted on a charge of homicide, and he was convicted of one of its lesser degrees. So successful was he, that the expression—" Prentiss couldn't clear him "—was a hyperbole that expressed the desperation of a criminal's fortunes.

Mr. P. was employed only in important cases, and generally as associate counsel, and was thereby relieved of much of the preliminary preparation which occupies so much of the time of the attorney in getting a case ripe for trial. In the Supreme and Chancery Courts he had, of course, only to examine the record and prepare his argument. On the circuit his labors were much more arduous. The important criminal and civil causes which he argued, necessarily required consultations with clients, the preparation of pleadings and proofs, either under his supervision, or by his advice and direction; and this, from the number and difficulty of the cases, must have consumed time and required application and industry.

At the time of which I speak, his long vigils and continued excitement did not enfeeble his energies. Indeed, he has been known to assert, that he felt brighter, and in better preparation for forensic debate, after sitting up all night in company with his friends than at any other time. He required less sleep, probably, than any man in the State, seldom devoting to that purpose more than three or four hours in the twenty-four. After his friends had retired at a late hour in the night, or rather at an early hour in the morning, he has been known to get his books and papers and prepare for the business of the day.

His faculty of concentration drew his energies, as through a lens, upon the subject before him. No matter what he was engaged in, his intellect was in ceaseless play and motion. Alike comprehensive and systematic in the arrangement of his thoughts, he reproduced without difficulty what he had once conceived.

Probably something would have still been wanting to explain his celerity of preparation for his causes, had not partial nature gifted him with the lawyer's highest talent, the *acumen* which, like an instinct, enabled him to see the points which the record presented. His genius for generalizing saved him, in a moment, the labor of a long and tedious reflection upon, and collation of, the several parts of a narrative. He read with great rapidity; glancing his eyes through a page he caught the substance of its contents at a view. His analysis, too, was wonderful. The chemist does not reduce the contents of his alembic to their elements more rapidly or surely than he resolved the most complicated facts into primary principles.

His statements—like those of all great lawyers—were clear, perspicuous and compact; the language simple and sententious. Considered in the most technical sense, as forensic arguments merely, no one will deny that his speeches were admirable and able efforts. If the professional reader will turn to the meagre reports of his arguments in the cases of *Ross* v. *Vertner*, 5 How. 305; *Vick et al.* v. *The Mayor and Aldermen of Vicksburg*, 1 How. 381; and *The Planters' Bank* v. *Snodgrass et al*, he will, I think, concur in this opinion.

Anecdotes are not wanting to show that even in the Supreme Court he argued some cases of great importance, without knowing any thing about them till the argument was commenced. One of these savors of the ludicrous. Mr. Prentiss was retained, as associate counsel, with Mr. (now Gen.) M—,

at that time one of the most promising as now one of the
most distinguished, lawyers in the State. During the session
of the Supreme Court, at which the case was to come on,
Mr. M— called Mr. P.'s attention to the case, and proposed
examining the record together; but for some reason this was
deferred for some time. At last it was agreed to examine
into the case the night before the day set for the hearing.
At the appointed time, Prentiss could not be found. Mr.
M— was in great perplexity. The case was of great importance ; there were able opposing counsel, and his client and
himself had trusted greatly to Mr. P.'s assistance. Prentiss
appeared in the court-room when the case was called up. The
junior counsel opened the case, reading slowly from the record all that was necessary to give a clear perception of its
merits ; and made the points, and read the authorities he had
collected. The counsel on the other side replied. Mr. P.
rose to rejoin. The junior could scarcely conceal his apprehensions. But there was no cloud on the brow of the speaker ; the consciousness of his power and of approaching victory sat on his face. He commenced, as he always did, by
stating clearly the case, and the questions raised by the facts.
He proceeded to establish the propositions he contended for,
by their reason, by authorities, and collateral analogies, and
to illustrate them from his copious resources of comparison.
He took up, one by one, the arguments on the other side, and
showed their fallacy ; he examined the authorities relied upon
in the order in which they were introduced, and showed their
inapplicability, and the distinction between the facts of the

cases reported and those in the case at bar; then returning to the authorities of his colleague, he showed how clearly, in application and principle, they supported his own argument. When he had sat down, his colleague declared
that Prentiss had taught him more of the case than he had
gathered from his own researches and reflection.

Mr. Prentiss had scarcely passed a decade from his majority when he was the idol of Mississippi. While absent
from the state his name was brought before the people for
Congress; the State then voting by general ticket, and elect-
ing two members. He was elected, the sitting members
declining to present themselves before the people, upon the
claim, that they were elected at the special election, ordered
by Governor Lynch, for two years, and not for the called
session merely. Mr. Prentiss, with Mr. Word, his colleague
went on to Washington to claim his seat. He was admitted
to the bar of the House to defend and assert his right. He
delivered then that speech which took the House and the
country by storm; an effort which if his fame rested upon it
alone, for its manliness of tone, exquisite satire, gorgeous
imagery, and argumentative power, would have rendered his
name imperishable. The House, opposed to him as it was
in political sentiment, reversed its former judgment, which
declared Gholson and Claiborne entitled to their seats, and
divided equally on the question of admitting Prentiss and
Word. The speaker, however, gave the casting vote against
the latter, and the election was referred back to the people.

Mr. Prentiss addressed a circular to the voters of Mississippi, in which he announced his intention to canvass the State. The applause which greeted him at Washington, and which attended the speeches he was called on to make at the North, came thundering back to his adopted State. His friends—and their name was legion—thought before that his talents were of the highest order; and when their judgments were thus confirmed—when they received the indorsement of such men as Clay, Webster, and Calhoun, they felt a kind of personal interest in him : he was *their* Prentiss. They had first discovered him—first brought him out—first proclaimed his greatness. Their excitement knew no bounds. Political considerations, too, doubtless had their weight. The canvass opened—it was less a canvass than an ovation. He went through the State—an herculean task—making speeches every day, except Sundays, in the sultry months of summer and fall. The people of all classes and both sexes turned out to hear him. He came, as he declared, less on his own errand than theirs, to vindicate a violated constitution, to rebuke the insult to the honor and sovereignty of the State, to uphold the sacred right of the people to elect their own rulers. The theme was worthy of the orator, the orator of the subject.

This period may be considered the golden prime of the genius of Prentiss. His real effective greatness here attained its culminating point. He had the whole State for his audience, the honor of the State for his subject. He came well armed and well equipped for the warfare. Not content with challenging his competitors to the field, he threw down the

gauntlet to all comers.   Party, or ambition, or some other
motive, constrained several gentlemen—famous before, notorious afterwards—to meet him.   In every instance of
such temerity, the opposer was made to bite the dust.

The ladies surrounded the rostrum with their carriages,
and added, by their beauty, interest to the scene.   There
was no element of oratory that his genius did not supply.
It was plain to see whence his boyhood had drawn its romantic inspiration.   His imagination was colored and imbued with
the light of the shadowy past, and was richly stored with the
unreal but life-like creations, which the genius of Shakspeare
and Scott had evoked from the ideal world.   He had linger-
ed, spell-bound, among the scenes of mediæval chivalry.   His
spirit had dwelt, until almost naturalized, in the mystic
dream-land they peopled—among paladins, and crusaders,
and knights-templars ; with Monmouth and Percy—with
Bois-Gilbert and Ivanhoe, and the bold McGregor—with the
cavaliers of Rupert, and the iron enthusiasts of Fairfax.   As
Judge Bullard remarks of him, he had the talent of an Italian
improvisatore, and could speak the thoughts of poetry with the
inspiration of oratory, and in the tones of music.   The fluency of his speech was unbroken—no syllable unpronounced—
not a ripple on the smooth and brilliant tide.   Probably he
never hesitated for a word in his life.   His diction adapted
itself, without effort, to the thought ; now easy and familiar,
now stately and dignified, now beautiful and various as the
hues of the rainbow, again compact, even rugged in sinewy
strength, or lofty and grand in eloquent declamation.

His face and manner were alike uncommon.   The turn of the head was like Byron's ; the face and the action were just what the mind made them.   The excitement of the features, the motions of the head and body, the gesticulatian he used, were all in absolute harmony with the words you heard.   You saw and took cognizance of the general effect only; the particular instrumentalities did not strike you; they certainly did not call off attention to themselves.   How a countenance so redolent of good humor as his at times, could so soon be overcast, and express such intense bitterness, seemed a marvel.   But bitterness and the angry passions were, probably, as strongly implanted in him as any other sentiments or qualities.

There was much about him to remind you of Byron : the cast of head—the classic features—the fiery and restive nature—the moral and personal daring—the imaginative and poetical temperament—the scorn and deep passion—the deformity of which I have spoken—the satiric wit—the craving for excitement, and the air of melancholy he sometimes wore —his early neglect, and the imagined slights put upon him in his unfriended youth—the collisions, mental and physical, which he had with others—his brilliant and sudden reputation, and the romantic interest which invested him, make up a list of correspondencies, still further increased, alas ! by his untimely death.

With such abilities as we have alluded to, and surrounded by such circumstances, he prosecuted the canvass, making himself the equal favorite of all classes.   Old democrats were,

seen, with tears running down their cheeks, laughing hyster-
ically ; and some, who, ever since the formation of parties,
had voted the democratic ticket, from coroner up to governor,
threw up their hats and shouted for him.   He was returned
to Congress by a large majority, leading his colleague, who
ran on precisely the same question, more than a thousand
votes.

The political career of Mr. Prentiss after this time is
matter of public history, and I do not propose to refer to it.

After his return from Congress, Mr. Prentiss continued
to devote himself to his profession ; but, subsequently to 1841
or 1842, he was more engaged in closing up his old business
than in prosecuting new.   Some year or two afterwards, the
suit which involved his fortune was determined against him
in the Supreme Court of the United States ; and he found
himself by this event, aggravated as it was by his immense
liabilities for others, deprived of the accumulations of years
of successful practice, and again dependent upon his own ex-
ertions for the support of himself and others now placed under
his protection.   In the mean time, the profession in Mississippi had become less remunerative, and more laborious.
Bearing up with an unbroken spirit against adverse fortune,
he determined to try a new theatre, where his talents might
have larger scope.   For this purpose, he removed to the city
of New Orleans, and was admitted to the bar there.   How
rapidly he rose to a position among the leaders of that
eminent bar, and how near he seemed to be to its first
honors, the country knows.   The energy with which he

addressed himself to the task of mastering the peculiar jurisprudence of Louisiana, and the success with which his efforts were crowned, are not the least of the splendid achievements of this distinguished gentleman.

The danger is not that we shall be misconstrued in regard to the rude sketch we have given of Mr. Prentiss in any such manner as to leave the impression that we are prejudiced against, or have underrated the character of, that gentleman. We are conscious of having written in no unkind or unloving spirit of one whom, in life, we honored, and whose memory is still dear to us; the danger is elsewhere. It is two-fold : that we may be supposed to have assigned to Prentiss a higher order of abilities than he possessed ; and, in the second place, that we have presented, for undistinguishing admiration, a character, some of the elements of which do not deserve to be admired or imitated—and indeed, which are of most perilous example, especially to warm-blooded youth. As to the first objection, we feel sure that we are not mistaken, and even did we distrust our own judgment we would be confirmed by Sharkey, Boyd, Wilkinson, Guion, Quitman, to say nothing of the commendations of Clay, Webster, and Calhoun, " the immortal three," whose opinions as to Prentiss's talents would be considered extravagant if they did not carry with them the *imprimatur* of their own great names. But we confess to the danger implied in the second suggestion. With all our admiration for Prentiss—much as his memory is endeared to us—however the faults of his character and the irregularities of his life may be palliated by the

10

peculiar circumstances which pressed upon idiosyncracies of temper and mind almost as peculiar as those circumstances, —it cannot be denied, and it ought not to be concealed, that the influence of Prentiss upon the men, especially upon the young men of this time and association, was hurtful. True, he had some attributes worthy of unlimited admiration, and he did some things which the best men might take as examples for imitation.   He was a noble, whole-souled, mag-nanimous man : as pure of honor, as lofty in chivalric bear-ing as the heroes of romance : but, mixed with these brilliant qualities, were vices of mind and habit, which made them more dangerous than if they had not existed at all : for vice is more easily copied than virtue : and in the partnership between virtue and vice, vice subsidizes virtue to its uses. Prentiss lacked regular, self-denying, systematic application. He accomplished a great deal, but not a great deal for his capital : if he did more than most men, he did less than the task of such a man : if he gathered much, he wasted and scat tered more.   He wanted the great essential element of a true, genuine, moral greatness : there was not—above his intellect and the bright army of glittering faculties and strong powers of his mind—above the fierce host of passions in his soul—a *presiding spirit of Duty.*   Life was no trust to him : it was a thing to be enjoyed—a bright holiday season—a gala day, to be spent freely and carelessly—a gift to be decked out with brilliant deeds and eloquent words and all gewgaws of fancy—and to be laid down bravely when the evening star should succeed—the bright sun and the dews begin to fall softly upon the green earth. True, he labored more than most men: but he labored as he frolicked—because his mind could not be idle, but burst into work as by the irrepressible instinct which sought occupation as an outlet to intellectual excitement: but what he accomplished was nothing to the measure of his powers. He studied more than he seemed to study,—more, probably, than he cared to have it believed he studied. But he could accomplish with only slender effort, the end for which less gifted men must delve, and toil, and slave. But the imitators, the many youths of warm passions and high hopes, ambitious of distinction—yet solicitous of pleasure—blinded by the glare of Prentiss's eloquence, the corruscations of a wit and fancy through which his speeches were borne as a stately ship through the phosphorescent waves of a tropical sea—what example was it to *them* to see the renown of the Forum, the eloquence of the Hustings, the triumphs of the Senate associated with the faro-table, the midnight revel, the drunken carouse, the loose talk of the board laden with wine and cards? What Prentiss effected they failed in compassing. Like a chamois hunter full of life, and vigor, and courage, supported by the spear of his genius—potent as Ithuriel's—Prentiss sprang up the steeps and leaped over the chasms on his way to the mount where the " proud temple" shines above cloud and storm ; but mediocrity, in assaying to follow him, but made ridiculous the enterprise which only such a man with such aids could accomplish. And even he, not wisely or well: the penalty came at last, as it must ever come for a violation of

natural and moral laws.   He lived in pain and poverty droop-
ing in spirit, exhausted in mind and body, to lament that
wasting of life, and health, and genius, which, unwasted, in
the heyday of existence, and in the meridian lustre of his un-
rivalled powers, might have opened for himself and for his
country a career of usefulness and just renown scarcely paralleled by the most honored and loved of all the land.

If to squander thus such rare gifts were a grievous fault,
grievously hath this erring child of genius answered it.
But painfully making this concession, forced alone by the
truth, it is with pleasure we can say, that, with this deduc-
tion from Prentiss's claims to reverence and honor, there yet
remains so much of force and of brilliancy in the character
—so much that is honorable, and noble, and generous—so
much of a manhood whose robust and masculine virtues are
set off by the wild and lovely graces that attempered and
adorned its strength, that we feel drawn to it not less to admire than to love.

In the midst of his budding prospects, rapidly ripening
into fruition, insidious disease assailed him.   It was long
hoped that the close and fibrous system, which had, seemingly, defied all the laws of nature, would prove superior to
this malady.   His unconquerable will bore him up long
against its attacks.   Indeed it seemed that only death itself
could subdue that fiery and unextinguishable energy.   He
made his last great effort, breathing in its feeble accents but
a more touching and affecting pathos, and a more persuasive
eloquence, in behalf of Lopez, charged with the offence of

fitting out an expedition against Cuba. So weak was he, that he was compelled to deliver it in a sitting posture, and was carried, after its delivery, exhausted from the bar.

Not long after this time, in a state of complete prostration, he was taken, in a steamboat, from New-Orleans to Natchez, under the care of some faithful friends. The opiates given him, and the exhaustion of nature, had dethroned his imperial reason; and the great advocate talked wildly of some trial in which he supposed he was engaged. When he reached Natchez, he was taken to the residence of a relation, and from that time, only for a moment, did a glance of recognition fall—lighting up for an instant his pallid features—upon his wife and children, weeping around his bed. On the morning of —— died this remarkable man, in the 42d year of his age. What he *was*, we know. What he *might have been*, after a mature age and a riper wisdom, we cannot tell. But that he was capable of commanding the loftiest heights of fame, and marking his name and character upon the age he lived in, we verily believe.

But he has gone. He died, and lies buried near that noble river which first, when he was a raw Yankee boy, caught his poetic eye, and stirred, by its aspect of grandeur, his sublime imagination : upon whose shores first fell his burning and impassioned words as they aroused the rapturous applause of his astonished auditors. And long will that noble river flow out its tide into the gulf, ere the roar of its current shall mingle with the tones of such eloquence again—eloquence, as full and majestic, as resistless and sublime, and as wild in its sweep as its own sea-like flood,

> —— "the mightiest river
> Rolls mingling with his fame for ever."

The tidings of his death came like wailing over the State, and we all heard them, as the toll of the bell for a brother's funeral.   The chivalrous felt, when they heard that "young Harry Percy's spur was cold," that the world had somehow grown commonplace; and the men of wit and genius, or those who could appreciate such qualities in others, looking over the surviving bar, exclaimed with a sigh—

> "The blaze of wit, the flash of bright intelligence,
> The beam of social eloquence,
> Sunk with HIS sun."

THE BAR OF THE SOUTH-WEST.

THE citizens of an old country are very prone to consider the people of a newly settled State or Territory as greatly their inferiors : just as old men are apt to consider those younger than themselves, and who have grown up under their observation, as *their* inferiors. It is a very natural sentiment. It is flattering to pride, and it tickles the vanity of senility —individual and State—to assign this status of elevation to self, and this consequent depression to others. Accordingly, the Englishman looks upon the American as rather a green-horn, gawky sort of a fellow, infinitely below the standard of John Bull in every thing, external and internal, of character and of circumstance ; and no amount of licking can ·thrash the idea out of him. As Swedenborg says of some religious dogmas held by certain bigots—it is glued to his brains. So it is with our own people. The Bostonian looks down upon the Virginian—the Virginian on the Tennesseeian—the Tennesseeian on the Alabamian—the Alabamian on the Mississippian—the Mississippian on the Louisianian—the Louisianian on the Texian—the Texian on

New Mexico, and, we suppose, New Mexico on Pandemonium.

It may be one of the perversions of patriotism, to create and foster invidious and partial discriminations between different countries, and between different sections of the same country : and especially does this prejudice exist and deepen with a people stationary and secluded in habit and position. But travel, a broader range of inquiry and observation, more intimate associations and a freer correspondence, begetting larger and more cosmopolitan views of men and things, serve greatly to soften these prejudices, even where they are not entirely removed. That there is *some* good country even beyond the Chinese wall, and that all not within that barrier are not quite " outside barbarians," the Celestials themselves are beginning to acknowledge.

There is no greater error than that which assigns inferiority to the bar of the South-West, in comparison with that of any other section of the same extent in the United States. Indeed, it is our honest conviction that the profession in the States of Tennessee, Alabama, Mississippi and Louisiana, are not equalled, as a whole, by the same number of lawyers in any other quarter of the Union,—certainly in no other quarter where commerce is no more various and largely pursued.

The reasons for this opinion we proceed to give. The most conclusive mode of establishing this proposition would probably be by comparison; but this, from the nature of the case, is impossible. The knowledge of facts and men is wanting, and even if possessed by any capable of instituting the comparison, the decision would, at last, be only an opinion, and would carry but little weight, even if the capacity and fairness of the critic were duly authenticated to the reader.

It is a remarkable fact, that the great men of every State in the Union, were those men who figured about the time of the organization and the settling down of their several judicial systems into definite shape and character. Not taking into the account the Revolutionary era—unquestionably the most brilliant intellectual period of our history—let us look to that period which succeeded the turmoil, embarrassment and confusion of the Revolution, and of the times of civil agitation and contention next following, and out of which arose our present constitution. The first thing our fathers did was to get a country; then to fix on it the character of government it was to have; then to make laws to carry it on and achieve its objects. The men, as a class, who did all this, were lawyers : their labors in founding and starting into motion our constitutions and laws were great and praiseworthy : but after setting the government agoing, there was much more to do ; and this was to give the right direction and impress to its jurisprudence. The Statutes of a free country are usually but a small part of the body of its law—and the common law of England, itself but a judicial enlargement and adaptation of certain vague and rude principles of jurisprudence to new wants, new necessities and exigencies, was a light rather than a guide, to the judges of

10*

our new systems, called to administer justice under new and widely different conditions and circumstances.   The greatest talent was necessary for these new duties.   It required the nicest discrimination and the soundest judgment to determine what parts of the British system were opposed to the genius of the new constitution, and what parts were inapplicable by reason of new relations or differing circumstances.   The great judicial era of the United States—equally great in bar and bench—was the first quarter of this century.   And it is a singular coincidence that this was the case in nearly every, if not in every, State.   Those were the days of Marshall and Story and Parsons, of Kent and Thompson and Roane, of Smith and Wythe and Jay, and many other fixed planets of the judicial system, while the whole horizon, in every part of the extended cycle, was lit up by stars worthy to revolve around and add light to such luminaries.   Mr. Webster declared that the ablest competition he had met with, in his long professional career, was that he encountered at the rude provincial bar of back-woods New Hampshire in his earlier practice.

And this same remarkable preëminence has characterized the bar of every new State when, or shortly after emerging from, its territorial condition and first crude organization; the States of Tennessee, Kentucky, Alabama, Mississippi and Louisiana forcibly illustrate this truth, and we have no question but that Texas and California are affording new expositions of its correctness.

A fact so uniform in its existence, must have some solid

principle for its cause. This principle we shall seek to ascertain. It is the same influence, in a modified form, which partly discovers and partly creates great men in times of revolution. Men are fit for more and higher uses than they are commonly put to. The idea that genius is self-conscious of its powers, and that men naturally fall into the position for which they are fitted, we regard as by no means an universal truth, if any truth at all. Who believes that Washington ever dreamed of his capacity for the great mission he so nobly accomplished, before with fear and trembling, he started out on its fulfilment? Probably the very ordeal through which he passed to greatness purified and qualified him for the self-denial and self-conquest, the patience and the fortitude, which made its crowning glory. To be great, there must be a great work to be done. Talents alone are not distinction. For the Archimedean work, there must be a fulcrum as well as a lever. Great abilities usually need a great stimulus. What dormant genius there is in every country, may be known by the daily examples of a success, of which there was neither early promise nor early expectation.

In a new country the political edifice, like all the rest, must be built from the ground up. Where nothing is at hand, every thing must be made. There is work for all and a necessity for all to work. There is almost perfect equality. All have an even start and an equal chance. There are few or no factitious advantages. The rewards of labor and skill are not only certain to come, but they are certain to come at once. There is no long and tedious novitiate. Talent and

energy are not put in quarantine, and there is no privileged
inspector to place his *imprimatur* of acceptance or rejec-
tion upon them.   An emigrant community is necessarily a
practical community; wants come before luxuries—things
take precedence of words; the necessaries that support life
precede the arts and elegancies that embellish it.   A man
of great parts may miss his way to greatness by frittering
away his powers upon non-essentials—upon the style and
finish of a thing rather than upon its strength and utility—
upon modes rather than upon ends.   To direct strength
aright, the aim is as essential as the power.   But above all
things, success more depends upon self-confidence than any
thing else; talent must go in partnership with will or it cannot do a business of profit.   Erasmus and Melancthon were
the equals of Luther in the closet; but where else were
they his equals ?   And where can a man get this self-reliance
so well as in a new country, where he is thrown upon his
own resources; where his only friends are his talents;
where he sees energy leap at once into prominence; where
those only are above him whose talents are above his;
where there is no *prestige* of rank, or ancestry, or
wealth, or past reputation—and no family influence, or de-
pendants, or patrons; where the stranger of yesterday is
the man of mark to-day; where a single speech may win
position, to be lost by a failure the day following; and
where amidst a host of competitors in an open field of rivalry, every man of the same profession enters the course
with a race-horse emulation, to win the prize which is glitter-

ing within sight of the rivals. There is no stopping in such a crowd : he who does not go ahead is run over and trodden down. How much of success waits on opportunity ! True, the highest energy may make opportunity; but how much of real talent is associated only with that energy which appropriates, but which is not able to create, occasions for its display. Does any one doubt that if Daniel Webster had accepted the $1,500 *clerkship* in New Hampshire, he would not have been *Secretary* of State ? Or if Henry Clay had been so unfortunate as to realize his early aspirations of earning in some backwoods county his $333 33 per annum, is it so clear that Senates would have hung upon his lips, or Supreme Courts been enlightened by his wisdom ?

The exercise of our faculties not merely better enables us to use them—it strengthens them as much; the strength lies as much in the exercise as in the muscle; and the earlier the exercise, after the muscle can stand it, the greater the strength.

Unquestionably there is something in the atmosphere of a new people which refreshes, vivifies and vitalizes thought, and gives freedom, range and energy to action. It is the natural effect of the law of liberty. An old society weaves a network of restraints and habits around a man; the chains of habitude and mode and fashion fetter him : he is cramped by influence, prejudice, custom, opinion; he lives under a feeling of *surveilance* and under a sense of *espionage*. He takes the law from those above him. Wealth, family, influence, class, caste, fashion, coterie and adventitious circumstances of all sorts, in a greater or less degree, trammel him; he acts not so much from his own will and in his own way, as from the force of these arbitrary influences; his thoughts and actions do not leap out directly from their only legitimate head-spring, but flow feebly in serpentine and impeded currents, through and around all these impediments. The character necessarily becomes, in some sort, artificial and conventional; less bold, simple, direct, earnest and natural, and, therefore, less effective.

What a man does well he must do with freedom. He can no more speak in trammels than he can walk in chains; and he must learn to think freely before he can speak freely. He must have his audience in his mind before he has it in his eye. He must hold his eyes level upon the court or jury —not raised in reverence nor cast down in fear. For the nonce, *the* speaker is the teacher. He must not be sifting his discourse for deprecating epithets or propitiating terms, nor be seeking to avoid being taken up and shaken by some rough senior, nor be afraid of being wearisome to the audience or disrespectful to superiors : bethinking him of exposure and dreading the laugh or the sneer, when the bold challenge, the quick retort, the fresh thought, the indignant crimination, the honest fervor, and the vigorous argument are needed for his cause. To illustrate what we mean—let us take the case of a young lawyer just come to the bar of an old State. Let us suppose that he has a case to argue. He is a young man of talent, of course—*all* are. Who make his audience ? The old judge, who, however mild a mannered man he may be, the youth has looked on, from his childhood, as the most awful of all the sons of men. Who else ? The old seniors whom he has been accustomed to regard as the ablest and wisest lawyers in the world, and the most terrible satirists that ever snapped sinews and dislocated joints and laid bare nerves on the rack of their merciless wit. The jury of sober-sided old codgers, who have known him from a little boy, and have never looked on him except as a boy, most imprudently diverted by parental vanity from the bellows or the plough-handles, to be fixed as a cannister to the dog's tail that fag-ends the bar :—that jury look upon him,—as he rises stammering and floundering about, like a badly-trained pointer, running in several directions, seeking to strike the cold trail of an idea that had run through his brain in the enthusiasm of ambitious conception the night before :—these, his judges, look at him or from him with mingled pity and wonder ; his fellow-students draw back from fear of being brought into misprision and complicity of getting him into this insane presumption ; and, after a few awkward attempts to propitiate the senior, who is to follow him, he catches a view of the countenances of the old fogies in whose quiet sneers he reads his death-warrant ; and, at length, he takes his seat, as the crowd rush up to the veteran who *is to do* him—like a Spanish rabble to an *auto da fe*. What are his feelings ? What or who can describe his mortification ? What a vastation of pride and self-esteem that was ? The speech he made was not the speech he had conceived. The speech he had in him he did not *deliver ;* he

" aborted " it, and, instead of the anticipated pride and joy of
maternity, he feels only the guilt and the shame of infanticide.

Alack-a-day ! Small is the sum of sympathy which is
felt by the mass of men for the woes and wounds of juvenile vanity and especially for the woes of professional vanity.
From the time of Swift, who pilloried Bettsworth to eternal ridicule, and of Cobbett, who, with rude contempt,
scoffed at the idea of being blamed for " crushing a lawyer in the egg," but few tears of commiseration have been
shed for the poor " Wind-seller," cut down in his raw and
callow youth. And, yet, I cannot help, for the soul of me,
the weakness which comes into my eyes, when I see, as I
have seen, a gallant youth, full of ardor and hope, let down,
a dead failure,—on his first trial over the rough course of
the law. The head hung down—the cowed look of timid
deprecation—the desponding carriage—tell a story of deep
wounds of spirit—of hopes overcast, and energies subdued,
and pride humbled—which touches me deeply. I picture
him in the recesses of his chamber, wearing through the
weary watches of the night—grinding his teeth in impatient
anguish,—groaning sorrowfully and wetting his pillow with
bitter tears—cursing his folly, and infatuation, and his hard
fate—envying the hod-carrier the sure success of his humbler
lot, and his security against the ill fortune of a shameful failure, where failure was exposed presumption.

I have felt, in the intensity of my concern for such an
one, like hazarding the officiousness of going to him, and ad-
vising him to abandon the hang-dog trade, and hide his
shame in some obscurer and honest pursuit.

And, rough senior, my dear brother, think of these things when your fingers itch to wool one of the tender neophytes—and forbear. I crave no quarter for the lawyer, full-grown or half-grown; he can stand peppering—it is his vocation, Hal—he is paid for it; but for the lawyerling I plead; and to my own urgency in his behalf, I add the pathetic plea of the gentle Elia in behalf of the roast-pig— "Barbecue your whole hogs to your palate, steep them in shalots, stuff them with the plantations of the rank and guilty garlic; you cannot poison *them* or make them stronger than they are—but consider, *he* is a weakling—a flower."

But *revenons à nos moutons.*

But suppose the debutant does better than this; suppose he lets himself out fully and fearlessly, and has something in him *to* let out; and suppose he escapes the other danger of being ruined by presumption, real or supposed; he is duly complimented:—"he is a young man of promise— there is some 'come out' to that young man; some day he will be something—if—if " two or three peradventures don't happen to him. If he is proud,—as to be able to have accomplished all this he must be,—such compliments grate more harshly than censure. He goes back to the office; but where are the clients? They are a slow-moving race, and confidence in a young lawyer " is a plant of slow growth." Does he get his books and " scorn delights and live laborious days," for the prospect of a remote and contingent, and that at best, but a poorly remunerating success ? Does he cool his hot blood in the ink of the Black-letter, and spin his toils with the industry and forethought of the patient spider that is to be remunerated *next* fly-season, for her pains, and sit, like *that* collecting attorney, at the door of the house, waiting and watching until *then*, for prey? If so, he is a hero indeed; but what years of the flower of his life are not spent in waiting for the prosperous future, in the vague preparation which is not associated with, or stimulated by, a present use for, and direct application to a tangible purpose of what he learns! Where one man of real merit succeeds, how many break down in the training; and even where success *is* won, how much less that success than where talent, like Pitt's, takes its natural position at the start, and, stimulated to its utmost exercise, fights its way from its first strivings to its ultimate triumphs—each day a day of activity and every week a trial of skill and strength; learning all of law that is evolved from its practice, and forced to know something, at least, of what the books teach of it; and getting that larger and better knowledge of men which books cannot impart, and that still more important self-knowledge, of which experience is the only schoolmaster.

In the new country, there are no seniors: the bar is all Young America. If the old fogies come in, they must stand in the class with the rest, if, indeed, they do not "go foot." There were many evils and disadvantages arising from this want of standards and authority in and over the bar—many and great — but they were not of long continuance, and were more than counterbalanced by opposite benefits.

It strikes me that the career of Warren Hastings illustrates my idea of the influence of a new country and of a new and responsible position over the character of men of vigorous parts. In India, new to English settlement and institutions, he well earned the motto, " *Mens æqua in arduis*," inscribed over his portrait in the council chamber of Calcutta : but after he returned to England, amidst the difficulties of his impeachment, his policy ignored all his claims to greatness, had it alone been considered : the genius that expatiated over and permeated his broad policy on the plains of Hindostan seemed stifled in the conventional at mosphere of St. Stephen's.

While we think that the influence of the new country upon the intellect of the professional *emigré* was highly beneficial, we speak, we hope, with a becoming distrust, of its moral effect. We might, in a debating club, tolerate some scruple of a doubt, whether this violent disruption of family ties — this sudden abandonment of the associations and influence of country and of home — of the restraints of old authority and of opinion — and this sudden plunge into the whirling vortex of a new and seething population — in which the elements were curiously and variously mixed with free manners and not over-puritanic conversation — were efficient causes of moral improvement : we can tolerate a doubt as to whether the character of a young man might not receive something less than a pious impression, under these circumstances of temptation, when that character was in its most malleable and fusible state. But we leave this moral problem to be solved by those better able to manage it, with this single observation, that if the subject *were* able to stand the trial, his moral constitution, like his physical after an attack of yellow fever, would be apt to be the better for it. We cannot, however, in conscience, from what we have experienced of a new country with " flush fixins " annexed, advise the experiment. We *have* known it to fail. And probably more of character would have been lost if more had been put at hazard.

In trying to arrive at the character of the South-Western bar, its opportunities and advantages for improvement are to be considered. It is not too much to say that, in the United States at least, no bar ever had such, or so many : it might be doubted if they were *ever* enjoyed to the same extent before. Consider that the South-West was the focus of an emigration greater than any portion of the country ever attracted, at least, until the golden magnet drew its thousands to the Pacific coast. But the character of emigrants was not the same. Most of the gold-seekers were mere gold-diggers—not bringing property, but coming to take it away. Most of those coming to the South-West brought property — many of them a great deal. Nearly every man was a speculator; at any rate, a trader. The treaties with the Indians had brought large portions of the States of Alabama, Mississippi and Louisiana into market; and these portions, comprising some of the most fertile lands in the world, were settled up in a hurry. The Indians claimed lands under these treaties—the laws granting pre-emption rights to settlers on the public lands, were to be construed, and the litigation growing out of them settled, the public lands afforded a field for unlimited speculation, and combinations of purchasers, partnerships, land companies, agencies, and the like, gave occasion to much difficult litigation in after times. Negroes were brought into the country in large numbers and sold mostly upon credit, and bills of exchange taken for the price; the negroes in many instances were unsound—some as to which there was no title; some falsely pretended to be unsound, and various questions as to the liability of parties on the warranties and the bills, furnished an important addition to the litigation: many land titles were defective; property was brought from other States clogged with trusts, limitations, and uses, to be construed according to the laws of the State from which it was brought: claims and contracts made elsewhere to be enforced here: universal indebtedness, which the hardness of the times succeeding made it impossible for many men to pay, and desirable for all to escape paying: hard and ruinous bargains, securityships, judicial sales; a general looseness, ignorance, and carelessness in the public officers in doing business; new statutes to be construed; official liabilities, especially those of sheriffs, to be enforced; banks, the laws governing their contracts, proceedings against them for forfeiture of charter; trials of right of property; an elegant assortment of frauds constructive and actual; and the whole system of chancery law, admiralty proceedings; in short, all the flood-gates of litigation were opened and the pent-up tide let loose upon the country. And such a criminal docket! What country could boast more largely of its crimes? What more splendid rôle of felonies! What more terrific murders! What more gorgeous bank robberies! What more magnificent operations in the land offices! Such McGregor-like levies of black mail, individual and corporate! Such superb forays on the treasuries, State and National! Such expert transfers of balances to undiscovered bournes! Such august defalcations! Such flourishes of rhetoric on ledgers auspicious of gold which had departed for ever from the vault! And in INDIAN affairs!— the very mention is suggestive of the poetry of theft—the romance of a wild and weird larceny! What sublime conceptions of super-Spartan roguery! Swindling Indians by the nation! (*Spirit of Falstaff, rap!*) Stealing their land by the township! (*Dick Turpin and Jonathan Wild! tip the table!*) Conducting the nation to the Mississippi river, stripping them to the flap, and bidding them God speed as they went howling into the Western wilderness to the friendly agency of some sheltering Suggs duly empowered to receive their coming annuities and back rations! What's Hounslow heath to this? Who Carvajal? Who Count Boulbon?

And all these merely forerunners, ushering in the Millennium of an accredited, official Repudiation; and IT but vaguely suggestive of what men could do when opportunity and capacity met — as shortly afterwards they did— under the Upas-shade of a perjury-breathing bankrupt law!— But we forbear. The contemplation of such hyperboles of mendacity stretches the imagination to a dangerous tension. There was no end to the amount and variety of lawsuits, and interests involved in every complication and of enormous value were to be adjudicated. The lawyers were compelled to work, and were forced to learn the rules that were involved in all this litigation.

Many members of the bar, of standing and character, from the other States, flocked in to put their sickles into this abundant harvest. Virginia, Kentucky, North Carolina and Tennessee contributed more of these than any other four States ; but every State had its representatives.

Consider, too, that the country was not so new as the practice. Every State has its peculiar tone or physiognomy, so to speak, of jurisprudence imparted to it, more or less, by the character and temper of its bar. That had yet to be given. Many questions decided in older States, and differently decided in different States, were to be settled here ; and a new state of things, peculiar in their nature, called for new rules or a modification of old ones. The members of the bar from different States had brought their various notions, impressions and knowledge of their own judicature along with them ; and thus all the points, dicta, rulings, offshoots, quirks and quiddities of all the law, and lawing, and law-mooting of all the various judicatories and their satellites, were imported into the new country and tried on the new jurisprudence.

After the crash came in 1837—(there were some *premonitory fits* before, but *then* the *great convulsion* came on)

—all the assets of the country were marshalled, and the suing material of all sorts, as fast as it could be got out, put into the hands of the workmen. Some idea of the business may
be got from a fact or two : in the county of Sumpter, Alabama, in one year, some four or five thousand suits, in the
common-law courts alone, were brought ; but in some other
counties the number was larger ; while in the lower or river
counties of Mississippi, the number was at least double.
The United States Courts were equally well patronized in
proportion—indeed, rather more so.   The white *suable* population of Sumpter was then some 2,400 men.   It was a merry
time for us craftsmen ; and we brightened up mightily, and
shook our quills joyously, like goslings in the midst of a
shower. We look back to that good time, " now past and
gone," with the pious gratitude and serene satisfaction with
which the wreckers near the Florida Keys contemplate the
last fine storm.

It was a pleasant sight to profesional eyes to see a whole
people let go all holds and meaner business, and move off to
court, like the Californians and Australians to the mines :
the " pockets" were picked in both cases.   As law and lawing soon got to be the staple productions of the country, the
people, as a whole the most intelligent—in the wealthy counties—of the rural population of the United States, and, as a
part, the *keenest* in all creation, got very well " up to trap"
in law matters ; indeed, they soon knew more about the delicate mysteries of the law, than it behooves an honest man to
know.

The necessity for labor and the habit of taking difficulties by the horns is a wonderful help to a man ; no one knows what he can accomplish until he tries his best ; or how firmly he can stand on his own legs when he has no one to lean on.

The range of practice was large. The lawyer had to practise in all sorts of courts, State and Federal, inferior and Supreme. He had the bringing up of a lawsuit, from its birth in the writ to its grave in the sheriff's docket. Even when not concerned in his own business, his observation was employed in seeing the business of others going on ; and the general excitement on the subject of law and litigation, taking the place, in the partial supension of other business, of other excitements, supplied the usual topics of general, and, more especially, of professional conversation. If he followed the circuit, he was always in law : the temple of Themis, like that of Janus in war, was always open.

The bar of every country is, in some sort, a representative of the character of the people of which it is so important an "institution." We have partly shown what this character was : after the great Law revival had set in, the public mind had got to be as acute, excited, inquisitive on the subject of law, as that of Tennessee or Kentucky on politics : every man knew a little and many a great deal on the subject. The people soon began to find out the capacity and calibre of the lawyers. Besides, the multitude and variety of lawsuits produced their necessary effect. The talents of the lawyers soon adapted themselves to the nature and exigencies of the service required of them, and to the tone and temper of the juries and public. Law had got to be an every-day, practical, com- mon-place, business-like affair, and it had to be conducted in the same spirit on analogous principles. Readiness, preci- sion, plainness, pertinency, knowledge of law, and a short-hand method of getting at and getting through with a case, were the characteristics and desiderata of the profession. There was no time for wasting words, or for manœuvring and skirmishing about a suit; there was no patience to be expended on exor- diums and perorations: few jurors were to be humbugged by demagogical appeals ; and the audience were more con- cerned to know what was to become of the negroes in suit, than to see the flights of an ambitious rhetoric, or to have their ears fed with vain repetitions, mock sentimentality, or tumid platitudes. To start *in medias res*—to drive at the centre—to make the home-thrust—to grasp the hinging point —to give out and prove the law, and to reason strongly on the facts—to wrestle with the subject Indian-hug fashion— to speak in plain English and fervid, it mattered not how rough, sincerity, were the qualities required : and these qual- ities were possessed in an eminent degree.

Most questions litigated are questions of law : in nine cases out of ten tried, the jury, if intelligent and impartial, have no difficulty in deciding after the law has been plainly given them by the court : there is nothing for a jury to do but to settle the facts, and these are not often seriously con- troverted, in proportion to the number of cases tried in a new country ; and the habit of examining carefully, and arguing fully, legal propositions, is the habit which makes the lawyer. Nothing so debilitates and corrupts a healthy taste and healthy thought, as the habit of addressing ignorant juries; it corrupts style and destroys candor; it makes a speech, which ought to be an enlightened exposition of the legal merits of a cause, a mere mass of " skimble skamble stuff," a compound of humbug, rant, cant and hypocrisy, of low, demagoguism and flimsy perversions—of interminable wordiness and infinite repetition, exaggeration, bathos and vituperation—frequently of low wit and buffoonery—which " causes the judicious to grieve," " though it splits the ears of the goundlings." I do not say that the new bar was free from these traits and vices : by no manner of means : but I do say that they were, as a class, much freer than the bar of the older States out of the commercial cities. The reason is plain : the new dogs hadn't learned the old tricks; and if they had tricks as bad, it was a great comfort that they did not have the same. If we had not improvement, we had, at least, variety ; but, I think, we had improvement.

There was another thing : the bar and the community—as all emigrant communities—were mostly young, and the young men cannot afford to play the pranks which the old fogies safely play behind the domino of an established reputation. What is ridiculous, in itself or in a young man, may be admired, or not noticed, in an older leader with a prescriptive title to cant and humbug; it is *lese majesty* to take him off, but the juniors with us had no such immunity. If he tried such tricks he heard of it again ; it was rehearsed in

his presence for his benefit—if he made himself *very* ridiculous, he was carried around the circuit, like a hung jury in
old times, for the especial divertisement of the brethren. A
respectable old snob like Mr. Buzzfuz, shrouded like Jack
the Giant Killer, in a mantle of dignity that forbade approach,
if it did not hide the wearer from attack, never could hear
what his " d—d good-natured friends" thought of his performances in the department of humbug or cant; but this was,
by no means, the case with such an one in our younger community.

Again, it is flattering to human nature to know that these
forensic tricks are not spontaneous but acquired, and a young
bar cannot, all at once, acquire them. It requires experience, and a monstrous development of the organs of Reverence and Marvellousness in the audience to practise them
with any hope of success, and these bumps were almost entirely wanting in the craniums of the new population around,
all of whose eye-teeth were fully cut, and who, standing
knee-deep in exploded humbugs, seemed to wear their eyes
stereotyped into a fixed, unwinking *qui vive :* the very expression of their countenances seemed to be articulate with
the interrogatory, " who is to be picked up next ? " It stops
curiously the flow of the current when the humbugger sees
the intended humbuggee looking him, with a quizzical 'cute-
ness, in the eye, and seeming to say by the expression of his
own, " Squire, do you see any thing green here ? "

The business of court-house speaking began to grow too
common and extensive to excite public interest; the novelty

of the thing, after a while, wore off. A stream of sound poured over the land like the trade winds ; men now, as a general thing, only came to court because they had business there, and staid only until it was accomplished. It is other-wise in the old country as it had been in the new. It is one of the phenomena of mind that quiet and otherwise sensible men, come from their homes to the county seat to listen to the speeches of the lawyers,—looking over the bar and dropping the under jaw in rapt attention, when some foren-sic Boreas is blowing away at a case in which they have no interest or concern, deserting, for this queer divertisement, the splitting of their rails and their attention to their bul-locks ; or, if they needed some relaxation from such pursuits, neglecting their arm-chairs in the passage with the privilege of reading an old almanac or listening to the wind whistling through the key-hole. When a thing gets to be a work-day and common place affair, it is apt to be done in a common-place way, and the parade, tinsel, and fancy fireworks of a holiday exercise or a gala-day fête are apt to be omitted from the bill and the boards.

It is a great mistake to suppose that a lawyer's strength lies chiefly in his tongue ; it is in the preparation of his case—in knowing what makes the case—in stating the case accurately in the papers, and getting out and getting up the proofs. It requires a good lawyer to make a fine argument ; but he is a better lawyer who saves the necessity of making a fine argument, and prevents the possibility of his adversa-ry's making one.

These practical requirements and habits had the effect of driving from the bar that forensic nuisance, "a pretty speaker;" Fourth-of-Julyisms fled to the stump or the national anniversary barbecues; they were out of place in those prosaic times and proceedings. A veteran litigant having a tough lawsuit, had as little use for a flowery orator, letting off his fancy pyrotechnics, as he had for Juno's team of peacocks for hauling his cotton to market.

Between the years 1833 and 1845, the bar was most numerous, and, we think, on the whole, most able. The Supreme Court bar of Mississippi was characterized by signal ability. It may well be doubted if so able and efficient a bar ever existed at any one period of the same duration, in a Southern State: not that the bar was made up of Wickhams, Leighs, Johnsons, and Stanards, nor of Clays, Crittendens, Rowans, and Wickliffes; nor, possibly, that there were any members of the Jackson bar equal to these great names of the Richmond and Frankfort bars; yet those who have heard the best efforts of Prentiss, Holt, Walker, Yerger, Mays, and Boyd, may be allowed to doubt the justness of that criticism which would deny a place to them among lawyers even so renowned as the shining lights of the Virginia and Kentucky forums. But we meant to say, that if this claim be ignored, yet the Mississippi bar, if not so distinguished for individual eminence, made up the deficiency by a more generally-diffused ability, and a larger number of members of inferior, though only a shade inferior, distinction.

As some proof of the ability of the South-western bar, it may be stated, that we had not unfrequently an advent into the new country of lawyers of considerable local reputation in the older States—men who, in their own bailiwicks, were mighty men of war—so distinguished, indeed, that on the first bruiting of a lawsuit, the litigants, without waiting for the ferry-boat, would swim Tar river, or the Pedee, or French Broad, to get to them, under the idea that who got to them first would gain the case. But after the first bustle of their coming with the fox-fire of their old reputations sticking to their gowns, it was generally found, to the utter amazement of their friends who had known them in the old country, that the new importation would not suit the market. They usually fell back from the position at first courteously tendered them, and, not unfrequently, receded until, worked out of profitable practice, they took their places low down in the list, or were lost behind the bar, among the spectators. There is something doubtless in transplantation—something in racing over one's own training-paths—something in first firing with a rest, and then being compelled to fire off-hand amid a general flutter and confusion; but, making all this allowance, it hardly accounts fully for the result. For we know that others, against these disadvantages, sustained themselves.

Nor was there, nor is there, any bar that better illus-trates the higher properties or nobler characteristics which have, in every State, so much ennobled the profession of the law, than that of the South-West, a class of men more fearless or more faithful, more chivalrous, reliable or trustworthy, more loyal to professional obligations, or more honorable in inter-professional intercourse and relations.   True, there were exceptions, as, at all times and every where, there are and will be.   Bullying insolence, swaggering pretension, underhanded arts, low detraction, unworthy huckstering for fees, circumvention, artful dodges, ignoring engagements, facile obliviousness of arrangements, and a smart sprinkling, especially in the early times of pettifogging, quibbling and quirking, but these vices are rather of persons than of caste, and not often found; and, when they make themselves apparent, are scouted with scorn by the better members of the bar.

We should be grossly misunderstood if we were construed to imply that the bar of the South-West, possessing the signal opportunities and advantages to which we have adverted, so improved them that all of its members became good lawyers and honorable gentlemen.   Mendacity itself could scarcely be supposd to assert what no credulity could believe.   All the guano of Lobos could not make Zahara a garden.   In too many cases there was no sub-soil of mind or morals on which these advantages could rest.   As Chief Justice Collier, in Dargan and Waring, 17 Ala. Reports, in language, marrying the manly strength and beauty of Blackstone to the classic elegance and flexible grace of Stowell, expresses it, " the claim of such," so predicated, " would be *pro tanto* absolutely void, and, having nothing to rest on, a court of equity " (or law) " could not impart to it vitality.

Form and order *has* been given to chaos, but an appeal to equity " (or law) " to breathe life into a nonentity, which is both intangible and imperceptible, supposes a higher power—one which no human tribunal can rightfully exercise. *Æquitas scquitur legem.*" This view is conclusive.

We should have been pleased to say something of the bench, especially of that of the Supreme Court of Alabama and Mississippi, but neither our space nor the patience of the reader will permit.

A writer usually catches something from, as well as communicates something to, his subject. Hence if, in the statements of this paper, we shall encounter the incredulity of some old fogy of an older bar, and he should set us down as little better than a romancer in prose, we beg him to consider that we have had two or three regiments of lawyers for our theme—and be charitable.

THE HON. FRANCIS STROTHER.

I NIB my pen and impart to it a fine hair-stroke, in order that I may give the more delicate touches which can alone show forth the character of this distinguished gentleman. It is no ordinary character, and yet it is most difficult to draw. There are no sharp angles, no salient points which it is impossible to miss, and which serve as handles whereby to hold up a character to public view. The lines are delicate, the grain fine, the features regular, the contour full, rounded and perfectly developed, nowhere feeble or stunted, and nowhere disproportioned. He is the type of a class, unfortunately of a small class; more unfortunately of a class rapidly disappearing in the hurly-burly of this fast age of steam pressure and railway progress: a gentleman of the Old School with the energy of the New.

If I hold the pencil in hand in idle reverie, it is because my mind rests lovingly upon a picture I feel incapable of transcribing with fidelity to the original: I feel that the coarse copy I shall make will do no justice to the image on the mind; and, therefore, I pause a moment, to look once more at the original before it is obscured by the rude counterpart.

Fifteen years ago—long years crowded with changes and events—such changes as are only effected in *our* country within so short a period,—the savage disappearing—the frontier-man following on to a further border—that border, like the horizon, widening and stretching out towards the sinking sun, as we go on;—*then* the rude settlement, *now* the improved neighborhood, with its school-houses and churches; the log cabin giving way to the mansion,—the wilderness giving way to the garden and the farm; fifteen years ago, I first saw him. He was then, so far as I can remember, what he is now:—no perceptible change has occurred in any outward or inner characteristic, except that now a pair of spectacles occasionally may be found upon his nose, as that unresting pen sweeps in bold and beautiful chirography across his paper; a deeper tinge of gray may be seen in his hair, and possibly too, his slight, but graceful and well-knit form may be a trifle less active than of old. I put these as possibilities—not as matters I can note.

The large, well-developed head—the mild, quiet, strong face—the nose, slightly aquiline—the mouth, firm yet flexible—the slightly elongated chin—the shape of the head oval, and protruding largely behind the ears in the region that supplies the motive powers, would not have conveyed a right meaning did not the blue eyes, strong yet kind, beaming out the mingled expression of intelligence and benignity, which, above all other marks, is the unmistakable, uncounterfeit-

able outward sign of a true gentleman, relieve and mellow
the picture. The voice kind, social, gentle—and the whole
manner deferential, simple, natural and winning—self-poised,
modest, friendly, and yet delicate and gracefully dignified.
Dignified is scarcely an apt word in the vulgar meaning attached to it; for there was no idea of self, much less of pretension or affectation connected with his manner or bearing.
But there was, towards high and low, rich and poor, a genuine and unaffected kindness and friendliness, which every
man who approached him felt had something in it peculiarly
sweet towards him ; and made the most unfriended outcast
feel there was, at least, *one* man in the world who felt an interest in and sympathy for him and his fortunes. Towards
the young especially was this exhibited, and by them was it
appreciated. A child would come to him with the feeling
of familiarity and a sense of affectionate consideration ; and
a young man, just coming to the bar, felt that he had found
one who would be glad to aid him in his struggles and en-
courage him in difficulty. Were this rare manner a thing of
art and but a manual gone through with—put on for effect—
it could not have been long maintained or long undiscovered.
But it was the same all the time—and the effect the same.
We need scarcely say that the effect was to give the subject
of it a popularity well nigh universal. It was a popularity
which during years of active life in all departments of business affairs, public and private—all the strifes of rivalry and
collisions of interest never shook. The fiercest oppositions
of party left him uninjured in fame or appreciation : indeed

no party ties were strong enough to resist a popularity so deep and wide.

He had passed through the strong temptations which beset a man in a new country, and *such* a country, unscathed, unsoiled even by suspicion, and ever maintained a reputation above question or challenge. It were easy to have accumulated an immense fortune by an agency for the Indians in securing their claims under the treaty of 1830; and he was offered the agency with a compensation which would have made him a millionnaire; he took the agency but rejected the fortune.

He was the genius of labor. His unequalled facility in the dispatch of business surprised all who knew its extent. Nothing was omitted—nothing flurried over—nothing bore marks of haste, nothing was done out of time. System—order—punctuality waited upon him as so many servants to that patient and indomitable industry. He had a rare tact in getting at, and in getting through, a thing. He saw at once the point. He never missed the joint of the argument. He never went to opening the oyster at the wrong end. He never turned over and over a subject to find out what to do with it or how to commence work. He caught the *run* of the facts—moulded the scheme of his treatment of them—saw their right relations, value and dependence, and then started at once, in ready, fluent and terse English, to put them on paper or marshal them in speech. His power of statement was remarkable, especially of written statement. He could make more out of a fact than most men out of two :

and immaterial matters he could so dove-tail and attach to other matters, that they left an impression of a great deal of plausibility and pertinency.

He loved labor for its own sake as some men love ease. There was no part of office-work drudgery to him. He carried his writing materials about with him as some men their canes: and that busy pen, at a moment's notice, was speeding over the paper, throwing the g's and y's behind at a rapid rate.

A member of Congress—he was in the House, defending the Pre-emption System, out of it, attending to some business before the departments ; in again, writing with a pile of letters before him ; in the committee room, busy with *its* business : again, before the Secretary of War, arguing some question about the Dancing Rabbit Treaty, 14th article :— and then consulting the Attorney General, so that persons who had no knowledge of his ubiquitous habits, seeing him at one of these places, would have been willing to have sworn an *alibi* for him if charged with being that morning at any other.

Returning to the practice, it was the same thing. The management and care of his own property—his attention to a large family and household affairs—these things would have made some inroads upon another's time, but these and a large practice, extended over many courts and several of the wealthiest counties of the State, at a time when every man was a client, did not seem to press upon him. He could turn himself from one subject to another with wonderful ease : the hinges of his mind moved as if oiled, in any direction. Trying an important case in the Circuit Court, as the jury retired and the Court was calling some other case, he would propose to the opposite counsel to go down into the Orphan's Court, and try a case there, involving a few thousands; and that dispatched, might be found in the Chancery office preparing a suit for trial there; which finished, he would hear the result of the law case, and, by the meeting of Court, have (if decided adversely) a bill of exceptions ready, of a sheet or two of foolscap, or a bill for an injunction to take the case into Chancery. At night, he would be ready for a reference before the Master of an account of partnership transactions of vast amount; and, as he walked into Court next morning, would merely call by to file a score or two of exceptions; and, in all the time, would carry on his consultations and prepare the cases coming on for trial, and be ready to enjoy a little social conversation with his brethren. In all this, there was no bustle, hurry, parade, fuss, or excitement. He moved like the Ericsson motor, without noise, the only evidence that it was moving being the progress made.

He was never out of temper, never flurried, never excited. There was a serious, patient expression in the eyes, which showed a complete mastery of all things that trouble the nervous system. Even when he complained—as he often did— it was not a testy, ill-natured, peevish grumbling, but seemingly the complaint of a good, gentle nature, whose meekness was a little too sternly tried. He never abused anybody. He had no use for sarcasm or invective. Even when prosecuting for crime a heinous criminal, he used the language of civility, if not of kindness. Indeed, he seemed to seek a conviction from a sheer feeling of consideration for the prisoner. He would cross-examine a swift or perjured witness in a tone of kindness which seemed anxious to relieve him from embarrassment; and plying with great tact question after question, would, when the witness faltered and stammered or broke down, seem to feel a lively sentiment of commiseration for his unfortunate predicament. In commenting upon his testimony, he would attribute his unhappy course to any thing but wilful misstatement—to strange hallucination, prejudice, an excitable temperament, want of memory, or even to dreaming: but still the right impression was always left, if in no other way, by the elaborate disclaimers and apologies, that, with such persistent and pertinacious over-kindness, he made for the delinquent

There was business skill in every thing he did. His arguments were clear, brief, pointed—never wandering, discursive or episodical—never over-worked, or over-laden, or over-elaborated. He took all the points—took them clearly, expressed them neatly and fully—knew when to press a point and when to glide over it quickly, and above all—what so few know—he knew when he was done. His tone was that of animated conversation, his manner courteous, respectful, impressive and persuasive: never offending good taste, never hurried away by imprudence or compromising his case by a point that could be made to reach it; and probably making as few imprudent admissions as any member of the bar.

But in many of these points he was equalled; in one he was not—his tact in drawing papers. In a paper showing for a continuance or for a change of venue, the skill with which the facts were marshalled and conclusions insinuated was remarkable. Like shot-silk the light glanced over and along the whole statement, though it was often hard to find precisely where it was or what made it; yet, if admitted, a little emphasis or a slight connection with extraneous matter would put his adversary's case in a dangerous position.

A more pliant, facile, complying gentleman than the Hon. Francis, it was impossible to find on a summer's day,—so truthful, so credulous, so amiably uncontroverting. It seemed almost a pity to take advantage of such simplicity, to impose upon such deferential confidence! Such innocence deserved to be respected, and like the Virgin in the fable, sleeping by the lion, one would think that it ought to carry in its trusting purity a charm against wrong from the most savage brutality or the most unscrupulous mendacity. This view of the subject, I am forced to say, does not quite represent the fact. The Hon. Francis *was* very limber—but it was the limberness of whalebone, gum-elastic, steel springs and gutta percha—limber because tough—easily bowed, but impossible to be broken or kept down. He had great suavity—but it was only the *suaviter in modo*. Substantially and essentially he was *fortiter in re*—mechanically he was *suaviter in modo :* the *suaviter* was only the running gear by which he worked the *fortiter*. In his own private affairs no man was more liberal and yielding, or less exacting or

pertinacious; professionally, his concessions took the form
of, and exhausted their energies in beneficent words, benignant seemings and gracious gestures. But his manner was
inimitably munificent. Though he gave nothing, he went
through the motions of giving most grandly; empty-handed
you felt that you were full; you mistook the filling of your
ears for some substantial benefit to your client; there was
an affluence of words, a lingual and manual generosity which
almost seemed to transpose the figures on the statement
which he proposed as a settlement. With a grand self-abne-
gation, he would allow you to continue a cause when his side
was not ready to try it, and would most blandly merely insist on your paying the costs, magnanimously waiving further advantage of your situation. He would suffer you to
take a non-suit with an air of kindness calculated to rivet a
sense of eternal obligation. No man revelled in a more
princely generosity than he when he gave away nothing.
And to carry out the self-delusion, he *took* with the air of
giving a bounty. Before his manner of marvellous concession all impediments and precedence vanished. If he had
a case at the end of the docket, he always managed to get it
tried first : if the arrangement of the docket did not suit his
convenience, his convenience changed it by a sort of not-be-
fore understood, but taken-for-granted general consent of
the bar. There was such a matter-of-course about his polite
propositions, that for a good while, no one ever thought of
resisting them ; indeed, most lawyers, under the spell of his
infatuating manners, half-recollected some sort of agreement

which was never made. In the trial of a cause he would slip in testimony on you in such a cozy, easy, insinuating fashion, that you were ruined before you could rally to oppose it. Even witnesses could not resist the graciousness and affectionateness of his manner, the confidence with which he rested on their presumed knowledge :—they thought they must know what he evidently knew so well and so authentically.

He lifted great weights as the media do heavy tables without any show of strength.

The Hon. Francis had no doubts. He had passed from this world of shadows to a world of perfect light and knowledge. He had the rare luck of always being on the right side : and then he had all the points that could be made on that side clearly in his favor, and all that could be made against him were clearly wrong. He was never taken off his guard. If a witness swore him out of court, he could not swear him out of countenance. He expected it. His case was better than he feared. In the serene confidence of unshakable faith in his cause, brickbats fell on his mind like snowflakes, melting as they fell, and leaving no impression. If he had but one witness, and you had six against him, long after the jury had ceased listening and when you concluded, he would mildly ask you if that was *all* your proof, and if you proposed going to the jury on that ?

But if the Hon. Francis had no doubts, he had an enormous development of the organ of wonder. He had a note of admiration in his eye as large as a ninepin. He wondered that a party should have brought *such* a suit; that another had set up such a defence; that the counsel should have taken such a point; that the court should have made such a ruling (with great deference), and he wondered that the Supreme Court had sustained it. *Nil admirari* was not his maxim.

I was a little too fast when I said he was never taken by surprise. He was once—indeed twice. Casually looking at some papers Blass held in his hand, as an important case was being called for trial, he saw what he took to be a release of the action by one of the nominal plaintiffs: in order to avoid the effect of this paper, he applied for a continuance, which it was never difficult for him to obtain. Finding out afterwards his mistake, he moved to set aside the order of continuance. It required a lion-like boldness to make and assign the grounds of the motion: this effort he essayed with his usual ingenuity. He commenced by speaking of Blass's high character—that he had been deceived by the real and implied assurance of B.—that he acquitted B. of all intentional impropriety: he entered into a most elaborate disclaimer of all injurious imputation: he spoke only of the effect: he had only seen hastily a paper endorsed as a release: he should be surprised if the gentleman would hold him to the order taken under such circumstances of mistake—a mistake which had misled him, and which he took the earliest opportunity of correcting. "In other words," said B., "you peeped into my hand and mistook the card, and now you want to renig because your eyes fooled you." "Ahem!" said S., "I have already stated the facts." "Well," said B., pulling out the paper, "I will let you set aside the order if you promise to go to trial." "No," S. answered, "I believe not: on further reflection, perhaps it might be irregular."

On another occasion he had been cross-examining an Irishman, and the Hibernian desiring to come prepared to make a display in affidavit elocution, had written out his testimony at length : but having got drunk he had dropped the MS., which being found by the client of Mr. S., was put into his hands. Mr. S. opened the paper and inquired of the witness, "Mr. McShee, did you ever see this paper before : have the kindness to look at it ?" The witness snatched up the paper and answered quickly, "Sure, yes—it's mine, Misther Strother, I lost it meself, and where is the $5 bill I put in it ? "

Being pressed for time, one morning, Mr. S. entered a barber's shop in Mobile, where he saw a brother lawyer of the Sumter bar, Jemmy O., highly lathered, sitting in much state in the chair waiting for tho bar*berium* to sharpen his blade. Mr. S. addressed his old acquaintance with great warmth and cordiality—requested him to keep his seat—begged him not to be at all uneasy on his account—protested that he was not in his way—he could wait—not to think of putting him to trouble—pulled off his cravat—it was no intrusion—not at all—by no means—politely disclaimed, affirmed and protested—until J. O., thinking that Mr. S. somehow had precedence, got up and insisted on Mr. S. taking the chair, to which Mr. S., like Donna Julia, "vowing he would ne'er consent, consented"—was duly shaved—

all the while protesting against it—and went out, leaving J.
O. to think he was the politest man he had ever met with.

When J. O. afterwards found out that S. had no precedence, he said he had been taught a new chapter of law—
the title by disclaimer.

At length the Hon. Mr. Strother got his hands full.
He got at last to the long wished for enjoyment which was
to reward the trials of his earlier years. He was made commissioner of the State Banks of Alabama. He had it all
to himself. No partner shared with him this luxurious re-
past. Such a mass and mess of confusion—such a bundle
of heterogeneous botches; in which blundering stupidity,
reckless inattention, and both intelligent and ignorant rascality had made their tracks and figures, never before was
seen. He was to bring order out of chaos—reconcile dis-
crepancies—supply whole pages of ledgers—balance unbal-
anceable accounts—understand the unintelligible—collect
debts involved in all mazes of legal defences, or slumbering
cozily in chancery—to bring all sorts of agents to all sorts
of settlements—to compromise bad debts—disencumber
clogged property—to keep up a correspondence like that
of the Pension Bureau—and manage the finances of the
State government. The State trembled on the verge of Repudiation; if the assets of the banks were lost, the honor
of the State was gone. The road through the Bank operations was like the road through Hounslow heath, every step
a robbery. To bring the authors to their responsibility—to
hunt up and hunt down absconding debtors and speculators

—to be every where at once—to be in Boston, Mobile, New Orleans, New-York—and then to keep up his practice in several counties just for holiday refreshment, were some of the labors he performed.

He succeeded wonderfully. He kept untarnished the honor of the State. He restored its solvency, and, clothed with such vast trusts, greater than were ever before confided, perhaps, in the South-West to a. single man, he discharged them with a fidelity which can neither be exaggerated nor denied. He, like Falstaff, " turned diseases to commodity :" the worthless assets of the Banks were turned into State Bonds ; and the State, relieved of the pressure upon her resources, rose up at once to her place of honor in the sisterhood of States, and shone, with a new and fresher lustre, not the least in that bright galaxy. Relieved of her embarrassments, in no small degree through the instrumentality of the distinguished citizen, whose name shines through the *nom de guerre* at the head of this article, improvements are going on, mingling enterprise with patriotism, and giving forth the most auspicious prospects for the future. It is, therefore, not out of place to give some passing notice of one more instrumental than any other in redeeming the State from the *Flush Times*, in the course of our hasty articles illustrative of that hell-carnival

MR. TEE AND MR. GEE.

ONE of the most distinguished lawyers in the State of Mississippi, was W. Y. Gee, Esq.   He was distinguished not less for his legal learning than for the acuteness and subtlety of his intellect.   He was fond of exercising his talents in legal speculations, and was pleased when some new and difficult point was presented for solution.   John S. Tee, Esq., was not of that sort.   *He* was a man of facts and figures, and practical and stern realities.   He cared nothing about a lawsuit except for the proofs and what appeared on the back of the execution, and thought the best *Report* ever made of a case was that made by the sheriff.   He was completely satisfied if the Fi-fa was.   He was doing a large collecting business ; he prided himself more on the skill with which he worked on a promissory note than he would have done if he had pinned Pinkney, like a beetle, to the wall, in *McCollough* vs. *The State of Maryland*, or made Webster "take water" in the great Dartmouth College case. What seemed to him " the perfection of human reason," was not the common law, but that part of the Statute law which gave the remedy by attachment, and which statute was, as he was fond of saying, "to be liberally construed in favor of justice and for the prevention of fraud:" and he thought the perfection of professional practice under the "perfection of reason," was, to get a skulking debtor fixed so as to give an opportunity for starting the remedy after him, and thus securing a bad or doubtful debt out of property which might otherwise be "secreted," or squandered in paying *other* debts, for which the debtor might have a sickly fancy.

Squire Tee was a great favorite of Northern creditors, and deservedly. He clung to them through thick and thin, through good report and through bad report, in hard times and in easy times, and through all times. He "kept his loyalty, his love, his zeal" in a perpetual fervor. His confidence in them was unbounded. Nothing could either increase or diminish it. He would have sacrificed his own interest to theirs—he did, no doubt, frequently: and the more he gave of service to their cause—by the usual law of charity—the more he was capable of giving—the widow's cruse of oil grew by the giving to two widows' cruses of oil.

Among other things, he practised an intimate acquaintance with the facts of his case. No man was more sedulous in the preparation of proofs. He knew that however well a case was put up on the papers, it was of but little avail if it was not also well put up in the evidence. He liked evidence—a plenty of it, and good what there was of it: better too much than not enough;—he liked to converse

12

with the witnesses himself—to know exactly what they would prove: it pleased him to hear them rehearse, and then it prepared him for the coming on of the piece when he could act as prompter. He was an amateur in evidence; he loved it as an antiquarian an old fossil—as a machinist a new invention—as a politician a new humbug; it was a thing to be admired for itself—it had both an intrinsic and an extrinsic value. Receiving many claims when the times were at the hardest, he found himself frequently opposed by the ablest counsel of the State; and the incident we are to relate of him occurred on one of those occasions.

It should have been stated that, as in collecting cases, many of the clients lived at a great distance from the debtor, the attorney acted, in such instances, as the general agent of the creditor, to a great extent: and, in preparing a case for trial, had to do the work of both client and counsel. Mr. Tee was often brought into correspondence with the debtors afterwards to be made defendants. Opportunities afforded by such relations, it will readily be perceived, could very easily be improved into occasions for eliciting such facts as would, in no few instances, be very useful evidence on the trial. In this way, Mr. Tee's research and industry had been rewarded by a vast amount of useful information of which his duty to his clients made him not at all penurious, when it became their interest to have it turned into testimony. He had a good memory, a good manner, an excellent voice and a fine person; and he knew of no more pleasing way of putting to account a good memory, a good manner, an excellent voice and a fine person, than in delivering testimony in open court for a Northern client. He had one advantage over most witnesses; he knew something about the facts before he heard the parties' statements : he paid the most particular attention with the view of having matters definitely fixed in his mind, and then, being a lawyer and a good judge of the article proof, he was able to refer his statement to the proper points, and to know the relevancy and bearing of the facts on the case. He was fluent, easy, unembarrassed, though somewhat earnest of manner and speech, and had a lively talent for affidavit, elocution and a considerable power of compendious, terse and vigorous narrative in that department of forensic eloquence. It affords us pleasure to be able to pay this deserved meed of justice to an old friend and associate. *Some* men are niggardly of praise. Not so this author.

This marked fidelity to the interests of his clients had made Mr. Tee somewhat familiar with the witness box, and the result had almost universally been a speedy disposal of the matter involved in the controversy in favor of his client.

The bar, not always the most confiding of men, nor the least querulous, had begun to find fault with this *euthanasia*, as Mr. C. J. Ingersoll, in his Bunyan-like style, expresses it : they wanted a lawsuit to die the old way, and not by chloroform process,—the old bull-baiting fashion—fainting off from sheer exhaustion, or overpowered by sheer strength and lusty cuffs, kicking and fighting to the last. And so they *complained* and *averred* it was to their *great damage, where-fore they sued* Tee to *discontinue proceedings* of this sort, but *he refused, and possibly, still refuses.*

A suit had been brought by Tee for a leading house in New-York, in the U. S. Court, on a bill of exchange drawn or indorsed by a merchant, and W. Y. Gee, Esq., employed to defend it. The amount was considerable, but the case promised to be more interesting as involving a new and difficult point in the Law Merchant upon the question of notice.

The case had been opened for the plaintiff—the bill, protest, depositions, foreign statutes, and so forth, read, and one or two witnesses examined. The Court had taken a recess for dinner—it being understood or taken for granted that the plaintiff had closed his case. The defendant either had no witnesses or else preferred submitting the case without them, the point on which Mr. Gee relied having been brought out by an unnecessary question propounded by Tee to his own witness.

After the meeting of the Court, Mr. Gee, who was a little near-sighted, was seen before the bar, leisurely arranging a small library of books he had collected, and by the aid of which he was to argue the point on the notice. Having accomplished this to his satisfaction, he leaned his head on his hand and was absorbed in profound cogitation—like an Episcopal clergyman before the sermon. The court interrupted him in this meditation by announcing its readiness to proceed with the cause. Gee rose and remarked to the Court that the defence was one of pure law, and he should raise the only question he meant to make by a demurrer to the plaintiff's evidence. " Not until the plaintiff gets through his proof, I reckon," said Mr. Tee. " Why, I thought you had rested," replied Mr. Gee. " Yes," said Tee, " I did rest a little, and am now tired resting, and will proceed to labor—Clerk, SWEAR ME."

Gee jumped from his seat and rushed towards Tee— " Now Tee," said he—" just this one time, if you please, forbear, for Heaven's sake—come now, be reasonable—it is the prettiest point as it stands I ever saw—the principle is really important—don't spoil it, Tee." But Tee, fending Gee off with one hand, held out the other for the book. Gee grew more earnest—" Tee, Tee, old fellow—I say now, look here, Tee, don't do this, *this* time—just hold off for a minute— come, listen to reason—now come, come, let *this* case be an exception—you *said* you were through—if you will just stand off I won't demur you out any more."

But Tee was not to be held off—he repeated, " Clerk, swear me, I must discharge my professional duties."

Gee retired in disgust, not waiting to hear the result— barely remarking, that if it came to *that*, Tee would cover the case like a confession of judgment and the statute of *Jee-fails* besides. We believe he was not mistaken; for his *affidavy* carried the case sailing beyond gun-shot of Gee's batteries.

Gee contented himself with giving notice to Tee that he

should require him for the future to give him notice when he meant to testify in his cases, as he wished to be saved the trouble of bringing books and papers into Court.   To which Tee replied he might consider a *general* notice served upon him *then*.

SCAN. MAG.

PATRICK MCFADGIN found himself indicted in the Circuit Court of Pickens County, for indulging in sundry Hibernian pastimes, whereby his superflux of animal and ardent spirits exercised themselves and his shillaly, to the annoyance of the good and peaceable citizens and burghers of the village of Pickensville, at to wit, in said county.

One Squire Furkisson was a witness against the afore said Patrick, and, upon his evidence chiefly, the said McFadgin was convicted on three several indictments for testing the strength of his shillaly on the craniums of as many citizens; albeit, Patrick vehemently protested that he was only in fun, " and afther running a rig on the boys for amusement, on a sportive occasion of being married to a female woman —his prisint wife."

A more serious case was now coming up against Pat, having its origin in his drawing and attempting to fire a pistol, loaded with powder and three leaden bullets, which pistol the said Patrick in his right hand then and there held, with intent one Bodley then and there to kill and murder contra-

ry to the form of the statute (it being highly penal to murder a man in Alabama contrary to the form of the statute).

To this indictment Patrick pleaded "Not guilty," and,
the jury being in the box, the State's Solicitor proceeded to
call Mr. Furkisson as a witness.   With the utmost innocence,
Patrick turned his face to the Court and said, "Do I understand yer Honor that Misther Furkisson is to be a witness
fornent me agin?"   The judge said dryly, it seemed so.
"Well, thin, yer Honor, I plade guilty sure, an' ef yer
Honor plase, not becase I *am* guilty, for I'm as innocent as
yer Honor's sucking babe at the brist—but jist on the account of saving Misther Furkisson's *sowl*."

AN EQUITABLE SET-OFF.

An enterprising young gentleman of the extensive family of Smith, rejoicing in the Christian prefix of Theophilus, and engaged in that species of traffic for which Kentucky is famous, to wit, in the horse-trading line, tried his wits upon a man in the same community of the name of Hickerson, and found himself very considerably *minus* in the operation; the horse he had swapped turning out to be worth, by reason of sundry latent defects, considerably less than nothing.

Smith waited, for some time, for an opportunity of righting himself in the premises; preferring to be discreetly silent on the subject of his loss, such accidents being looked upon, about that time, by those with whom he most associated, more as a matter of ridicule than sympathy. At length Mr. Hickerson, in the course of one of his trading forays in the neighboring village, had got a fine mule, and brought him home, well-pleased with his bargain. A favorable opportunity now presented itself for Mr. Smith to obtain his revenge. He adopted the following plan: He sent a complaisant friend, a Mr. Timothy Diggs, over to Hickerson's one Sunday morning, with instructions. Mr. Diggs, riding leisurely beyond Mr. Hickerson's premises, caught sight of the mule, and, turning towards the house, saw Mr. Hickerson, who was sitting in the porch calmly enjoying those exhilarating reflections which come across the mind of a jockey after a good trade. " Halloo, Hickerson," said he, " I see you have got Jones's big mule— Jones came near selling him to me, but I got item in time, and escaped." " Why," said Hickerson, " was any thing the matter with the mule?" " Yes," said Diggs; " however, I don't know myself that there was much, only this; that the mule does very well except in the full of the moon, and then he takes fits which last about a week, hardly ever longer ; and then such rearing and charging, and biting and kicking ! he's like all possessed—nobody and nothing can manage him. Now, the best you can do is to go down to Smith's, and trade him off with him for a bran-new sorrel horse he's got. " Well," said Hickerson, " I'll do *that* sure. Hold on, and keep dark, old fellow, and see how I'll crack him."

Hickerson accordingly fixed up his mule, and rode over to Mr. Smith's, and after much chaffering, and many mutual compliments, in the French style, to their respective animals, the new sorrel, that had been fixed up for Mr. Hickerson's special benefit, and had all the diseases that horseflesh is heir to, and some it gets by adoption, was exchanged for the mule.

It was not long before Mr. Hickerson, finding Mr. Smith in company with some of the young gentlemen who could relish humor of this sort, ventured to relate this amusing incident; but when Mr. Smith, who had quietly awaited the termination of the narrative and the laughter growing thereout, in his turn gave in the counter-plot, Mr. Hickerson's sensibilities became greatly excited; and seeking to right himself by the law, on the facts coming out, found that Mr. Smith had only obtained an equitable set-off, and that he could not plead his own turpitude to regain what he had lost in trying to *come* the old soldier over another man.

A COOL REJOINDER.

A MR. KILLY, who was in the habit of *imbibing* pretty freely, at a court held in one of the counties of North Alabama, upon a case being called, in which K. found he could not get along for want of proof, was asked by the court what course he would take in the matter. "Why," said K., "if it please your honor, I believe *I will take water*" (a common expression, signifying that the person using it would take a nonsuit). Judge A. was on the bench, and was something of a wag in a dry way, and had his pen in his hand ready to make the entry.

"Well," said the Judge, "brother K., if you do, you will astonish your stomach most mightily."

A HUNG COURT.

Most of our readers have heard of a hung jury, but have they ever heard of a hung court? If not, I beg leave to introduce them to an instance of it, and show how it came about, and how it got unhung.

A justice of the peace in Alabama has jurisdiction in cases of *debt*, to the extent of fifty dollars; and there are two justices for every captain's beat. It was usual, when a case of much interest came on, for one justice to call in the other as associate. On one occasion, the little town of Splitskull, in ——— County, was thrown into a flutter of excitement, by a suit brought by one Smith against one Johnston, for forty dollars, due on a trade for a jack-ass, but payment of which was resisted, on the plea that the jackass turned out to be valueless. The parties—the ass excluded—were brothers-in-law, and the "connection" very numerous; the ass, too, was well known, and shared the usual fate of notoriety—a great deal of good, and a some-what greater amount of bad, repute. The issue turned upon the worth of the jack, and his standing in the community. Partisan feeling was a good deal aroused—the community grew very much excited—several fights arose from the matter, and it was *said* that a constable's election had been decided upon the issue of jackass *vel non ;* and—but we doubt this—it was even reported that a young lady in the neighborhood had discarded a young gentleman for the part he took in favor of the quadruped, differing widely, as she did—no doubt honestly—on the merits of the question, from her swain. Unfortunately, politics at that time were raging wildly; and the name of the jack being *Dick* Johnson, and one of the parties being a whig and the other a democrat, that disturbing element was thrown in. But it is only fair to say, that the excitement on the actual merits of the subject, to a considerable extent, blotted out party lines; so that I cannot say that the ass was seriously injured by politics—few are. This controversy got into the church; but the church had soon to drop it—two of the preachers having got to fisticuffs, and made disclosures on each other, &c., &c., the danger being that it would break up the congregation.

It got, at length, into the lawyers' hands; and then, of course, all hopes of a settlement of the controversy, except in one way, were at end.

After the parties employed their lawyers, the note of busy preparation rang more loudly throughout the excitement. Forty witnesses a side were subpœnaed. The people turned out as to a muster. The pro-ass party, and the anti-ass party, made themselves busy in getting things ready for trial. The justices preserved an air of mysterious and dignified impartiality, and all attempts to sound them on the question proved abortive. Little Billy Perkins, who taught a singing school in the neighborhood, and who had many arts and many opportunities for ingratiating himself with the wife and daughters of Squire Crousehorn, *did* get, he used afterwards to boast, some little item, in a private way, as to the leaning of that jurist; and, on the strength of it, laid a wager of a set of singing books and a tuning-fork, against twenty bushels of corn, *vs.* the ass: but the wary Squire Rushong, who was a bachelor, kept his own counsel, and even kept away from all the quiltings and shuck-ings, for fear his secret might be wormed out of him by some seducing Delilah; or else, that he might, by refusing to compromise his judicial character, compromise his matri-monial prospects. But it *was said* that the Squire was sweet on Miss Susan Smith; and it was easy enough to see, that to take part against the ass, in the present aspect of affairs, was the same as to give up all hopes of Miss Susan, or, what was tantamount with the prudent Squire—any in-choate rights or prospective interests in her father's estate. And it *was whispered* about by some of the anti-ass party, that, considering how cold Miss Susan had been to the Squire before, there was something suspiciously sweet in the way she smiled on him as he helped her into the ox-wagon from the church door, when she was about leaving for home. But I dare say this was mere imagination. The plaintiff, Smith, was fortunate enough to employ Tom B. Devill, an old lawyer who had great experience in the courts of the county, especially in such fancy cases as the present; and was justly distinguished throughout all that neck of woods, for having the most " LIBELLIOUS " tongue in all that region : while the rival faction were thrown upon young Ned Boller, a promising disciple in the same department of the profession ; and who was considered as a " powerful judge of law," especially of " statue law," but who had not the same experience in the conduct of such important and delicate litigation. Great was the exultation of the pro-assites, when it was announced that their messenger—though the others had got to the court-house first—had seen the Squire Tom B. before their adversary ; the pro-assite messenger, by sharp foresight, having made his way straight to the grocery where Tom was, and the other, by a strange mistake as to his whereabouts, going to his office to find him.   The pro-assites swore there was no use in carrying the thing further— it was as good as decided already—for " Tom B. Devill could *shykeen* and bullyrag Ned Boller's shirt off, and give him two in the game. "   Anti-ass stock fell in the market, and there was even some feeler put out for a " *comp*."—but the proposition was indignantly rejected.

The canvassing of the witnesses, and preparations for trial, played the very mischief with the harmony of the settlement.   The people had come in from one of the older Southern States, for the most part, and were known to each other, and had been for many years, and before they had come out :—unfortunately, being known has its disadvantages as well as advantages. Such revelations! Some had run off for debt, some for stealing—some had done one thing, some another; and even the women were not spared—and, of the rising generation—but I spare these details.

The plaintiff, knowing the advantage of having a persecuted individual in view of the evidence, had brought Dick Johnson under a *subpœna duces tecum*, on the ground; and the groom, Hal Piles, made him go through the motions very grandly—rearing up—braying his loudest, and kicking up other rustics, indicating a great flow of *animal* spirits, and great *vivacity* of manners. Accompanying all which performances, Hal's ready witticisms—which he had picked up at his various stands—though not remarkable for refinement, seemed to excite no little merriment in the crowd around, well qualified to appreciate and enjoy such rhetorical flourishes and intellectual entertainment.

The trial came on. It lasted several days. The place of the trial was the back-room of the grocery, the crowd standing outside or in the front-room; but this not affording space enough, it was adjourned to the grove in front of the meeting-house; and ropes drawn around an area in front for the lawyers, Court, and witnesses. The case was carried through, at last, even to the arguments of the learned barristers; but these we cannot give, as we were not present at the trial, and might do injustice to the eminent counsel, by reporting their speeches second-hand. It is enough to say, that old Devill did his best, and fully sustained his reputation; while Boller not only met the expectations of his friends, but acquitted himself in the blackguarding line so admirably, that even old Tom B. Devill asked the protection of the Court: an appeal he had never made before.

At length the case was put to the justices, and they withdrew to consider of their judgment. They remained out, in consultation, for a good while. The anxiety of the crowd and the parties was intense, and kept growing, the longer they staid out. A dozen bets were taken on the result; and fourteen fights were made up, to take place as soon as the case was decided. At least twenty men had deferred getting drunk, until they could hear the issue of this great suit.

The justices started to return to their places—and " here they come," being cried out, the crowd (or rather crowds scattered about the hamlet) came rushing up from all quarters to hear the news.

Silence being ordered by the constable, you might have seen a hundred open mouths (as if hearing were taken in at that hole) gaping over the rope against which the crowd pressed. Justice Crousehorn hemmed three times, and then, with a tremulous voice, announced that the " Court ar hung," —one and one. Now here was a fix. What was to be done? In vain the " Digest " was looked into; in vain " Smith's Justice " was searched. Nothing could be found to throw light on the matter. The case had to be tried: if decided either way, "there was abundance of authority," as Rushong well suggested, to show that the defeated party could appeal: but here there was no judgment. Ned Boler insisted that the defendant had really gained the case, as the plaintiff must show himself entitled to judgment before he could get it; and likened it to a case of failure of proof: but, on this point, the Court divided again. Tom B. Devill argued that *the plaintiff* was entitled to judgment, as he had the justice issuing the warrant in his favor, and the associate was only called in as vice-justice, or, at most, as supplementary, and supernumerary, and advisory: and likened it to the case of a President of the United States differing from his cabinet. But here the Court divided again.

The crowd outside now raised a terrible row, disputing as to who had won the bets—the betters betting on particular side's winning, contending that they had not lost, as such a thing as a hung court "wasn't took into the *calcu*."—but their adversaries claimed that the bet was to be literally construed.

At length a brilliant idea struck Mr. Justice Crousehorn—which was, that his brother Rushong should sit and give judgment alone, and then, afterwards, that he, Crousehorn, should sit and grant a new trial. Accordingly, this was agreed to. Justice Rushong took the bench, and Squire Crousehorn retired. The former then gave judgment for the plaintiff; which the crowd, not knowing the arrangement, hearing, the pro-assites raised a deafening shout of triumph, in which Dick Johnson joined with one of his loudest and longest brays. But brother Crousehorn, taking the seat of justice, speedily checked these manifestations of applause, by announcing he had granted a new trial, which caused the anti-assites to set up a counter-shout, in which Richard also joined. So the cause was gotten back again to where it was before, and then was continued for further proceedings.

But what was to be done with the case *now?* If tried again, the same result would happen, and there was no election of new justices for eighteen months; the costs, in the mean time, amounting to an enormous sum. The lawyers now got together, and settled it. Each party was to pay his own costs—Tom B. Devill took the jackass for his fee, and was to pay Ned Boller ten dollars of his fee, and the forty dollar note was to be paid to the plaintiff: an arrangement whereby the parties only lost about fifty dollars a-piece, besides the amount in controversy. But the heart-burnings and excitement the great trial left, were incapable of com-promise, and so they remain to this day.

But this trial was the making of Ned Boller. His practice immediately rose from $75 to $350 a year. And to this day, so strong was the effect of his speech, that when the Splitskullers want an hyperbole to express a compliment for a speech, they say it was "nearly equal to Ned Boller's great speech against the jackass."

SAMUEL HELE, ESQ.

I CANNOT omit Sam from my gallery of daubs. I should feel
a sense of incompleteness, grieving the conscience with a feeling of duty undischarged and opportunities neglected, such
as Cave Burton would have felt had he risen from table with
an oyster-pie untouched before him.

Of all the members of the bar, Sam cultivated most the
faculty of directness. He could tolerate nothing less than
its absence in others. He knew nothing of circumlocution.
He had as soon been a tanner's horse, and walked all his life
pulled by a pole and a string, around a box, in a twenty-foot
ring, as to be mincing words, hinting and hesitating, and picking out soft expressions. He liked the most vigorous words;
the working words of the language. He thought with remarkable clearness; knew exactly what he was going to say;
meant exactly what he said; and said exactly what he meant.
A sea-captain with his cargo insured, would as soon have
made a " deviation" and forfeited the insurance, as Sam, especially when in pursuit of a new idea, would have wandered
for a minute from his straight course.   His sense was strong,

discriminating, and relevant. Swift was not more English in
his sturdy, peremptory handling of a subject, than Sam; nor
more given to varnish and mollifying. He tore the feathers
off a subject, as a wholesale cook at a restaurant does the plu-
mage off a fowl, when the crowd are clamorously bawling for
meat. Sam was well educated and well informed. But his
memory had never taken on more matter than his mind assimi·
lated. He had no use for any information that he could not
work into his thought. He had a great contempt for all prejudices except his own, and was entirely uncramped by other
people's opinions, or notions, or whims, or fancies, or desires.
The faculty of veneration was not only wanting, but there
was a hole where there ought to have been a bump. *Prestige*
was a thing he didn't understand. *Family* he had no idea
of, except as a means of procreation, and he would have respected a man as much or as little, if, improving on the modern
spirit of progress, he had been hatched out in a retort by a
chemical process, as if he had descended from the Plantagenets,
with all the quarterings right, and no bar sinister. He had
no respect for old things, and not much for old persons.
Established institutions he looked into as familiarly as into a
horse's mouth, and with about as much respect for their age.
He would, if he could, have wiped out the Chancery system, or
the whole body of the common law, " the perfection of human
reason," as he would an ink blot dropped on the paper as he
was draughting a bill to abolish them. He had no tender·
ness for the creeds or superstitions of others. A man, ten-
der-toed on the matter of favorite hobbies, had better not be

in Sam's neighborhood.   If he cherished any mysteries and
tendernesses of belief that the strong sunlight of common sense
caused to blink in the eyes, Sam was no pleasant companion
to commune with ; for Sam would drag them from the twi-
light as he would an owl, into noonday, and laugh at the
figure they cut in the sunshine.   A delicately-toned spiritu-
alist felt, when Sam was handling his brittle wares, as a fine
lady would feel, on seeing a blacksmith with smutty fingers
taking out of her box, her complexion, laces and finery.

Doctor Samuel Johnson objected to some one " that there
was no salt in his talk;" he couldn't have said that of Sam's
discourse.   It not only contained salt, but salt-petre : for
probably, as many vigorous, brimstone expressions proceeded from Sam's mouth, as from any body else's, the peculiar
patron of brimstone fireworks only excepted.

The faculty of the *wonderful* did not hold a large place
on Sam's cranium.   He believed that every thing that was
marvellous was a lie, unless he told it himself; and sometimes
even then, he had his doubts.   He only wondered on one subject ; and that was, that there always happened to be about
him such " a hell of a number of d—d fools;" and this wonder was constant, deriving new strength every day ; and he
wondered again at his inability to impress this comfortable
truth upon the parties whom he so frequently, in every form
and every where, and especially in their presence, sought to
make realize its force and wisdom, by every variety of illustration; by all the eloquence of earnest conviction and solemn
asseveration.

If Sam had a sovereign contempt for any one more than another, it was for Sir William Blackstone, whom he regarded as " something between a sneak and a puke," and for whose superstitious veneration of the common law he felt about the same sympathy that Gen. Jackson felt for Mr. Madison's squeamishness on the subject of blood and carnage, which the hero charged the statesman with not being able " to look on *with composure* "—(he might as well have said, pleasure).

Squire Sam was of a good family—a circumstance he a good deal resisted, as some infringement on his privileges. He would have preferred to have been born at large, without any particular maternity or paternity; it would have been less local and narrow, and more free and roomy, and cosmopolitan.

There had once been good living in the family. This is evident from the fact that Sam had the gout; which proof, indeed, except vague traditions, which Sam rejected as unworthy of a sensible man's belief, is the only evidence of this matter of domestic economy. Sam thought particularly hard of this; he considered it a monstrous outrage, that the only portion of the prosperous fortunes of his house which fell to his share, should have been a disease which had long survived the causes of it. As his teeth were set on edge, he thought it only fair he should have had a few of the grapes.

Sam's estimate of human nature was not extravagant. He was not an optimist. He had not much notion of human perfectibility. He was not apt to be carried away by his feelings into any very overcharged appreciation either of particular individuals or the general race. I never heard him say what he thought would eventually become of most of them; but it was very evident, from the tenor of his unstinted talk, what he thought *ought* to become of them, if transmundane affairs were regulated by principles of human justice.

The particular community in which the Squire had set up his shingle was not, even in the eyes of a more partial judgment than he was in the habit of exercising upon men, ever supposed to be colonized by the descendants of the good Samaritan ; and if they continued perverse, and persevered in iniquity, it was not Sam's fault—he did *his* duty by them. He cursed them black and blue, by night and by day. He spared not. In these divertisements he exercised his faculties of description, prophecy and invective, largely. The humbugs suffered. Sam vastated them, as Swedenborg says they do with them in the other world, until he left little but a dark, unsavory void, in souls, supposed by their owners to be stored up, like a warehouse, with rich bales of heavenly merchandise. He pulled the dominos from their faces, and pelted the hollow masks over their heads lustily. These pursuits, laudable as they may be, are not, in the present constitution of village society, winning ways ; and therefore I cannot truly say that Sam's popularity was universal ; nor did it make up by intensity in particular directions, what it lacked of diffusion. Indeed, I may go so far as to say, that it was remarkable neither for surface nor depth.

It is a profound truth, that the wounds of vanity are galling to a resentful temper, and that few people feel much obliged to a man who, purely from a love of truth, convinces the public that they are fools or knaves; or who excites a doubt in themselves touching the right solution of this problem of mind and morals. Hence I may be allowed to doubt whether Sam's industry and zeal in these exercises of his talents—whatever effect they may have had on the community—essentially advanced this gentleman's personal or pecuniary fortunes. However, I am inclined to think that this result, so far from grieving, rather pleased the Squire. Having formed his own estimate of himself, he preferred that that estimate should stand, and not be shaken by a coincidence of opinion on the part of those whose judgments in favor of a thing he considered was pretty good *prima facie* evidence against it.

Sam's disposition to animadvert upon the community about him, found considerable aggravation in a state of ill health ; inflaming his gout, and putting the acerbities and horrors of indigestion to the long account of other provocatives, of a less physical kind, to these displays. For a while, Sam dealt in individual instances; but this soon grew too tame and insipid for his growing appetite; for invective is like brandy—the longer it is indulged in, the larger and stronger must be the dose. Sam began to take them wholesale ; and he poured volley after volley into the devoted village, until you would have thought it in a state of siege.

13

There had, a few days before, been a new importation from Yankeedom—not from its factory of calicoes, but from its factory of school-teachers. The article had been sent to order, from one of the interior villages of Connecticut. The Southern propensity of getting every thing from abroad, had extended to school-mistresses,—though the country had any number of excellent and qualified girls wishing such employment at home,—as if, as in the case of wines, the process of importing added to the value. It was soon discovered that this article was a bad investment, and would not suit the market. Miss Charity Woodey was almost too old a plant to be safely transplanted. What she had been in her youth could not be exactly known; but if she ever had any chàrms, their day had long gone by. I do not mean to flatter her when I say I think she was the ugliest woman I ever saw—and I have been in places where saying that would be saying a good deal. Her style of homeliness was peculiar only in this—that it embraced all other styles. It is a wonderful combination which makes a beautiful woman; but it was almost a miracle, by which every thing that gives or gilds beauty was withheld from her, and every thing that makes or aggravates deformity was given with lavish generosity. We suppose it to be a hard struggle when female vanity can say, hope, or think nothing in favor of its owner's personal appearance; but Miss Charity had got to this point: indeed, the power of human infatuation on this subject—for even *it* is not omnipotent—could not help her in this matter. She did not try to conceal it, but let the matter pass.

as if it were a thing not worth the trouble of thinking about.

Miss Charity was one of those "strong-minded women of New England," who exchange all the tenderness of the feminine for an impotent attempt to attain the efficiency of the masculine nature; one of that fussy, obtrusive, meddling class, who, in trying to *double-sex* themselves, *unsex* themselves, losing all that is lovable in woman, and getting most of what is odious in man.

She was a bundle of prejudices—stiff, literal, positive, inquisitive, inquisitorial, and biliously pious. *Dooty*, as she called it, was a great word with her. Conscience was another. These were engaged in the police business of life, rather than the heart and the affections. Indeed, she considered the affections as weaknesses, and the morals a sort of drill exercise of minor duties, and observances, and cant phrases. She was as blue as an indigo bag. The starch, strait-laced community she came from, she thought the very tip of the ton; and the little coterie of masculine women and female men—with its senate of sewing societies, cent societies, and general congress of missionary and tract societies—the parliaments that rule the world. Lower Frothingham, and Deacon Windy, and old Parson Beachman, and all the young Beachmans, constituted, in her eyes, a sort of Puritanic See, before which she thought Rome was in a state of continual fear and flutter.

She had come out as a missionary of light to the children of the South, who dwell in the darkness of Heathenesse. It was not long—only two days—before she began to set every thing to rights. The whole academy was astir with her activity. The little girls, who had been petted by their fathers and mothers like doll-babies, were overhauled like so much damaged goods by her busy fingers, and were put into the strait-jacket of her narrow and precise system of manners and morals, in a way the pretty darlings had never dreamed of before. *Her* way was the Median and Persian law that never changed, and to which every thing must bend. Every thing was wrong. Every thing must be put right. Her hands, eyes, and tongue were never idle for a moment, and in her microscopic sense of *doo*ty and conscience, the little peccadilloes of the school swelled to the dimensions of great crimes and misdemeanors.

It was soon apparent that she would have to leave, or the school be broken up. Like that great reformer Triptolemus Yellowby, she was not scant in delivering her enlightened sentiments upon the subject of matters and things about her, and on the subject of slavery in particular; and her sentiments on this subject were those of the enlightened coterie from which she came.

The very consideration with which, in the unbounded hospitality and courtesy to woman in the South-West, she was treated, only served to inflame her self-conceit, and to confirm her in her sense of what her *doo*ty called on her to do, for the benefit of the natives; especially to reforming things to the standard of New England insular habitudes.

A small party was given one evening, and she was invited. She came. There were some fifteen or twenty persons of both sexes there; among them our friend Sam, and a few of the young men of the place. The shocking fact must be related, that, on a sideboard in the back parlor was set out something cold, besides *solid* refreshments, to which the males who did not belong to the " Sons" paid their respects. A little knot of these were laughing and talking around Sam, who, as usual, was exerting himself for the entertainment of the auditors, and, this time, in good humor. Some remarks were made touching Miss Charity, for whose solitary state—she was sitting up in the corner by herself, stiff as steelyards—some commiseration was expressed; and it was proposed that Sam should entertain her for the evening. And it was suggested to Sam that he should try his best to get her off, by giving her such a description of the country as would have that effect. " Now," said one of them, " Sam, you've been snarling at every thing about you so long, suppose you just try your best this time, and let off all your surplus bile at once, and give us some peace. Just go up to her, and let her have it strong. Don't spare brush or blacking, but paint the whole community so black, that the Devil himself might sit for the picture." Sam took a glass, and tossing it off, wiped his mouth, after a slight sigh of satisfaction, and promised, with pious fervor, that, " by the blessing of Heaven, he would do his best."

One of the company went to Miss Charity, and, after speaking in the highest terms of Sam, as a New England man, and as one of the most intellectual, and reliable, and frank men in the country, and one, moreover, who had conceived a lively regard for her, asked leave to introduce him; which having been graciously given, Sam (having first refreshed himself with another potation) was in due form introduced.

Miss Woodey, naturally desirous of conciliating Squire Hele, opened the conversation with that gentleman, after the customary formalities, by saying something complimentary about the village. "And you say, madam," replied Sam, "that you have been incarcerated in this village for two weeks; and how, madam, have you endured it? Ah, madam, I am glad, on some accounts, to see you here. You came to reform: it was well. Such examples of female heroism are the poetry of human life. They are worth the martyrdom of producing them. I read an affecting account the other day of a similar kind—a mother going to Wetumpka, and becoming the inmate of a penitentiary for the melancholy satisfaction of waiting upon a convict son."

Miss Woodey.—"Why, Mr. Hele, how you talk! You are surely jesting."

Sam.—"Madam, there are some subjects too awfully serious for jest. A man had as well jest over the corruptions and fate of Sodom and Gomorrah—though, I confess, the existence of this place is calculated to excite a great deal of doubt of the destruction of those cities, and has, no doubt, placed a powerful weapon in the hands of infidelity throughout the immense region where the infamy of the place is known."

Miss W.—" Why, Mr. Hele, I have heard a very different account of the place. Indeed, only the other evening, I
heard at a party several of the ladies say they never knew
any village so free from gossip and scandal."

Sam.—" And so it is, madam. Men and women are free
of that vice. I wish it were otherwise. It would be a sign
of improvement,—as a man with fever when boils burst out
on him,—an encouraging sign. Madam, the reason why
there is no scandal here is, because there is not character
enough to support it. Reputation is not appreciated. A
man without character is as well off as a man with it. In
the dark all are alike. You can't hurt a man here by saying any thing of him; for, say what you will, it is less than
the truth, and less than he could afford to publish at the
court-house door, and be applauded for it by the crowd.
Besides, madam, every body is so busy with his own villany,
that no one has time to publish his neighbor's."

Miss W.—" Really, Mr. Hele, you give a poor account
of your neighbors. Are there no honest men among
them ? "

Sam.—" Why,—y–e–s,—a few. The lawyers generally
acknowledge, and, as far as circumstances allow, practise, in
their *private* characters, the plainer rules of morals; but,
really, they are so occupied in trying to carry out the villany
of others, they deserve no credit for it; for they have no
time to do any thing on private account. There is also *one*
preacher, who, I believe, when not in liquor, recognizes a
few of the rudiments of moral obligation. Indeed, some

think he is not blamable for getting drunk, as he does it only in deference to the public sentiment. I express no opinion myself, for I think any man who has resided for ten years in these suburbs of hell, ought modestly to decline the expression of any opinion on any point of ethics for ever afterwards.

Miss W.—" But, Mr. Hele, if all this villany were going on, there would be some open evidence of it. I have not heard of a case of stealing since I've been here."

Sam.—" No, madam; and you wouldn't, unless a stranger came to town with something worth stealing; and perhaps not then; for it is so common a thing that it hardly excites remark. The natives never steal from each other—I grant them that. The reason is plain. There are certain acquisitions which, with a certain profession, are sacred. ' Honor among,' &c.—you know the proverb. Besides, the thief would be sure to be caught: ' Set a '—member of a certain class—you know *that* proverb, too. Moreover, all they have got they got, directly or indirectly, in that way— if getting a thing by purchase without equivalent, or taking it without leave is stealing, as any where else out of Christendom, except this debatable land between the lower regions and the outskirts of civilization, it is held to be. And to steal from one another would be repudiating the title by which every man holds property, and thus letting the common enemy, the true owner, in, whom all are interested in keeping out. Madam, if New-York, Mobile, and New Orleans were to get their own, they might inclose the whole town, and label the walls "the lost and stolen office." When a Tennesseean comes to this place with a load of bacon, they consider him a prize, and divide out what he has as so much prize money. They talk of a Kentucky hog-drover first coming in in the fall, as an epicure speaks of the first shad of the season."

Miss W.—"The population seems to be intelligent and—"

Sam (with Johnsonian oracularity).—"*Seems*—true; but they are not. Whether the population first took to rascality, and that degraded their intellects, or whether they were fools, and took to it for want of sense, is a problem which I should like to be able to solve, if I could only find some one old enough to have known them when they first took to stealing, or when they first began playing the fool; but that time is beyond the oldest memory. I can better endure ten rascals than one fool; but I am forced to endure both in one. I see, in a recent work, a learned writer traces the genealogy of man to the monkey tribe. I believe that this is true of this population; for the characteristic marks of a low, apish cunning and stealing, betray the paternity: but so low are they in all better qualities, that, if their respectable old ancestor the rib-nosed baboon, should be called to see them, he would exclaim, with uplifted paws, 'Alas, how degenerate is my breed!' For they have left off all the good instincts of the beast, and improved only on his vices."

Miss W.—"I have heard something of violent crimes,

13*

murders, and so forth, in the South-West, but I have never
heard this particular community worse spoken of—"

Sam.—" Madam, I acquit them of all crimes which require any boldness in the perpetration.   As to assassination,
it occurs only occasionally,—when a countryman is found
drunk, or something of the sort; and even assaults and batteries are not common.   These occur only in the family circle ; such as a boy sometimes whipping his father when the
old man is intoxicated, or a man whipping his wife when
she is infirm of health : except these instances, I cannot say,
with truth, that any charge of this kind can be substanti-
ated.   As to negroes—'

Miss W.—" Do tell me, Mr. Hele—how do they treat
them?   Is it as bad as they say ?   Do—do—they,—really,
now—"

Hele.—" Miss W., this is a very delicate subject; and
what I tell you must be regarded as entirely confidential.
Upon this subject there is a secrecy—a chilling mystery of
silence—cast, as over the horrors and dungeons of the in-
quisition.   The way negroes are treated in this country
would chill the soul of a New Holland cannibal.   Why,
madam, it was but the other day a case occurred over the
river, on Col. Luke Gyves's plantation.   Gyves had just
bought a drove of negroes, and was marking them in his
pen,—a slit in one ear and an underbit in the other was
Luke's mark,—and a large mulatto fellow was standing at
the bull-ring, where the overseer was just putting the number

on his back with the branding-iron, when the nigger dog, seeing his struggles, caught him by the leg, and the negro, mad with the pain,—I don't think he did it intentionally,— seized the branding-irons, and put out the dog's—a favorite Cuba bloodhound—left eye. They took the negro down to the rack in the plantation dungeon-house, and, sending for the neighbors to come into the entertainment, made a Christ-mas frolic of the matter. They rammed a powder-horn down his throat, and lighting a slow match, went off to wait the result. When gone, Col. Gyves bet Gen. Sam Potter one hundred and fifty dollars that the blast would blow the top of the negro's head off; which it did. Gen. Sam re-fused to pay, and the case was brought into the Circuit Court. Our judge, who had read a good deal more of Hoyle than Coke, decided that the bet could not be recovered, because Luke bet on a certainty; but fined Sam a treat for the crowd for making such a foolish wager, and adjourned court over to the grocery to enjoy it."

Miss W.—" Why, Mr. Hele, it is a wonder to me that the fate of Sodom does not fall upon the country."

Sam.—" Why, madam, probably it would, if a single righteous man could be found to serve the notice. However, many think that its irredeemable wickedness has induced Heaven to withdraw the country from its jurisdiction, and remit it to its natural, and, at last, reversionary proprietors, the powers of hell. It subserves, probably, a useful end, to stand as a vivid illustration of the doctrine of total de-pravity.

Miss W.—" But, Mr. Hele,—do tell me,—do they *now* part the young children from their mothers—poor things ? "

Sam.—" Why, no,—candidly,—they do *not* very much, now. The women are so sickly, from overwork and scant feeding and clothing, that the child is worth little for the vague chance of living. But when cotton was fifteen cents a pound, and it was cheaper to take away the child than to take up the mother's time in attending to it, they used to send them to town, of a Sunday, in big hamper baskets, for sale, by the dozen. The boy I have got in my office I got in that way—but he is the survivor of six, the rest dying in the process of raising. There was a great feud between the planters on this side of Sanotchie, and those on the other side, growing out of the treatment of negro children. Those who sold them off charged the other siders with inhumanity, in drowning theirs, like blind puppies, in the creek; which was resented a good deal at the time, and the accusers denounced as abolitionists. I did hear of one of them, Judge Duck Swinger, feeding his nigger dogs on the young varmints, as he called them ; but I don't believe the story, it having no better foundation than current report, public belief, and general assertion."

Miss W. (sighing).—" Oh, Mr. Hele ! are they not afraid the negroes will rise on them ? "

Sam.—" Why, y–e–s, they do occasionally, and murder a few families,—especially in the thick settlements,—but less than they did before the patrol got up a subscription among the planters to contribute a negro or two apiece, every month or so, to be publicly hung, or burned, for the sake of example. And, to illustrate the character of the population, let me just tell you how Capt. Sam Hanson did at the last hanging. Instead of throwing in one of his own negroes, as an honest ruffian would have done, he threw in yellow Tom, a free negro; another threw in an estate negro, and reported him dead in the inventory; while Squire Bill Measly painted an Indian black and threw him in, and hung him for one of his Pocahontas negroes, as he called some of his half-breed stock."

Miss W.—"Mr. Hele! what is to become of the rising generation—the poor children—I do feel so much for them —with such examples ?"

Sam.—" Madam, they are past praying for—there is one consolation. Let what will become of them, they will get less than their deserts. Why, madam, such precocious villany as theirs the world has never seen before : they make their own fathers ashamed of even *their* attainments and proficiency in mendacity; they had good teaching, though. Why, Miss Woodey, a father here never thinks well of a child until the boy cheats him at cards : then he pats him on the head, and says, ' Well done, Tommy, here's a V. ; go, buck it off on a horse-race next Sunday, and we'll go snooks— and, come, settle fair, and no cheating around the board.' The children here at twelve years have progressed in villany beyond the point at which men get, in other countries, after a life of industrious rascality. They spent their rainy Sundays, last fall, in making a catechism of oaths and profanity for the Indians, whose dialect was wanting in those accomplishments of Anglo-Saxon literature. There is not a scoundrel among them that is not ripe for the gallows at fourteen. At five years of age, they follow their fathers around to the dram-shops, and get drunk on the heel-taps."

Miss W.—" The persons about here don't look as if they were drunk."

Sam.—" Why, madam, it is refreshing to hear you talk in that way. No, they are *not* drunk. I wish they were. It would be an astonishing improvement, if dissipation would only recede to that point at which men get drunk. But they have passed that point, long ago. I should as soon expect to see a demijohn stagger as one of them. Besides, the liquor is all watered, and it would require more than a man could hold to make him drunk: but the grocery keeper defends himself on the ground, that it is only two parts water, and he never gets paid for more than a third he sells. But I never speak of these small things; for, in such a godless generation, venial crimes stand in the light of flaming virtues. Indeed, we always feel relieved when we see one of them dead drunk, for then we feel assured he is not stealing."

Miss W.—" But, Mr. Hele, is there personal danger to be apprehended—by a woman?—now—for instance—expressing herself freely ? "

Sam.—" No, madam, not if she carries her pistols, as they generally do *now*, when they go out. They are usually insulted, and sometimes mobbed. They mobbed a Yankee school-mistress here, some time ago, for saying something against slavery; but I believe they only tarred and feathered her, and rode her on a rail for a few squares. Indeed, I heard some of the boys at the grocery, the other night, talk of trying the same experiment on another; but *who* it was, I did not hear them say."

Here Sam made his bow and departed, and, over a plate of oysters and a glass of hot stuff, reported progress to the meeting whose committee he was, but declined leave to sit again.

The next morning's mail-stage contained two trunks and four bandboxes, and a Yankee school-mistress, ticketed on the Northern line; and, in the hurry of departure, a letter, addressed to Mrs. Harriet S——, was found, containing some interesting memoranda and statistics on the subject of slavery and its practical workings, which I should never thought of again had I not seen something like them in a very popular fiction, or rather book of fictions, in which the slaveholders are handled with something less than feminine delicacy and something more than masculine unfairness.

[Sam takes the credit of sending Miss Charity off, but Dr. B., the principal, negatives this: he says he had to give her three hundred dollars and pay her expenses back to get rid of her; and that she received it, saying she intended to return home and live at ease, the balance of her life, on the interest of the money.]

JOHN STOUT ESQ., AND MARK SULLIVAN.

MARK SULLIVAN was imprisoned in the Sumter county jail, having changed the venue and place of residence from Washington county, where he had committed a murder. John Stout was an old acquaintance of Mark's, and being of a susceptible nature when there was any likelihood of a fee, was not a man to stand on ceremony or the etiquette of the profession. He did not wait to be sent for, but usually hurried post-haste to comfort his friends, when in the disconsolate circumstances of the unfortunate Mark. John had a great love for the profession, and a remarkable perseverance under discouraging circumstances, having clung to the bar after being at least twice stricken from the roll, for some practices indicating a much greater zeal for his clients than for truth, justice, or fair dealing : but he had managed to get reinstated on promises of amendment, which were, we fear, much more profuse than sincere. John's standard of morality was not exalted, nor were his attainments in the profession great; having confined himself mostly to a class

of cases and of clients better suited to give notoriety than
enviable reputation to the practitioner. He seemed to have
a separate instinct, like a carrion crow's, for the filthy; and
he snuffed up a tainted atmosphere, as Swedenborg says
certain spirits do, with a rare relish. But with all John's
industry and enterprise, John never throve, but at fifty years
of age, he was as seedy and threadbare in clothes as in
character. He had no settled abode, but was a sort of Calmuc Tartar of the Law, and roamed over the country generally, stirring up contention and breeding dirty lawsuits,
fishing up fraudulent papers, and hunting up complaisant
witnesses to very apocryphal facts.

Well, on one bright May morning, Squire Stout presented
himself at the door of the jail in Livingston, and asked ad-
mittance, professing a desire to see Mr. Mark Sullivan, an
old friend. Harvey Thompson, the then sheriff, admitted
him to the door within, and which stood between Mark and
the passage. John desired to be led into the room in which
Mark was, wishing, he said, to hold a private interview
with Mark as one of Mark's counsel; but Harvey pe-
remptorily refused—telling him, however, that he might talk
with the prisoner in his presence. The door being thrown
back, left nothing but the iron lattice-work between the
friends, and Mark, dragging his chain along, came to the
door. At first, he did not seem to recognize John; but
John, running his hand through the interstices, grasped
Mark's with fervor, asking him, at the same time, if it were
possible that he had forgotten his old friend, John Stout.

Mark, as most men in durance, was not slow to recognize any friendship, real or imaginary, that might be made to turn out to advantage, and, of course, allowed the claim, and expressed the pleasure it gave him to see John.   John soon got his *hydraulics* in readiness,—for sympathy and pathetic eloquence are wonderfully cheap accessories to rascality,— and begun applying his handkerchief to his eyes with great energy.   " Mark, my old friend, you and I have been friends many a long year, old fellow; we have played many a game of seven up together, Mark, and shot at many a shooting match, Mark, and drunk many a gallon of ' red-eye ' together ;—and to think, Mark, my old friend and companion, that I loved and trusted like a brother, Mark, should be in this dreadful fix,—far from wife, children, and friends, Mark,—it makes a child of me, and I can't— control—my feelings."   (Here John wept with considerable vivacity, and doubled up an old bandanna handkerchief and mopped his eyes mightily.)   Mark was not one of the crying sort.   He was a Roman-nosed, eagle-eyed ruffian of a fellow, some six feet two inches high, and with a look and step that the McGregor himself might feel entitled him to be respected on the heather.

So Mark responded to this lachrymal ebullition of Stout's a little impatiently : " Hoot, man, what are you making all that *how-de-do* for ?   It aint so bad as you let on.   To be sure, it aint as pleasant as sitting on a log by a camp fire, with a tickler of the reverend stuff, a pack of the documents and two or three good fellows, and a good piece of fat deer meat roast-

ing at the end of a ramrod; but, for all that, it aint so bad
as might be: they can't do nothing with me: it was done
fair,—it was an old quarrel.   We settled it in the old way:
I had my rifle, and I plugged him fust—he might a knowed
I would.   It was devil take the hindmost.   It wasn't my
fault he didn't draw trigger fust—they can't hurt me for it.
But I hate to be stayin' here so long, and the fishin' time
comin' on, too—it's mighty hard, but it can't be holped, I
suppose."   (And here Mark heaved a slight sigh.)

"Ah, Mark," said John, "I aint so certain about that;
that is, unless you are particular well defended.   You see,
Mark, it aint now like it used to be in the good old times.
They are getting new notions now-a-days.   Since the penitentiary has been built, they are got quare ways of doing
things,—they are sending gentlemen there reg'lar as pig-
tracks.   I believe they do it just because they've got an idea
it helps to pay taxes.   When it used to be neck or nothin',
why, one of the young hands could clear a man; but now it
takes the best sort of testimony, and the smartest sort of
lawyers in the market, to get a friend clear.   The way things
are goin' on now, murdering a man will be no better than
stealin' a nigger, after a while."

"Yes," said Mark., "things is going downwards,—there
aint no denyin' of that.   I know'd the time in old Washington, when people let gentle*men* settle these here little matters their own way, and nobody interfered, but minded their
own business.   And now you can't put an inch or two of
knife in a fellow, or lam him over the head a few times with

a light-wood knot, but every little lackey must poke his nose
into it, and *Law, law, law*, is the word,—the cowardly, nasty
slinks; and then them lawyers must have their jaw in it,
and bow, bow wow, it goes; and the ju*ror*, they must have
their say so in it; and the sher*rer*, he must do something,
too; and the old cuss that grinds out the law to 'em in the
box, he must have his *how-de-do* about it; and then the witnesses, they must swear to ther packs of lies—and the lawyers git to bawlin' and bellerin', like Methodist preachers at
a camp meetin'—allers quarrellin' and no fightin'—jawin'
and jawin' back, and sich eternal lyin'—I tell you, Stout, I
won't stay in no such country. When I get out of here, I
mean to go to Texas, whar a man can see some peace, and
not be interfered with in his private consarns. All this
come about consekens so many new settlers comin' in the
settle*ment*, bringin' their new-fool ways with 'em. The fust
of it was two preachers comin' along. I told 'em 'twould
never do—and if my advice had been tuk, the thing could
a been stopped in time; but the boys said they wanted to
hear the news them fellers fotch'd about the Gospel and
sich—and there was old Ramsouser's mill-pond so handy,
too!—but it's too late now. And then the doggery-keepers
got to sellin' licker by the drink, instead of the half-pint,
and a dime a drink at that; and then the Devil was to pay,
and NO *mi*stake. But they cant hurt me, John. They'll
have to let me out: and ef it wasn't so cussed mean, I'd
take the law on 'em, and sue 'em for damages; but then it
would be throw'd up to my children, that Mark Sullivan tuk

the law on a man; and, besides, Stout, I've got another way of settlin' the thing up,—in the old way,—ef my life is spared, and Providence favors me. But that aint nothin' to the present purpose. John, where do you live now?"

John.—" I'm living in Jackson, Mississippi, now, Mark; and hearing you were in distress, I let go all holds, and came to see you. Says I, my old friend Mark Sullivan is in trouble, and I must go and see him out; and says my wife: ' John Stout, you pretend you never deserted a friend, and here you are, and your old friend Mark Sullivan, that you thought so much of, laying in jail, when you, if any man could, can get him clear.' Now, Mark, I couldn't stand that. When my wife throw'd that up to me, I jist had my horse got out, and travelled on, hardly stopping day or night, till I got here. And the U. S. Court was in session, too, and a big lawsuit was coming on for a million of dollars. I and Prentiss and George Yerger was for the plaintiff, and we were to get five thousand dollars, certain, and a hundred thousand dollars if we gained it. I went to see George, before I left, and George said I must stay—it would never do. Says he, ' John,'—he used always to call me John,—' you know,'—which I did, Mark,—that our client relies *on you*, and you must be here at the trial. *I* can fix up the papers, and Prent. can do the fancy work to the jury; but when it comes to the heavy licks of the law, John, you are the man, and *no mistake.*' And just then Prentiss come in, and, after putting his arm and sorter hugging me to him,—which was Prent.'s way with his intimate friends,—says, ' John, my old friend, you have to follow on our side, and you must mash Sam Boyd and Jo Holt into Scotch snuff; and you'll do it, too, John: and after gaining the case, we'll have a frolic that will suck the sweet out of the time of day.' And then Yerger up and tells Prentiss about my going off; and Prentiss opened his eyes, and asked me if I was crazy; and I told him jist this: says I, 'Prent, you are a magnanimous man, that loves his friend, aint you?' and Prentiss said he hoped he was. And then said I, 'Prentiss, Mark Sullivan is *my* friend, and in jail, away from his wife and children, and nobody to get him out of that scrape; and may be, if I don't go and defend him—there is no knowing what may come of it; and how could I ever survive to think a friend of mine had come to harm for want of my going to him in the dark, dismal time of his distress.' (Here John took out the handkerchief again, and began weeping, after a fashion Mr. Alfred Jingle might have envied, even when performing for the benefit of Mr. Samuel Weller.) 'No,' said I, 'Sergeant Prentiss, let the case go to h—l, for me;—John Stout and Andrew Jackson never deserted a friend, and never will.' Said Prentiss, 'John, I admire your principles; give us your hand, old fellow; and come, let us take a drink;'—for Prent. was always in the habit of treating his noble sentiments—George wasn't. Well, Mark, you see I came, and am at your service through thick and thin."

"Yes," said Mark, "I'm much obleeged to you, John, but I'm afeered I can't afford to have you,—you're too dear an article for my pocket; besides, I've got old John Gayle, and I reckon he'll do."

"Why," said John, "I don't dispute, Mark, but that the old Governor *is* some punkins,—you might have done worse. I'll not disparage any of my brethren. I'll say to his back what I've said to his face. You might do worse than get old John—but, Mark, two heads are better than one; and though I may say it, when it comes to the genius licks of the law in these big cases, it aint every man in your fix can get such counsel. Now, Mark, money is money, and feelins is feelins; and I don't care if I do lose the case at Jackson. If you will only secure two hundred dollars to pay expenses, I am your man, and you're as good as cleared already."

But Mark couldn't or wouldn't come into these reasonable terms, and his friend Stout left him in no very amiable mood,—having quite recovered from the fit of hysterics into which he had fallen,—and Mark turned to Thompson, and making sundry gyrations with his fingers upon a base formed by his nose, his right thumb resting thereon, seemed to intimate that John Stout's proposition and himself were little short of a humbug, which couldn't win.

Mark, though ably and eloquently defended, was convicted at the next court, and was sentenced to the penitentiary for life. And Stout, speaking of the result afterwards, said he did not wonder at it, for the old rascal, after having sent for him all the way from Jackson, higgled with him on a fee of one thousand dollars, when he, in indignant disgust at his meanness, left him to his fate.

MR. ONSLOW.

IT is amusing to witness the excitement of the lawyers concerned in the trial of a long and severely-contested case, after the argument is concluded, and the judge is giving the jury charges as to the law. In Mississippi, the practice is for the counsel to prepare written charges after the case is argued, to be offered when the jury are about retiring from the box; and the Court gives or refuses them as it approves or disapproves of them,—sometimes altering them to suit its own views of the law.

On one occasion, a case was tried of some difficulty and complexity, involving the title to a negro, which had been run off from a distant part of the State, and sold in Noxubee county by a man, who had, previously to running him, mortgaged him to the plaintiff. The negro had been in the county for a good while before he was discovered; and the present holder had been sued—Mr. Onslow being the attorney for the mortgagee, and indeed it was understood, having some other rights in the litigation than those of counsel. The defendant had retained Henry G———y and James T.

H———, Esqrs., ingenious youth, who were duly and fully prepared, and especially willing, to exhaust all the law there was, and a good deal there wasn't, to defeat the plaintiff's recovery in the premises.

Mr. Onslow appeared alone. Indeed, he would have scorned assistance in such a proceeding. He had come on horseback from the Mississippi Swamp, on no other business than to attend to this case. His preparation was arduous and thorough—his zeal apostolic. No doubt he had made the pine-trees sweat rezinous tears, "voiding their rheum," and had made the very stumps ache, and the leaves quiver, as he journeyed on, rehearsing the great speech he intended to make in the to-be celebrated case of Hugginson *vs.* McLeod. He was a peculiar-looking man, was Mr. Onslow. Rising six feet in his stockings, large-boned, angular, muscular, without an ounce of surplus flesh, he was as active and as full of energy as a panther. His head was long and large, the features irregular and strongly-marked, face florid, eyes black, restless and glaring, mouth like a wolf-trap, and muscles twitching and shaking like a bowl of jelly, and hair a reddish-brown—about as much of it as Absalom carried, but of such independence of carriage that it stuck up all around, "like quills upon the fretful porcupine." He was a sort of walking galvanic battery ; charged full in every fibre with the electric current. If a man had run his hand over his hair in a dark room across the grain, the sparks would have risen as from the back of a black cat. We have not heard from him since the spiritual rappings, table tip·

14

pings, and movings were the vogue,—but we will go our old
hat against a julep, that if the spirits would not come at his
bidding, they have quit coming from the vasty deep, or closed
business, Mr. N. P. Tallmadge, or any other medium to the
contrary notwithstanding: and if he couldn't set a table
going by the odic force, the whole thing is a proved humbug.   He was a speaker of decided power,—indeed of tre-
mendous power.   When he spoke, he spoke in earnest.   He
went it with a most vigorous *vim*.   He had taken a cataract
and hurricane for his model.   Such a bellowing,—such a fiery
fury, of fuss and noise, would sink into a modest silence a
whole caravan of howling dervishes.   Jemmy T. thought he
could be heard when he let himself out two miles : I think
this extravagant,—I should think not more than a mile and
a half.   When he drew in a long breath, and bore his weight
on his voice, the very rafters seemed to move : but his voice
was not all.   He grew as rampant as a wolf in high oats,
—jumping up, rearing around, and squatting low, and sid-
ling about—forwards, backwards—beating benches—knocking the entrails out of law-books—running over chairs, and
clearing out the area for ten feet around him, whirling about
like a horse with the blind staggers ; while he quivered all over
like a galvanized frog.   He usually let off as much caloric
as would have fed the lungs of the Ericsson.

Innumerable were the points and half-points made during
the progress of the case, and Onslow was fortunate enough
to win on most of these.   At every ruling that was made
in his favor, he would suck in his breath with a long inspira-

tion, smile a spasmodic smile of grisly satisfaction, and smack his lips. He was in high feather, and on excellent terms with the judge, whose rulings he would indorse with marked *empressement*.

After he had bellowed his last, he took his seat; and the judge asked the counsel if they desired any charges.

Onslow rose, and told the Court he had a few. He drew out of his hat about six pages of foolscap, on which was written twenty-two charges, elaborately drawn out,— some of them long enough to have been divided into chapters,—and the whole might have been modified and indexed to advantage. The defendant's counsel, while Onslow was reading his charges, sent up to the bench a single instruction couched in a few words.

Onslow read his charge 1. in a loud and argumentative voice—the Court gave it: " Exactly, your honor," observed O., and so on to the 22d, which was also given, Onslow bowing and smiling, and his face glowing out, from anxiety to assurance, as the charge was read and given, like a lightning-bug's tail, giving light out of darkness.

After he got through reading the charges, he handed them to the judge. Hon. H. S. B. was on the bench—one of the best judges in the State. He turned to the jury: " Gentlemen," said he, " listen to the instructions the Court gives you in this case."

He then read the first instruction of Onslow, in a clear, decided tone; at the conclusion of it O. sighed heavily,— so with the next, and so on; Onslow all this time gazing

with rapt attention upon the judge, and his mouth motion-
ing with the judge's—like a school-boy writing O's in his
first copy—and at the end of every charge ejaculating,
" Exactly, your honor ! "

   After getting through these charges, the judge remarked :
" And now, gentlemen, I give you this charge for the defendant."   Onslow stopped breathing, as the judge slowly sylla-
bled out, " But notwithstanding—all—this—it being—an
admitted—fact—that—the mortgage—was—not—recorded
—in—Noxu—bee—county—you—must—fi—n—d for the
d—e—fen—dant."   As this was going on, Onslow was completely psychologized : he stared until his eyes looked as if
they would pop out—his lower jaw dropped—and putting
his hand to his head, involuntarily exclaimed—" Oh, hell !
your honor ! "

   He left in the course of ten minutes, to start on a return
journey of three hundred miles, in mid-winter, and *such*
roads—through the woods to the Mississippi Swamp.—
" *Phansy* his *phelinks.*"

JO. HEYFRON.

Judge Starling, of Mississippi, had become very sensitive because the lawyers insisted on arguing points after he
had decided them.   So he determined to put a stop to it.   But
Jo. Heyfron, an excellent lawyer, who had every thing of

the Emerald Isle about him, but its greenness,—was the wrong one for the decisive judicial experiment to be commenced on. Jo. knew too much law, and the judge too little, for an equality of advantages. On the occasion referred to, just as the judge had pronounced a very peremptory and a very ridiculous decision, Jo. got up in his deprecating way, with a book in his hand, and was about to speak, when the Judge thundered out, " Mr. Heyfron ! you have been practising, sir, before *this* Court long enough to know that when *this* Court has once decided a question, the propriety of its decision can only be reviewed in the High Court of Errors & Appeals ! Take your seat, sir ! "

" If your honor plase ! " broke out Jo., in a manner that would have passed for the most beseeching, if a sly twinkle in the off corner of his eye had not betokened the contrary,—" If your honor plase ! far be it from *me* to impugn in the slightest degray, the wusdom and prorietay of your honor's decision ! I marely designed to rade a few lines from the volume I hold in my hand, that your honor might persave how profoundly aignorant Sir Wulliam Blockstone was upon this subject."

The judge looked daggers, but spoke none ; and Heyfron sat down, immortal. His body is dead, but he still lives, for his brilliant retort, in the anecdotal reminiscences of the South-Western bar. The anecdote has already (in a different, but incorrect form) had the run of the newspapers.

OLD UNCLE JOHN OLIVE.

ATTENDING the Kemper Court one day, and engaged in a cause then going on, and which the adverse counsel was arguing to the jury (something in the nature of a suit for trespass for suing out execution and levying it on some corn reserved under the poor debtor's law), I saw this venerable old father in Israel playing bo-peep over the railing behind the bar, and giving me sundry winks and beckonings to come to him.

Uncle John was a gentleman of the old school, if, indeed, he was not before there was any school. He was some seventy or seventy-five years old, perhaps a little older. His physique was remarkable. He looked more like an antediluvian boy than a man. He was some four feet and a half or five feet high, rather large for that height, and tapering off with a pair of legs marking Hogarth's line of beauty, —an elegant curve, something on the style of a pair of pothooks. His beard and hair were grizzly gray, and the face oval, with a high front in the region of benevolence; but which, I believe, no one ever knew the sense of being placed there:

for all of Uncle John's benefactions together, would not have amounted to a supper of bones for a hungry dog. Uncle John's eyes were black or black-ish, with sanguine trimmings, as if lined by red fereting. He had a voice with a double wabble—and, especially when he tried it on the vowels, he ran up some curious notes on the gamut, and eked out the sound with a very useless expenditure of accent. Uncle John Olive belonged to the Baptist Church,—hard-shell division, but took it with the privilege: he had a thirst like the prairies in the dog-days, and it took nearly as much of the liquid to refresh it. But much as Uncle John loved the ardent restoratives, he loved money quite as well; and there was a continual warfare going on in Uncle John's breast between these aspiring rivals: but this led to a compromise. Uncle John treated both with equal impartiality: he drank very freely, but drank very cheap liquors, making up for any lack of quality, by no economy of quantity.

Uncle John's scheme of life was simple. It was but a slight improvement on Indian modes. He lived out in the woods, in a hut which an English nobleman would have considered poor quarters for his dogs. The furniture was in keeping, and his table was in keeping with the furniture. His whole establishment would probably have brought fifteen dollars. The entire civil list of the old gentleman could not have cost seventy-five dollars to answer its demands. He had no white person in his family except himself—and about fifteen negroes, of all sorts and sizes. He worked some six or seven hands, but being of a slow turn, and very old-fogyish in his notions, he did not succeed very well with them, either in governing them or making much of a crop: about a bale to the hand was the extent to which Uncle John ever went, even in the best seasons. But as he spent nothing except for some articles of the last necessity, he managed to lay up every year some few dollars, which he kept in specie, hid in a hole under a plank of the floor, in an old chest. This close economy and saving way of life, kept up for about fifty-five years, had at length made old Uncle John Olive worth some ten thousand dollars. He had made it wholly by parsimony. He was habitually and without exception the closest man I ever saw,—as close as the bark is to a tree, or as green is to a leaf.

He was dressed in home-made linsey, and as he went gandering it along, you would take him for the survivor of those Dutchmen whom Irving tells of, rolling the ninepins down the cave in the Kaatskill Mountains, when Rip Van Winkle went to see them; except that Uncle John did not carry the keg of spirits on his shoulder,—but generally in his belly.

A circle of a mile drawn around Uncle John would have embraced all he knew and more than he knew of this breathing world, its ways and works, and plan and order; except what he got item of at the market-town or at the court-house. All beyond that circle was mystery. Uncle John was a silent man,—he used his tongue for little except to taste his liquor,—and his eyes and ears were open always, though I suspect there must have been some stoppage in the way to the brain: for the more Uncle John heard and observed, the more he seemed not to know about matters seen and heard.   But a more faithful attention I never heard of. Uncle John was in the habit of attending court, and gave his special attention to the matters there carried on: the way he would listen to an argument on a demurrer or an abstract point of law, might be a lesson and example to the most patient Dutch commentator.   He would stare with a gaze of rapt attention upon the Court and Counsel, occasionally shifting one leg, and uttering a slight sigh as some one of them closed the argument; and stretching his head forward, and putting his hand behind his ear to catch the sound as the Court suggested something, though he never understood a single word of what was going on.   Towards the end of a long discussion, Uncle John would begin to flag a little, wiping the perspiration from his brow, as if the exercise of listening were very fatiguing—as, indeed, in not a few instances, it might well have been.

On the occasion referred to in the opening, Uncle John called me, and after the salutations, told me he wanted to see me right then on business of importance.   I should have said before that I had had some business of Uncle John's in hand, which I discharged entirely to his satisfaction; not charging the venerable old gentleman any thing, but getting my fee out of another person through whose agency the old man had got into the difficulty.   This being Uncle John's first and only lawsuit, though the matter was very simple, gave him a high opinion of my professional abilities.

14*

Indeed, next to his man Remus Simpson, the "foreman of the crap," whom he was in the habit of consulting on "difficult pints," I stood higher with Uncle John than any one else as "a raal judgmatical man." I hope I state the fact with a feeling of becoming modesty. In the way of law, Uncle John evidently thought the law would be behaving itself very badly, if it did not go the way I wished it; and looked to my opinion not so much as to what the law was, as what it was to be after I spoke the word.

I told Uncle John Olive that I was a good deal pressed for time just at that moment, as a case was going on in which I was concerned; but as it was he, Uncle John, I would spare him a few moments. And so I left Duncan to harangue the jury until I could confer with the old man, and took him into the vacant jury-room on the same floor, and shut the door. "Well," said I, "Uncle John, I hope nothing serious has happened—[which was a lie, for I was, in the then (and I might lay the fact with a *continuando*) depressed state of my fiscality,—I confess I was a little anxious for something to happen in order to relieve the same, and was just doing a little mental arithmetic; figuring up what I should charge the old man, whether a fifty or a hundred; but concluding to take the fifty, rather than hazard the chance of bluffing the old man off.]

"But," said the old man, "they is, *I* tell you. *B-a-a*-A-w-ling—Bawling, Virgil *C-a*-A-A-n-non won't do to tie to no way you can fix it—Bawling."

"Why," said I, "Uncle John, I must confess the conduct of that young man has not altogether—(here the sheriff called me at the door) but Uncle John, quick I'm called—"

" Well, Bawling, I reckon it don't make much odds about your going back—you've told that *juror* what they must do wonce, and I reckon they wont ha' a furgot it by this time, Bawling."

" Yes,—but they are obstinate *sometimes*, Uncle John, and I must go—quick now—Uncle John—You say Cannon did—what to you."

" Why, Bawling—Virgil Cannon—he had been a whippin' my nigger, Remus—Remus told me so hisself, and I kin prove it by Remus and sore-legged Jim—jest 'cause Remus sassed him—when he sassed Remus fust—when he, Virgil Cannon, should have said, as Remus heerd, that Virgil Cannon should ov said Remus stole his corn—I went to see Virgil Cannon, and ' Virgil Cannon,' says I,—jest in them words I said it, Bawling ; ' you nasty, stinking villain, what did you whip my nigger, Remus, fur ? ' And what you think Bawling, Virgil Cannon should have said ? " (here was a long emphatic stony stare.) " Why I don't know, Uncle John," replied I. " Why, Bawling, Virgil Cannon should ov said to me, says he, ' Go to h—ll, you d—d old bow-legged puppy, and kiss my foot '—Now, Bawling, what would you advise me to do, Bawling ? "

" Well," said I, " old man, *I* would advise you *not* to do it. Good-bye, I must go." And I left the old fellow stiff as a pillar staring at the place which I left.

I don't know how long he remained there—for I pitched into the case, and the way I made the fire fly from parties, witnesses and counsel, in the corn case, was curious.

EXAMINING A CANDIDATE FOR LICENSE.

SOME time in the year of Grace, 1837 or 8, during the session of the Circuit Court of N * * * * * * Mississippi, Mr. Thomas Jefferson Knowly made known to his honor, his (K.'s) respectful desire to be turned into a lawyer. Such requests, at that time, were granted pretty much as a matter of course. Practising law, like shinplaster banking or a fight, was pretty much a free thing; but the statute required a certain formula to be gone through, which was an examination of the candidate by the Court, or under its direction. The Judge appointed Henry G * * * and myself to put him through, a task we undertook with much pleasure. Jefferson, or Jeff, as he was called for short, had been lounging about the court-house for some time, refreshing his mind with such information as he could thus pick up on the trial of cases, and from the discussions of the bar in reference to the laws of his country. Having failed in the drygoods line at the cross-roads, he was left at leisure to pursue some other calling without being disturbed by any attention to his bill-book. He had taken up a favorable opinion of the law from the glimpses he had got of its physiognomy ; and, having borrow- ed an old copy of Blackstone, went to work to master its contents as well as he could. He had reached about thirty- five years when this hallucination struck him. He was a stout, heavy fellow—with a head that Spurzheim might have envied : though the contents thereof did not give any new proof of Spurzheim's theory. He was not encumbered with any learning. He had all the apartments of his memory un- filled and waiting to be stored with law. An owl-like grav- ity sat on him with a solemnity like the picture of sorrowing affection on a tombstone. He was just such a man as passes for a wonderful judge of law among the rustics—who usually mistake the silent blank of stupidity for the gravity of wis- dom.

We took Jefferson with us, in the recess of court, over to a place of departed spirits,—don't start, reader ! we mean, an evacuated doggery, grocery or juicery, as, in the elegant nomenclature of the natives, it was variously called ; the for- mer occupant having suddenly decamped just before court, by reason of some apprehensions of being held responsible for practising *his* profession without license.

Having taken our seats, the examiners on the counter, and the examinee on an empty whiskey barrel, the examina- tion began. My learned associate having been better grounded in the elemental learning of the books, into which his research was, as old H. used to say, " specially sarching,"

and being, besides, the State's attorney, was entitled to precedence in the examination; a claim I was very willing to
allow.   After some general questions, G. asked:

"Mr. Knowly, what is a *chose in action?*"

Knowly.—A chosen action? eh?—yes—exactly—just so
—a chosen action?   Why, a chosen action is—whare a man's
got a right to fetch two or three actions, and he chuses one
of 'em which he will fetch—the one that's chuse is the—chosen
action : that's easy, squire.

G.—Well, what is *a chose in possession?*

K.—A chosen possession?   A chosen possession—(*G.*—
Don't repeat the question—answer it, if you please.   *K.*—
Well—I won't—)

K.—A chosen possession?—Yes—exactly—jess so—
ahem—(here K. looked about for a stick, picked one up and
began whittling with a knife—then muttering absently)—" A
chosen possession?   Why, squire, if a man has two possessions to be chose, which he is to chuse as a guard*een* which
the estate have not been divided, and they come to a divide
of it in lots which the commissioners has set aside and prized,
and he chooses one of them possessions, *which* one he chooses,
that is the chosen possession.   That aint hard nuther.

G.—Mr. K. how many fees are there?

K.—How many fees?—why squire, several : doctor's fees,
lawyer's fees, sheriff's fees, jailer's fees, clerk's fees, both
courts, and most every body else's.

G.—What is the difference between a fee simple and a
contingent fee?

K.—The difference between a fee—(here G. told him not to repeat the question, K. promised he wouldn't, and resumed).

The difference between—yes—exactly—jess so. Why, squire—a simple fee is where a client gives his lawyer so much any how, let it go how it will; and a contingent fee is where he takes it on the sheeres, and no cure no pay.

G.—What are the marital rights of a husband at common law ?

K.— The martal rites ?—(smiling)—concerning of what, squire ?

G.—Her property ?

K.—Oh—*that*—why—yes—jess so—why, squire, he gets her track,—i. e., if he can without committing a tres*pass*—what's hers is his, and what's his is his own. Squire, I know'd that before ever I opened a law-book.

G.—Is the wife entitled to dower in the husband's lands if she survives him ?

K.—O—yes, squire—in course—I've seen that tried in Alabama; that is, squire, you understand if the estate is solvent to pay the debts.

G.— Suppose the husband's estate is insolvent—what then ?

K.—Why, then, in course not.

G.—Why not ?

K.—Why not ?—why, squire, it stands to reason : for then, you see, the husband might gather a whole heap of land, and then jest fraudently die to give his wife dower rights to his land.   I jest know plenty of men about here mean enough to do it, and jump at the chance.

G.—Has a man a *natural* right to dispose of his property by will ?

K.—Why, now, squire, concerning of that—my mind aint so clare as on tother pints—it strikes me sort a vague— something about a cow laying or that should have laid down in a place which she had a right, and another cow-beast, nor airy another havin' no rights to disturb her :—aint that *it*, squire ?

G.—Suppose, Mr. K., a tenant for life, should hold over after the termination of his estate, what kind of action would you bring against him ?

K.—Tenant for life—hold—termination of the state ?— ugh—um—jess so—Squire, aint that mortmain—the statue of mortmain—in Richard the 8th's time ?—Blackstone says something about *that*.

G.—Mr. K., if a man wants to keep his property in his family, how far can he make it descend to his children and grand-children, &c.

K.—Why as to that—something, squire, about all the candles burning—but, squire, I never could understand what burning candles had to do with it.

G.—What is an estate tail female, contingent on the happening of a past event, limited by contingent devise to the children of grantees after possibility of issue extinct, considered with reference to the statute *De Donis ?*

K.—Squire, the Devil himself couldn't answer that, and

I guess he's as smart as airy other lawyer—but I reckon it is—

G.—Well, Mr. K., what is the distinction between *Law* and *Equity?*

K.—Why, squire, Law is as it happens—'cordin' to proof and the way the juror goes; Eekity is jestis—and a man may git a devilish sight of law, and git devilish little jestis.

G.—Does Equity ever interfere with Law?

K.—Not that ever *I* seed, squire.

G.—Whose son is a bastard considered in law?

K.—Why, squire, that's further than I've got—*I've* ginerally seed that it was laid to the young man in the settle*ment* best able to pay over its main*tain*ance; and, I suppose, it would be *his son-in-law.*

G.—What is a libel?

K.—Why, squire, if a man gits another in a room, and locks the door on him, and makes him sign a paper certifying he's told a lie on him, the paper is *a lie-bill.*

G.—What is the difference between *Trespass* and *Case?*

K.—Why, squire, Tres*pass* ar when a man tres*pass*es on another.   Now, squire, your putting so many hard questions to *me*, that is a tres*pass.*

G.—Yes; and if the fellow can't answer a single one, *I* should say *he* was a Case.

Here the examination closed.   Jefferson walked slowly out of the grocery, and, after getting about thirty yards off on the green, beckoned me to him.

As I came towards him, he drew himself up with some dignity, took aim at a chip, about fifteen feet off, and squirted a stream of tobacco juice at it with remarkable precision. Said he, slowly and with marked gravity, " B——, you needn't make any report of this thing to the Judge. I believe I won't go in. I don't know as it's any harder than I took it at the fust—but, then, B——, ther's, so, d—d, much, more, of, it."

NOTES

In these informational notes, numbers refer to page and line of this volume.

1.9 *casus omissus*] Case of omission

4.7–8 *nati consumere fruges*] "Born to enjoy the fruits of the earth"; adapted from Horace, Epistle I, 2

6.28–7.2 Bolingbroke . . . Backwoods] In *Richard II*, Shakespeare characterizes Bolingbroke, the future Henry IV, as bluff, direct, and winning—a favorite of the common people. Hoosiers, inhabitants of Indiana, were often considered crude and unsophisticated.

7.12 "boys"] Common term for the fast set of sportsmen and gamblers

7.28 groceries] Backwoods euphemism for saloon; also referred to as *doggeries*

8.1–3 Adams' . . . memorial] In the 1830s in the House of Representatives, John Quincy Adams began introducing bundles of antislavery petitions, which southerners succeeded in tabling until 1844, when the gag rule was defeated. The Chartist memorial was a lengthy document presented to Parliament in 1838 by English radicals demanding democratic reforms.

8.20 Grymes . . . Mazereau] As a Whig, Etienne Mazureau, a Creole lawyer, orator, and state attorney general, was frequently opposed to Democrat John R. Grymes, onetime district attorney and aide to General Andrew Jackson in New Orleans.

9.4 Rapides . . . Coast] Rapides, a parish in central Louisiana, and the German Coast, an area within St. Charles and St. John the Baptist parishes thirty miles from New Orleans, were known for their valuable real estate.

9.6–7 Jack Hays] John Coffee Hays (1817–1883), who achieved a legendary reputation for bravery as a colorful colonel of the Texas Rangers, commanded a group under Zachary Taylor during the Mexican War (1846–1848).

9.17 Bowie's] James Bowie (1796–1836) was a Louisiana entrepreneur who moved to Texas around 1828, where he helped to organize the Republic of Texas; he died at the Alamo. The special heavy-bladed knife named for him was designed by his brother.

10.2 "perception and pernancy"] Legal term for the act of taking possession of anything; receipts, as rents or profits

10.21 Tammany] A political and patriotic society in New York City that by 1850 was identified with the Democratic party

11.13 V's and X's] Terms for five- and ten-dollar bills

11.23 "rosy" . . . "reaming suats"] The first is a corruption of *rosa solis* ("rose of the sun"), a liquor flavored with rosemary; "reaming swats" is Scottish for a foaming new ale.

11.28–12.1 Van Buren . . . Jackson] Andrew Jackson (1767–1845), seventh president of the U.S., and his successor, Martin Van Buren (1782–1862), are further examples of Bolus' name-dropping.

14.12 pressing invitations] Challenges to duel

15.3 Burke] Edmund Burke (1729–1797), the great Whig statesman who urged conciliation in England's difficulties with the American colonies, was known for his forensic skills.

15.24–25 D'Orsay . . . Murat] Alfred Guillaume, Count D'Orsay (1801–1852), handsome dandy known for his social elegance, was a lover of Lady Blessington at Gore House (see note to 16.14); Achille Murat (1801–1847), crown prince of Naples at the fall of the French Empire, fled with his entourage in 1823 to the U.S., where he became a popular author and celebrity.

16.5 White Sulphur or Saratoga] White Sulphur Springs in Virginia and Saratoga in New York were sites of fashionable spas.

16.13–14 Almack's . . . Gore House] Almack's was a fashionable London gambling club popular from about 1763 to 1840; Gore

House, the elegant London residence of Marguerite, Countess of Blessington (1789–1849), became a favorite gathering place for fashionable artists in the early nineteenth century.

16.23–24 Morgan] The *Illustrations of Masonry* was an exposé of the secrets of Freemasonry by William Morgan (1774–1826?), a central figure in anti-Masonic agitation in American politics of the late 1820s.

18.26 Tomlinson . . . Richard] The disillusioned and elegant highwayman in Bulwer-Lytton's *Paul Clifford* (1830), Augustus Tomlinson gives an apostrophe to London before he leaves England for greener pastures. The central figure in *Poor Richard's Almanack* (1733–1758) by Benjamin Franklin dispenses homey wisdom that links moral virtue and material success.

19.18 Ignatius] St. Ignatius of Loyola (1491–1556) was a Spanish military officer who enjoyed the world's luxuries before becoming a monk and founding the Society of Jesus.

19.22 Themistocles] This fifth-century B.C. Athenian military leader, when accused of embezzlement, fled into exile to escape apprehension.

23.9 Chesterfield and Beau Brummel] Both Philip Stanhope (1694–1773), Earl of Chesterfield, and George Bryan (Beau) Brummel (1778–1840) were known for their social graces and sartorial taste.

23.19 Warwicks] Richard Neville, Earl of Warwick (1428–1471), was known as the Kingmaker because of his role in deposing King Henry VI of England and enthroning Edward IV, against whom Warwick later turned and temporarily restored Henry VI.

23.28 Pocahontases] Some of the first families of Virginia proudly traced their descent from the marriage of Pocahontas, Chief Powhatan's daughter, and an English colonist, John Rolfe (1585–1622).

24.7 Henry, &c.] Old Kasm, that is, is a supporter of the Anti-Federalists, the conservative faction in Virginia politics.

39.21 Grotius] *De jure belli et pacis* by Hugo Grotius (1583–1645), Dutch jurist and author, is considered to be the foundation of modern international law.

43.8—9   Henry] The revolutionary statesman and orator, Patrick Henry (1736—1799), became a successful lawyer after failing as a merchant and farmer (see also note to 115.13).

43.28   Swain's Patent Vermifuge] A popular patent medicine for killing intestinal worms

44.7—8   *Abii, erupi, evasi*] Comic paraphrase of Cicero, *In Catilinam*, no. ii, sec. 1: "I fled, I broke out, I escaped"

45.4   *crim. con.*] Abbreviation for *criminal conversation*, the adulterous intercourse of a married woman, the grounds for a husband's lawsuit against his wife's sexual partner

47.4   Blackstone] Knowledge of the most comprehensive treatise on English law, the *Commentaries* of Sir William Blackstone (1723—1780), was one of the basic requirements for American lawyers.

47.17   *crimen falsi*] Forgery

48.11   *remotissima potentia*] "Remote source of power"

49.8—9   old Regulus] Defeated and taken prisoner by the Carthaginians, Marcus Atilius Regulus, the celebrated Roman general, was sent back to Rome to seek an exchange of prisoners; though unsuccessful, he returned as he promised to his captors in Carthage, where he was executed about 250 B.C.

50.17—18   Anacreon . . . Astor] The name of Anacreon, Greek lyric poet of the fifth century B.C., became gradually associated with lovemaking and drinking; John Jacob Astor (1763—1848), fur-trading entrepreneur who at his death was the richest man in America, was seen by his contemporaries as a ruthless operator whose only passion was amassing wealth.

50.21   *locus in quo*] "The place in which"—the locality where an act is alleged to have occurred

52.3   Themis] Greek goddess of law and order

54.3—4   *terra incognita*] "Unknown territory"

54.10   Prentiss] Seargent S. Prentiss (1808—1850), Mississippi lawyer famed for his oratory (see also note to 246.19—20 as well as the chapter devoted to him)

55.10—15   *venire . . . capias*] *Venire* ("to come") is the name of a writ directing the sheriff to assemble enough qualified citizens of his county to serve as jurors; *subpoena* ("under penalty") is a writ directing a witness to appear before a court to testify; *capias* ("that you take") is a basic writ directing the sheriff to take a defendant into custody.

56.23 Rousseau] Jean Jacques Rousseau (1712–1778), French philosopher and educator, argued that human nature in its primitive state is innocent and that it is gradually corrupted by society and history.

57.6 *void and voidable*] Terms indicating how applying the law is subject to circumstances: *void* refers to contracts that have no effect, such as illegal or criminal agreements; *voidable* contracts are valid and enforceable until they are disputed and set aside by a court.

57.19 *Shurkey*] During the Flush Times, William Lewis Sharkey (1797–1873), Mississippi lawyer, legislator, and senator, was chief justice of the state Court of Errors and Appeals.

60.9–10 Malgroucher . . . Ajax] In *Letters of Malachi Malagrouther* (1826), Sir Walter Scott satirized the British Parliament's efforts to prevent banks in Scotland from issuing their own currency; Mrs. Caudle, in Douglas Jerrold's *Mrs. Caudle's Curtain Lectures* (1846), is a nag who lectures her husband after they go to bed; Ajax, the Greek hero, was traditionally depicted from Sophocles to Shakespeare as obstinate, boastful, and arrogant in his self-confidence, despite his courage and great strength.

60.17–18 *non suit . . . assumpsit*] A *non suit* is a judgment given against a plaintiff when he is unable to prove his case or when he neglects to appear in court after the trial has been put at issue; *assumpsit* ("he has undertaken") is a form of action to recover damages for the nonperformance of a contract.

61.5 Vidocq] François Eugène Vidocq (1775–1857) was a famous French detective who, because he began his career as a thief, was especially adept at tracking down criminals.

61.8 Theseus] In Greek legend, Theseus, who was trapped in the labyrinth of Minos, found his way out by following a thread supplied by Ariadne.

63.27–28 *capias ad respondendum*] A writ in civil action for arrest and imprisonment of a defendant who, charged with inflicting injury, has failed to appear as directed in a process of attachment

67.23–24   cassock . . . gown] That is, Wash had exchanged the shadbelly, the distinctive coat of the preacher, for the black robes of the lawyer.

67.26   Dalgetty-like] In Sir Walter Scott's *A Legend of Montrose* (1819), Dugald Dalgetty is a former divinity student turned talkative soldier.

68.20   Phillips'] Wendell Phillips (1811–1884), lawyer, liberal reformer, and political agitator from Massachusetts, was famous for his florid speeches on behalf of abolition and women's rights.

73.5   *per se . . . propter se*] "As such" and "because of such"

73.12–13   *"Cœlum . . . currunt"*] "Those who travel change their skies, not their hearts."

76.4–8   Pleasants . . . "Ritchie] Hampden Pleasants (1797–1846), the most influential Whig newspaperman in Virginia, founded and edited for twenty-two years the *Constitutional Whig and Public Advertiser* in Richmond; he was killed in a duel with Thomas Ritchie, Jr. (1778–1854), an equally influential Democrat who edited the Richmond *Enquirer* for forty years.

76.7–8   *eo nomine*] "In that name"

76.12   *ab urbe condita*] "From the foundation of the city"—the era from which Romans computed time

76.24–25   Resolutions of 1798–99] The Resolutions, the immediate responses to the Federalists' Alien and Sedition Acts, asserted that the federal government possessed only limited powers.

79.11   *cui bono*] "For whose welfare"

79.15   *amor patriœ*] "Love of country"

80.28   Eclipse] The most famous racehorse of the eighteenth century

81.11   Webster] Daniel Webster (1782–1852), the American orator and statesman, was known for his solitary fishing trips.

84.17   Saxe-Weimar] Carl Bernhard, Duke of Saxe-Weimar (1792–1862), made a celebrated tour of the U.S. in 1825–26; his observations are recorded in *Travels through North America* (1828).

86.13–14   Governor-General of Bengal] When Robert, Lord Clive (1725–1774), English governor of Bengal, was recalled from India and charged by Parliament with financial irregularities, he described in detail the temptations to corruption that he resisted and exclaimed in a famous statement, "By God, Mr. Chairman, at this moment I stand astonished at my own moderation!"

87.6–7   *cacoethes accrescendi*] "Greed-ridden"

89.24–26   *fee tail . . . trusts*] *Fee tail* is the name given to any mutilated inheritance from which the designated heirs are cut off; *uses* refers to the benefit of properties the legal title to which is held by a person other than the one enjoying their profits; *trusts* refers to property interests held by one person for the benefit of another.

90.1   Tonans] "The Thunderer" is one of the epithets of the supreme god in Roman mythology; Baldwin here associates the source of Olympian judgment with President Andrew Jackson.

90.11–12   Specie Circular] President Jackson's executive order of 1836 required that government debts and purchases of public lands be paid in gold or silver rather than miscellaneous paper currency issued by local banks.

91.20   *auri sacra fames*] "Insatiable desire"

97.13   "Floats"] Certificates issued by the U.S. land office announcing their owners' intention to occupy a specified acreage on the public lands offered for settlement.

99.22   sora] The Carolina rail, a bird seen in marshy areas during its southward migration for the winter

108.6   Thurlow] The witticism of Charles James Fox (1749–1806), British Whig statesman—"No one ever was so wise as Thurlow looks"—was directed at the lord chancellor, Edward, First Baron Thurlow (1731–1806), who was known for his political intrigues and lack of principles.

108.18   Cromwell] In Thomas Carlyle's *On Heroes, Hero-Worship, and the Heroic in History* (1841), one of the earnest heroes is Oliver Cromwell (1599–1658), the English Puritan whose regime succeeded the revolution that deposed Charles I.

110.21   cutto] The now obsolete term for a seventeenth-century knife that was still in use during the Flush Times

115.13   Henry . . . Grundy] The reputation of the most famous orator of the American Revolution was enhanced in the early nineteenth century by William Wirt's *Sketches of the Life and Character of Patrick Henry,* which freely mixed facts and invention; Felix Grundy (1777–1840), who moved from Kentucky to Tennessee to improve his fortunes, became known as the most skillful criminal lawyer in the Old Southwest.

115.18   Pinkney] William Pinkney (1764–1822), revolutionary patriot and diplomat, senator, and U.S. attorney general

115.25   Museum] Phineas T. Barnum (1810–1891), showman and impresario, opened his American Museum in New York City in 1842. In addition to his natural history collections, it featured freaks and frauds because, as he declared, the public wanted to be humbugged.

118.26   Jonce Hooper's book] Johnson Jones Hooper's *Some Adventures of Captain Simon Suggs* (1845), a mock– campaign biography of an Alabama scoundrel, featured illustrations by Felix Darley (see also note to 238.19).

120.23   nolly prossy] *Nolle prosequi*: an agreement not to proceed further in a lawsuit

125.3   *pro falso clamore*] The court's direction to the plaintiff to pay a fine for bringing a false claim when he fails to recover judgment in his suit

130.2   "shykeenry"] Chicanery: to use tricks in litigation

133.16   *Jeo Fails*] *Jeofail*: a mistake in a pleading (see also note to 269.23–24)

157.26   *non constat*] "It is not certain"

160.28   Jenny Lind] For her American tour in 1850, Jenny Lind (1820–1887), the most celebrated singer of her day, demanded in her contract a music director and a baritone, Giovanni Belletti; in her concerts at the English court, the Swedish Nightingale often appeared with singers Giulia Grisi and Marietta Alboni and conductor Michael Costa, all Italians.

161.13   Wickliffe, &c.] Except for Henry Clay, the most influential and notable lawyer-politicians in Kentucky before the Civil War were John J. Crittenden (1787–1863), Benjamin Hardin (1784–1852), and Charles A. Wickliffe (1788–1869).

161.21   Plummer's speech] With his demagogic semi-literate speeches, Franklin E. Plummer (d. 1852), an audacious politician of eastern Mississippi, won great popularity by denouncing Natchez aristocrats.

161.28   Kunker's dog] Baldwin is referring to an episode in Johnson Jones Hooper's *A Ride with Old Kit Kuncker, and Other Sketches, and Scenes of Alabama* (1849).

162.25   Marshall . . . Wickliffe] Thomas A. Marshall (1794–1871), though he practiced in Bourbon County and later became chief justice of the Kentucky Court of Appeals, was a congressman in Washington, D.C., in 1834; Robert C. Wickliffe (1819–1895), who later moved to Louisiana and became its governor, was in 1834 only a boy of fifteen. By mangling chronology, Baldwin suggests that Cave Burton's name-dropping anecdotes of his legal exploits are stretchers.

167.4–5   Ireland, Emmet, Curran] Robert Emmet (1778–1803), involved in the 1803 Irish insurrection against English rule, was celebrated for his nationalistic speeches after his arrest; he was hanged before he could marry the daughter of John P. Curran (1750–1817), an Irish judge connected with the rising in 1798. That Cave Burton should be speaking of such irrelevant matters suggests his forensic style.

173.23   tic-doloreux] A nervous disorder that manifests itself in facial tics

177.10   *ex parte*] "From one side"

185.7   *quoud*] "As to"

188.5   *lincister*] Linkister: a linguist or interpreter

192.9   "who left . . . good"] For a performance of Edward Young's *Revenge* in New South Wales in 1790, an English convict transported for theft wrote a prologue in which this line appears.

196.6   "the star . . . way"] A popular misquotation of some lines from "On the Prospects of Planting Arts and Learning in America," a poem by Bishop George Berkeley (1685–1753).

197.5–6   Prentiss . . . and others] Baldwin lists here the lawyers who helped make Vicksburg and its environs the most politically influential part of Mississippi, both in the territorial years and immediately after statehood in 1817 (see also note to 246.19–20).

203.7   Playfair] John Playfair (1748–1819) was a Scottish mathematician and professor at the University of Edinburgh.

204.2   Wirt] William Wirt (1772–1834), U.S. attorney general and biographer of Patrick Henry, once wrote in a letter that "a lawyer must understand the particular facts and questions which arise in his cause, before genius has any materials to work upon."

207.15 Foote] Unionist senator and governor of Mississippi, Henry Stuart Foote (1804–1880) was also at one time U.S. surveyor general.

213.8 Clay, Webster, and Calhoun] The three most influential members of the U.S. Senate in the 1830s and 1840s were Henry Clay of Kentucky (1777–1852), Daniel Webster of Massachusetts (1782–1852), and John C. Calhoun of South Carolina (1782–1850).

214.16–18 Monmouth . . . Fairfax] Geoffrey of Monmouth (1100–1152?) was the English chronicler whose *Historia Regum Britanniae* inspired the Arthurian romances; Henry Percy, son of the first earl of Northumberland, was killed at the Battle of Shrewsbury in 1403; Bois-Gilbert and Ivanhoe are characters in Sir Walter Scott's *Ivanhoe*; Macgregor is the hero of Scott's *Rob Roy*; Rupert, Prince of the Palatinate (1619–1683), English naval commander in the Thirty Years' War, was defeated by Oliver Cromwell in the English Civil War; Thomas Fairfax (1612–1671), Parliamentary leader in the English Civil War, defeated Charles I in 1645.

217.20 Sharkey . . . Quitman] For William Lewis Sharkey see note to 57.19; for Samuel S. Boyd see note to 197.5–6; for Edward C. Wilkinson see note to 197.5; John Isaac Guion (1802–1855) was a prominent Whig and circuit court judge in Mississippi and law partner of S. S. Prentiss; for John A. Quitman see note to 197.5–6.

220.28 Lopez] Narciso López (1798–1851) was a Latin American general who in 1841 went to Cuba to fight against Spain but fled to the U.S. in 1849, where he organized three filibustering expeditions that illegally involved several prominent American politicians whose motive was the annexation of Cuba.

226.11–13 Marshall . . . Jay] John Marshall (1755–1835) was a Virginia jurist and chief justice of the U.S. Supreme Court; Joseph Story (1779–1845) was a Massachusetts jurist, justice of the U.S. Supreme Court, and professor of law at Harvard; Theophilus Parsons (1750–1813) was a Massachusetts jurist and justice of the state supreme court; James Kent (1763–1847) was a

New York jurist, state supreme court judge, and author of *Commentaries on American Law*; Smith Thompson (1768–1843) was a New York jurist, chief justice of the state supreme court, and justice of the U.S. Supreme Court; Spencer Roane (1762–1822) was a Virginia jurist and member of the Virginia assembly and senate; John Cotton Smith (1765–1845) was a governor of Connecticut; George Wythe (1726–1806) was a Virginia delegate to the Continental Congress, signer of the Declaration of Independence, and professor of law at the College of William and Mary; John Jay (1745–1829), New York statesman, served as U.S. minister to Spain, governor of New York, and the first chief justice of the U.S. Supreme Court.

228.14–15   Erasmus . . . Luther] Both Desiderius Erasmus (1466–1536), Dutch scholar and theologian, and Philipp Melanchthon (1497–1560), German reformer and professor, were influences on Martin Luther (1483–1546), the leader of the Protestant Reformation.

232.6–7   Swift . . . Cobbett] Jonathan Swift (1667–1745) lambasted Richard Bettesworth (*ca.* 1689–1741), an Irish member of Parliament, as "Booby Bettesworth" in several satiric poems; William Cobbett (1763–1835) was a political reformer whose inflammatory essays occasioned numerous lawsuits.

233.12   *revenons à nos moutons*] An acknowledgment of having digressed; literally, "let us return to our sheep" (*i.e.*, let us get back to the subject), a passage adapted from a French farce by Pierre Blanchet, *La Farce de Maistre Pierre Patelin* (*ca.* 1460)

234.12   Pitt] Baldwin probably has in mind not William Pitt, first Earl of Chatham (1708–1778), the most striking political figure in eighteenth-century England, but his precocious second son, William (1759–1806).

234.28–235.5   Hastings . . . *arduis*"] Warren Hastings (1732–1818), the British governor general of India, was forced to improvise political and military alliances in order to achieve fiscal efficiency; when he returned to England after some thirty-five years as administrator to face charges of corruption, he was acquitted after a seven-year trial. His motto, *Mens aequa in arduis*, means "calmness in difficulties."

238.5–22   McGregor-like levies . . . Boulbon] In this paragraph Baldwin compares the swindling during the Flush Times with notorious examples from the past. Sir Gregor MacGregor (*fl.* 1817), the Scottish adventurer in South America, after several freebooting exploits settled down as the ruler of the Poyais Indians in Central America and as cacique he took developmental loans from London banks that were never repaid; Dick Turpin and Jonathan Wild were eighteenth-century highwaymen, the subject of English ballads and novels; Hounslow Heath was an area near London noted as a gathering place for such highwaymen; Francisco de Carvajal (1464–1548), Spanish warrior who sought his fortune in Peru, was called the "demon of the Andes" because of his cruelty and grim humor; Simon Suggs is J. J. Hooper's fictional frontier sharper to whom Baldwin pays further tribute in "Simon Suggs, Jr."; and Gaston, Count Raousset de Boulbon (1817–1854), was highly publicized in California during the Flush Times as the affable but luckless leader of filibustering expeditions in Sonora.

240.25   "up to trap"] To be wary of danger

242.15   *in medias res*] To start "in the middle," a device common in epic poems

243.26   *lese majesty*] Lèse majesté: high treason

244.20   *qui vive*] "Who goes there?"—*i.e.*, an alert attitude

246.7–8   peacocks] In Roman mythology, Juno, wife of Jupiter and queen of the gods, was associated with the peacock.

246.14–16   Wickhams . . . Wickliffes] The first four names are of Virginia lawyers who made the Richmond bar famous: John Wickham (1765–1839), Benjamin W. Leigh (1781–1849), Chapman Johnson (1779–1849), and Robert S. Stanard (*fl.* 1830s); the next four were distinguished members of the Kentucky bar: Henry Clay (1777–1852), John J. Crittenden (1787–1863), John Rowan (1773–1853), and Charles A. Wickliffe (1788–1869).

246.19–20   Prentiss . . . Boyd] Baldwin cites these lawyers of his own generation in Mississippi as equals of those in Virginia and Kentucky: Seargent S. Prentiss (1808–1850), Joseph Holt (1807–1894), Robert J. Walker (1801–1869), George S. Yerger (1801–1860), Daniel Mayes (1792–1861), and Samuel S. Boyd (*fl.* 1830s).

248.22–23   Collier] Henry W. Collier (1801–1855) was chief justice of the Alabama Supreme Court until 1849, when he was elected governor.

248.24–25   Blackstone . . . Stowell] Sir William Blackstone (1723–1780), author of the *Commentaries*, articulated the first comprehensive survey of the English legal system; William Scott, Lord Stowell (1745–1836), member of Parliament and judge, was a respected interpreter of international law.

249.4–5   *Æquitas sequitur legem*] "Equity follows the law"— *i.e.*, equity has no power to change rights established by statute

255.18   Ericsson] John Ericsson (1803–1889), the Swedish inventor of the quiet caloric engine in 1833, emigrated to the U.S. in 1839; his greatest fame came with his turreted ironclad, the *Monitor*, launched in 1862.

257.24–25   *suaviter . . . re*] "Gentle in manner, vigorous in performance"

260.5   *Nil admirari*] The phrase comes from *Nil admirari prope res est una* from Horace, Epistle I: "Not to admire is the best."

264.12   Fi-fa] Abbreviation of *fieri facias* ("you cause it to be made"), an ordinary writ commanding the sheriff to levy the amount of judgment.

264.17   "take water"] Legal slang suggesting failure; to take a nonsuit

267.24   Ingersoll] Charles Jared Ingersoll (1782–1862) was a Philadelphia lawyer and Democratic congressman, diplomat, and author.

269.23–24   *Jee-fails*] In the statute of *jeofailes* the pleader, perceiving an error in form in the proceedings, acknowledges it and is at liberty to amend it.

269.25   *affidavy*] An affidavit is a statement reduced to writing and sworn to before an authorized officer of the court.

271   SCAN. MAG.] Abbreviation for *scandalum magnatum* ("slander of great men"); in earlier English law, derogatory words spoken against a judge or other officer of the realm were considered a more serious offense than was ordinary slander.

275.8   to *come*] Regional slang: to play a trick on another

277.4   *vel non*] "Or not"

279.21 *"comp."*] Compromise

280.7 *subpœna duces tecum*] A writ requiring a witness to appear in court with documents relevant to the case even if the witness is not himself a party to the suit.

285.18 Plantagenets] A line of English kings that ended with the death of Richard III in 1485.

288.18 vastated] Emanuel Swedenborg (1688–1772), Swedish scientist and philosopher, defined *vastation* as the process by which, for the regenerate, all things that hinder the operation of grace in the soul are removed; for the unregenerate, vastation is the deprivation of all goodness and truth, which leaves them prey to evil.

289.15–16 *prima facie*] "At first view"

293.6 "Sons"] Various chapters of the Sons of Temperance, a national reform organization, were sporadically active in the Old Southwest during the Flush Times.

299.14–15 Hoyle . . . Coke] Baldwin suggests that the judge was more familiar with the rules of gambling than with those of law. Edmond Hoyle (1672–1769) was the author of manuals on whist and other card games; Sir Edward Coke (1552–1634), author of the *Institutes*, was a legal theorist frequently cited in law cases in the U.S.

303.14–20 Mrs. Harriet S——] Harriet Beecher Stowe (1811–1896) was a Christian educator and novelist whose abolitionist principles in *Uncle Tom's Cabin* (1852) created a furor in the slaveholding South.

305.4–5 snuffed . . . relish] See Swedenborg's *True Christian Religion* (New York, 1909), n. 569.

305.8–9 Calmuc Tartar] The Kalmucks, a branch of the Mongolian peoples in China and Siberia, were nomadic tribesmen known for their primitive fierceness.

309.17 Prentiss . . . Yerger] For Prentiss, see note to 54.10; George S. Yerger (1801–1860), one of six lawyer-brothers, moved from Tennessee to Vicksburg in 1838, where he practiced until 1844, when he moved to Jackson.

310.2 Boyd . . . Holt] As with S. S. Prentiss and George Yerger earlier, Stout continues his name-dropping with two more lawyers prominent during the Flush Times (see note to 246.19–20).

310.28   Gayle] The old shyster's name-dropping is meant to identify him with the most renowned lawyers in the area; the prisoner, however, counters by claiming as his counsel John Gayle (1792–1859), who, as former governor of Alabama, U.S. congressman, and district court judge, is fully their equal.

314.4   Tallmadge] Nathaniel Pitcher Tallmadge (1795–1864), U.S. senator from New York, became a prominent convert to spiritualism, one of the many pseudosciences that flourished in the 1830s and 1840s.

315.4   *empressement*] Eagerness; promptness

325.9   Spurzheim] Kaspar Spurzheim (1776–1832), German popularizer of the pseudoscience of phrenology